The Liminal Shore

About the author

Alex Langstone was born and raised in the heart of Essex Witch Country, that low lying coastal region of atmospheric salt marsh, haunted trackway and deeply cut estuary. He has authored several books and essays about folklore, magic, and the spirit of place. You can contact the author via his blog at www.alexlangstone.com or find him on social media.

To Pete

The Liminal Shore
Witchcraft, Mystery & Folklore of the Essex Coast

Alex Langstone

Happy reading

Alex

27/3/22

TROY BOOKS

© 2021 Alex Langstone

First printing in hardback
March 2022

ISBN 978-1-909602-29-8

All rights reserved.
No part of this publication may be reproduced, stored within a retrieval system or transmitted in any form or by any means, electronic, mechanical, photocopying, scanning, recording or otherwise, without the prior written permission of the author and the publisher.

Any practices or substances described within this publication are presented as items of interest. The author and the publisher accept no responsibility for any results arising from their enactment or use. Readers are self-responsible for their actions.

Published by Troy Books
www.troybooks.co.uk

Troy Books Publishing
BM Box 8003
London WC1N 3XX

Cover images: Paul Atlas-Saunders
Cover design: Gemma Gary

Other Books by Alex Langstone

Bega and the Sacred Ring

Lucifer Bridge

Spirit Chaser

Menhir

From Granite to Sea

List of illustrations

Hatfield Peverel's sixteenth century Waterhouse family imp by Paul Atlas-Saunders.

Hatfield Peverel witch, Joan Waterhouse. Woodcut from the Elizabethan booklet published at the time of her execution in 1566 (artist unknown).

Hatfield Peverel witch, Agnes Waterhouse depicted in a woodcut from the Elizabethan booklet published at the time of her execution in 1566 (artist unknown).

St Osyth Dragon by Paul Atlas-Saunders.

Matthew Hopkins, notorious and psychotic witch finder (artist unknown).

Frontispiece of The Discovery of Witches by Matthew Hopkins, 1647. Elizabeth Clarke appears on the right alongside her witchcraft teacher Anne West and their familiars (artist unknown).

The three crowns of the Colchester legend, (based on the Colchester town coat of arms) by Paul Atlas-Saunders.

Easthorpe Sheela-na-Gig by Paul Atlas-Saunders.

Mersea Island Romano-British barrow by Paul Atlas-Saunders.

The Devil and his demon dogs, who haunt the saltmarshes around Salcott Creek and Tolleshunt Knights by Paul Atlas-Saunders.

Beeleigh Abbey, Maldon by William Henry Bartlett. Engraved by Charles Mottram. 1832

St Peter-ad-Muram built by Lindisfarne Celtic Christian monk Cedd on the marshes at Bradwell-on-Sea in 654 AD by Paul Atlas-Saunders.

Mundon Oak Grove by Paul Atlas-Saunders.

The ghostly Black Shuck by Paul Atlas-Saunders.

An example of an eighteenth-century Essex witch stick from Finchingfield in north-west Essex. Historically, comparable sticks would have undoubtedly been used by the Curren and other Essex Cunning folk. Illustrated by Paul Atlas-Saunders.

The Neolithic Dagenham Idol by Paul Atlas-Saunders.

James Murrell's hexagram protection sigil by Paul Atlas-Saunders.

James Murrell's Angelic pentagram protection sigil by Paul Atlas-Saunders.
South Ockendon green man by Paul Atlas-Saunders.

Contents

Foreword By David Southwell	13
Preamble	16
Enchanted Edgeland	20
Alchemists, Cunning Folk, and Witches	24
Part One: Tendring	35
1. Manningtree and Harwich	38
2. Witch Ghost Coast	60
3. Colne Estuary and Oldest Town	74
Part Two: Blackwater	94
4. Mysterious Isle	96
5. Devil Haunted Marshes	102
6. Ancient Port of Maldon	113
Part Three: Dengie	130
7. Sea Secrets	136
8. The Lonely Places of Marsh-Mystery	143
9. Hart Family and The Curren	153
Part Four: Thames	167
10. Mud Archipelago	169
11. Salt Marsh, Creek, and Riverside	194
12. Urban Shores	205

Photographs by the author between pages 120-121

"A more desolate region can scarce be conceived, and yet it is not without beauty. In summer, the thrift mantles the marshes with shot satin, passing through all gradations of tint from maiden's blush to lily white. Thereafter a purple glow steals over the waste, as the sea lavender bursts into flower, and simultaneously every creek and pool is royally fringed with sea aster. A little later the glass-wort, that shot up green and transparent as emerald glass in the early spring, turns to every tinge of carmine. When all vegetation ceases to live, and goes to sleep, the marshes are alive and wakeful with countless wild fowl. At all times they are haunted with sea mews and roysten crows, in winter they teem with wild duck and grey geese. The stately heron loves to wade in the pools, occasionally the whooper swan sounds his loud trumpet, and flashes a white reflection in the still blue waters of the fleets. The plaintive pipe of the curlew is familiar to those who frequent these marshes, and the barking of the brent geese as they return from their northern breeding places is heard in November."

'Mehalah' Sabine Baring Gould

Dedication

For my ancestors
who have lived by the tidal, salty rivers and the mysterious
marshy shores of Essex Witch Country for many generations.
Also, in memory of Jane Cook, 10th January 1947 – 7th
March 2018

Acknowledgments

With grateful thanks to: My wonderful husband Paul Atlas-Saunders, for the beautiful illustrations that enhance this work and for all his help and support; Caroline Blick for reading the manuscript and offering sensible suggestions; Claire Capon-Hawley for accompanying me on many esoteric and folkloric adventures in the 1980s; my brilliant publishers Jane Cox and Gemma Gary at Troy Books; Ian Dawson for the plentiful folkloric field-trips during the 1980s; Morag Embleton and all at www.oldknobbley.com, for allowing me to reproduce the delightful photograph of Mistley's ancient oak; Sheila Fletcher for invaluable help with manuscript checking; Dave Hunt - my late friend and mentor, who first set me on this path; my brothers, Jon and Tim and my sister Barb, for their help unlocking the past; David Southwell for writing the foreword and for creating the exquisitely mysterious, eerie and evocative world of Hookland; Val Thomas for proof reading the manuscript; Paul Weston for many mysterious Thameside adventures; and Carole Young for reminding me of some forgotten Essex lore. I would also like to mention the helpful staff at various institutions, in particular the remote archival assistance of Essex Record Office; Southend Museums Service; Hadleigh and Thundersley Community Archive; Mersea Museum online archive; and the Museum of Witchcraft & Magic online archive, which have all proved to be invaluable during a time of travel restrictions and lockdowns due to the Covid-19 pandemic. Finally, I would like to make mention of my late parents for revealing some of the secret spots on the liminal shore.

Every reasonable attempt has been made to contact the copyright holders of certain quotations and photographs found within this work. If any person or organisation subsequently contacts me with information concerning permissions or copyright information, we will gladly make the appropriate acknowledgments and amend future editions of this book.

foreword

Though we pretend otherwise, most writers have some insidious vanity at our core. We like being asked to contribute something to a fellow writer's work – it makes us feel as if someone actually believes our words have worth. However, it is a particular honour to be asked to write a foreword by an author whose work you adore. Even more when you know the book is one that others are going to love, going to regard as something special on the folklore section of their bookshelves.

Because folklore matters. Folklore is a moving, breathing thing that walks across any imposed notion of border. Folklore creates and also recreates a relationship with place, a sense of awe, a revelation of truth. It does so in tales that may be transmitted across seemingly impossible vastnesses of space and time. It's one of our cleverest, oldest inventions. Disparage folklore, disparage humanity.

For me folklore is a weaving of the past into the now. It's a thread stitching stories onto our souls, giving us navigation of the labyrinth of our ancestors. In tales and telling, it gives us cave-old eyes of wonder. Few subjects are more worthy of contemplation, few subjects provide such unbridled joy. Yet so often books on the topic kill it with ink-poisoning, butterfly-pin living lore, offer only words of ossification. Alex's work is always a refusal of such malarkey. He writes in such a way that none of a tale's life is lost in his telling.

One of the reasons for this is because Alex understands that place is the constant context of our stories, of our lives. Whether it is in cursed pier, strikingly-signed pub or feral church stretching up to peer over trees, landmarks store story like a battery. They are anchor for folklore, for long the remembrance of the land itself. More than that, place itself is composed of layers of memory. Any trek across the ghost soil always scuffs up stories. Alex's telling of folklore always feels walked. It feels harvested from the hedges and estuary edges. These are tales with mud and dust on their boots.

I too am a child of 1970s Essex. Like Alex I am a child of the bruised, coastal lip of Eastern England, of dares to walk the Broomway or run nine times counterclockwise around the boneyard to summon the Devil. As this book demonstrates with fierce grace, it is a landscape that makes a bone tattoo in you through stinging salt kisses and tides of mud. At the time when both Alex and I were young, it was also a place where before you even hit double digits, you would have walked through a whole English myth cycle of smuggler's tunnels, Black dogs running corpse roads, Royal ghosts, witchcraft and mystery.

All the strange stories I grew up surrounded by and which I try to channel into the Hookland project are presented here without the active misremembering I engage in. They are also presented with a rare lyricism. I am not surprised by this. Alex was the first person I ever knew who openly talked of being a poet – which in working-class Essex of the 1980s was just not a done thing – but to me was hugely inspiring. He is even able to use words I normally shun such as edgeland and liminal in ways which are not only apposite, but essential to understanding both Essex and its mysteries.

There is a lot of brave, beautiful and personal writing in The Liminal Shore. Instead of the stasis by ink-poisoning, Alex refuses to be bound to just offering the oldest and weirdest tales, but also surveys the evolution of folklore, reminds us of its modern traditions that parade our streets, populate the civic calendar with ritual and symbolism. This is much rarer in books on the subject than it should be. Alex also brings a sense of his own personal folkloric conversation with Essex and through it gives you a sense of how that landscape invites you to believe in salt sprites, in phantoms of the Legio XIV Gemina. Again, this is more scarce in this subject than you would imagine, as is his refusal to forget the context of class, to engage with the importance of trades and the harshness of rural living that are so clearly massive engines of much of the county's folklore.

In a book where mystery is so central, it is also brave to not offer easy answers, but allow readers to make their own determination. Where he has left space to trust in his readers, space for interpretation, it is not from lack of research. The Liminal Shore is filled with a sense not just of a lifetime of reading on its subjects, but countless conversations in local pubs where stories are currency, correspondences with those who have encountered some aspect of lore or are living within the place where a story was born.

In recent years many have tried to commodify the cunning and witchcraft that Essex is famous for. No-one owns this and Alex gives a masterful sense of how witch-soaked as well as ghost-soaked Essex can be. The cunning clung to my childhood environs. I grew up in the home of the 'last witch doctor of England', played in the boneyard of the 'last Master of Witches'. It was a palpable force you brushed against. I remember my mother pointing out which house on a lane into the woods was owned by someone from 'cunning stock'. "Never play knock-down against her door." It is an absolute delight to read a work that gives a sense of how much these subjects were familial and communal mythology that seemingly all Essex children of our era passed through.

With The Liminal Shore, Alex Langstone joins the likes of Arthur Morrison, Eric Maple and Charlotte Craven Mason in chronicling the folklore of Essex in work which has no expiry date. This book will be read in the decades to come, still delivering stabs of wonder and delight. It will still be offering – as you are about to find out – shortcuts and gates into the enfolding worlds of mystery, witchcraft and faerie as they border the county of my birth.

David Southwell
@HooklandGuide

preamble

There are more ghosts prowling between the Thames at Canvey and the Roman walls at Colchester than any other equivalent area in England. Generation after generation of Essex families have recounted the stories of these ghosts of the reclaimed marshlands.

'Jop Summers'

here is a book that I have always wanted to write. As a child of the 1970s, I found the folklore, legends, and tales of the coastline of Essex truly fascinating. Likewise, of the geography. If you look at a map of the south-eastern coast of the Isle of Britain, the Essex shore is easily identifiable. The muddled line of the seaboard blurs into the mud and marsh which seem to mysteriously hold the ancient spirits of the Trinovantian, Roman and later Saxon shore. This long and winding salty strand connects the estuary of London's great river, with the wide curve and bulk of East Anglia, whose own shores reveal the most easterly edge of Britain, terminating at that vast tidal and otherworldly entrance to fen-country, called the Wash.

Preamble

If you zoom in on a map of Essex, you will see a jagged and deeply serrated coastline, with muddy islands, discrete peninsulas, and river estuaries. I don't think that this coast has ever been described as a poet's coast, but out here on England's forgotten threshold you can find hidden places of enchantment, where landscape, saltmarsh and the dark sea demand poetry, which can quickly lead into otherworldly conversations. There are sites here that will conjure words from the elements with ease. This is 'other' Essex, where coastal-urban conceals enchantment and isolated rural marshland reveals the arcane.

This can, however, be an uncomfortable land, where its history reveals that the marshes were once home to the Essex Ague. Known as the cursed fever of the Essex marshes, this malarial disease was rife up until the late nineteenth century. The English mosquito, Anopheles atroparvus, loved to breed in the brackish rivulets of the coastal plain making the Essex shores particularly susceptible. Many of the marshmen adopted folk charms and remedies to try and suppress the debilitating effects of the Ague. Stinking worms, bed bugs, herbal powders, shoes lined with tansy leaves, or pills made from compressed spider's webs were all used in various ways to ward off the fever attacks. Luckily by 1880 the disease was better understood, and it gradually disappeared.

'Uncomfortable' barely describes the other, more hideous stain of history which marks this patch of shore. This coast was home to one of the most notorious witch-finders and illegal torturers within England's history. Aided and abetted by his evil accomplices, they reigned over a short but hideous age of terror, where women were not safe, unless married and monied.

Evidence of the more ancient pre-history of this region can be found as far back as 400,000 years in the Palaeolithic era. During 1911, historian and geologist Samuel Hazzledine Warren found a large assemblage of stone tools at Clacton-on-Sea, including the famous Clacton spear, a wooden hunting implement made of yew wood and shaped into a point. It was found within a foreshore exposure of Palaeolithic sediment along with shaped flint tools, some of which would have been used to carve the spear. This ancient artefact was used during a far distant age when mammoth, auroch and woodland rhinoceros shared the land alongside many prehistoric humans. It is believed that its owner was a member of species Homo heidelbergensis, who would have used it for hunting and gathering food. This artefact is now held at the Natural History Museum in London.

During the Neolithic period the building of the Springfield Cursus began. This rectilinear earthwork was discovered in 1979, and was built around 3000 BC. The earthen complex was around seven hundred metres long and forty metres wide. The site, which was probably built for ceremonial use, had a circle of fourteen upright timber posts some twenty-six metres in diameter at the north-eastern end, which would probably have been the focus for ritual and funerary rites. The cursus was built close to the northern bank of the river Chelmer, on a broad loop of the river, so it would have been easily accessible from the coast at Maldon. This site was in continuous use from the Neolithic and alterations and additions continued throughout the Bronze Age, and today is widely interpreted as a ritual landscape which included a mortuary enclosure, Neolithic enclosure, and a nationally important cursus monument.[1]

During the Iron Age many hill forts or fortified enclosures were constructed, roughly between 400 and 200 BC, including those at Danbury and Shoeburyness. During the later period of the Iron Age, the Celtic tribe of the Trinovantes was established across much of what is now Essex. After the Roman invasion, the land of the Trinovantes became a Roman client kingdom within the same geographical area, though skirmishes with the neighbouring tribe of the Catuvellauni became

---

1. megalithix.wordpress.com/2010/09/04/springfield-cursus-chelmsford

Preamble

more frequent. By 10 AD the Trinovantian capital, Camulodunum, had been claimed by the Catuvellauni, and this gave them the access they needed to trade with the continent via the coast.

For the purposes of this book, the geography of the Essex coast includes the hinterland of the estuaries up to, and occasionally beyond the navigable waters. For a quick and easy reference, the land featured in this book is the area to the east of the old Roman road, which is now the perpetually busy A12.

enchanted edgeland

There are two very differing aspects to the intriguing and low-lying coastline of Essex. The rural, bleak, remote and often isolated salt marsh allows a liminal escape from twenty-first century life. A place where sea lavender blooms and the salt-wind blows, sweeping across the haunted creeks, otherworldly islands, and saline estuaries.

The second side is that of urbanisation. The bustling towns, seaside resorts, and the land of half-forgotten holidays, where sand always made its way into your picnic. These are the towns where pleasure-piers can be found: those boardwalks of fun above the cool dark waters, often protruding further into the North Sea than they ought.

There are a few specific places on the Essex coast that hold particularly vivid childhood memories for me, during the early and mid-1970s. These were places that agitated my childhood mind, and later fascinated me as an adult, drawing me towards their mysteries and magic.

Top of the list is the port of Harwich, a fascinating place with a busy harbour. The old high lighthouse, standing in the centre of the town on the edge of St Helen's Green and built of brick, giving it a gaunt and somewhat sinister appearance, towers above the old dwellings of the longshoremen and sailors. This somewhat overpowering and long disused beacon, fired my imagination, allowing me a fleeting glimpse of the old wooden shipping vessels tied up by the jetty, creaking and groaning on the rise and fall of the tide. The deeply brooding and atmospheric maritime town of press-gangs, piracy and smuggling, Harwich has its roots as a medieval port with a ship building heritage, where the Mayflower is believed to have been built and where its captain, Christopher Jones lived.

A little to the south lies the so-called 'Essex Sunshine Coast', and it was here, at Holland-on-Sea, where a damp and salty beach hut became a welcome sight in the summer holidays, allowing longer visits and picnics to the sandy beach and encouraging us to explore the soft low cliffs along the foreshore. For closer to home day trips, Maldon promenade was just a short bus ride away. With its open-air swimming pool, wasp infested wooden ice-cream shacks and the majestic russet sails of the old Thames barges manoeuvring into port, it was an exciting maritime playground.

But it was on the eerie witch-land of the Dengie, by the seventh century chapel of St Peter-ad-Muram at Bradwell-juxta-Mare, where I was introduced to the idea of an enchanted coast at an early and impressionable age. This book has its roots at this isolated spot, known to the Romans as Othona. On the opposite coast of the Dengie peninsula, at the riverside port of Burnham-on-Crouch, the music of the marina has stayed with me, as a hauntological soundscape. The natural play of wind on halyard, allowed those ancient spirits of the sea an outlet for an eerie suite of music, that still evokes Burnham waterfront to this day. Southend-on-Sea is also remembered with affection, in part due to the once famous sea-front illuminations but mainly because of its unique pier railway, which proved to be an exciting and resonant way for a child of the 1970s to travel out across the wide expanse of the Thames estuary.

Whichever side of this coastline you seek, there is a vast canon of folklore, myth and legend, which lays hidden just below the surface of the work-a-day lives of the populations who call this shore home. This lore has permeated the landscape through centuries of history, and can give us a fascinating glimpse into the past, along this 350-mile-long shore. This surprisingly long coastline, with its deeply indented tidal estuaries, has provided a living and a way of life for hundreds of years, with fishing, farming, smuggling and wildfowling at the fore.

This coast has also given us some of the most interesting and fascinating tales of witchcraft and folk-magic, with famous names, such as Cunning Murrell of Hadleigh, Ursula Kemp of St Osyth and Mother Redcap of Wallasea Island. The stories of theirs, and others lives, have played out as the unusual folk on the edge of society, living on the salty frill of the land, outside of the everyday rules by which they would have been judged and sometimes hanged by their neighbours. These interesting liminal characters, each of them adds more intrigue, mystery, and all-to-often, horror, to the secret shore, a place where magic seeps in with each tide, reaching far inland through an intricate network of salty creeks. In these alluvial spots, the land relaxes into brine, and its eternal breath seeps out into the vast ocean of dreams. For it is at the edge, where the alchemical quality of estuary stirs the evocative mix of land-lore and sea-secrets.

Ghosts invade the very fabric of the region, seeping into the everyday existence of the inhabitants, both past and now. Folklore spawns on the frill of the land, and the misty shorelines of Essex reek with stories of its mysterious past. The broad, flat saltings teem with wild fowl. Here the curlew is king, whose eerie shrill cry cuts through the thick atmosphere of the mire. This is a feral landscape, where fleeting glimpses of the past and future arise unexpectedly, and where a feeling of unease often creeps in. To stand on the shoreline at dusk, maybe at Woodrolfe Creek or Barling Ness, can open doorways, allowing the spectral to feed the subconscious.

There have been others who came before, with their own visionary prose on this theme. Sabine Baring Gould, Vicar, folklorist, and antiquarian penned his epic tale of Mersea Island life in his novel Mehalah, full of folklore, marsh-atmosphere, and mystery. There was also ghost hunter and investigator of Essex folk-magic, Eric Maple, who in the 1950s gathered much remembered witch lore from the old Dengie and Rochford Hundreds. A couple of generations previous, saw Charlotte Craven Mason, who penned her collection on the folklore and social history of the southern part of Essex during the opening decade of the twentieth century and Arthur Morrison, author, journalist and art collector, who wrote such beautifully poetic descriptions of the salt marsh of Thameside Essex, in his novel about the life and adventures of Cunning Murrell. These and other collectors of lore and legend from the Essex shore have left us a folk-narrative rich legacy of this otherworldly coast of secretive islands, muddy creeks, and ghost laden marshes. I hope to be able to expand on this and bring the mystery and enchantment of the liminal shore, where marsh wizards and sea witches practised their craft, to a new audience in the twenty-first century.

alchemists, cunning folk, and witches

I was born and raised on the rural periphery of Hatfield Peverel, close to the threshold where Gypsy Lane and Maldon Road meet. The village lies in the centre of eastern Essex, not on the coast but closely neighbouring the salty hinterland that creeps inland from the edge. It was a landscape of gravel pits, rivers, barley, and woodland. All of these made up a rich and varied playground, where canal locks, combine harvesters and ancient footpaths evoke special places in my memory. I distinctly remember a first-hand account of how, during the Autumn of 1974, one of the local landowners had performed an act of environmental vandalism.[2] On one Autumnal afternoon, they had secretly brought in the bulldozers and removed the last remaining

---

2. Hatfield Peverel Review, November 1974, author's family archive.

section of ancient hedgerow from along Gypsy Lane, an historic footpath linking farms, settlements and the river on the eastern edge of the parish. You can still see traces of the footpath on modern maps, and it would have originally linked St Andrew's priory church, Lower Farm, Moor Gardens, Smallands Hall Farm, and across the shallow Blackwater valley towards Wickham Bishops and Beacon Hill. As a child I walked sections of this path almost daily, and along with my siblings; we often got wet whilst playing in the enchanted stream that flowed across the fertile valley towards its destination at the parish boundary, where it emptied into the River Blackwater.

I can still vaguely recall the old east Essex accent and dialect being spoken, but this was to virtually disappear within the span of my childhood, and by the 1980s it was all but gone. To hear this accent today, you will need to travel to the far north-east of the county, where Manningtree and Harwich appear to be the last bastions of the old inflections. But it can still occasionally be heard elsewhere on the coast; the tone and lilt sometimes re-emerges, often hidden within the pseudo-Cockney twang of Estuary English, now spoken by the masses.

The paternal strand of my family can trace its history to around three hundred years in Hatfield Peverel. Documents show that William Langstone was born in 1740 and married Mary Bunting at the priory church of St Andrew, in 1762. Since then, many generations have lived in the village. My maternal family hailed from Maldon and Colchester, two historic Essex ports, where I guess my fascination with this coast must originate.

Hatfield Peverel has a wealth of recorded folklore, which fascinated me as a child. On the long drive leading to the fine Georgian house of Crix there is an often-repeated folk-narrative of Shaen's Shaggy Dog. The dog was described as a large animal with glaring eyes and was said to frequently haunt the entrance of the drive. It was at this spot during the nineteenth century, that a driver of a timber wain once lashed out at him with his whip. The result was that the driver, horse, load, and cart were engulfed in a great fiery blaze which quickly and thoroughly reduced them to ashes.[3] It is a widely held belief that the spectre of the ghostly black dog of Crix Corner was finally exorcised by an act of spontaneous combustion at his first sighting of a motor car.[4]

There is a more recent account of this folklore, which originates from 13th September 1980. A couple were driving home, after dark, along the Terling road heading towards Crix, when a large black and white animal came hurtling down the left bank and hit the car with a loud thud. The animal then went underneath the car and let out a loud and sickening scream. The occupants of the car leapt out and grabbed a torch, fearful of what they may find. They looked underneath the car, and along each side of the vehicle, but nothing could be found. There were no animal remains, no damage to the car and nothing to indicate any sort of physical confirmation as to what they had witnessed. They later described the animal to the local police as the size of a cow, but looking more like a dog. Though as it was a very dark night, they couldn't be sure. A few years later the driver of the car read about Shaen's Shaggy Dog and felt that he may have experienced something similar.[5] Could this be the first and only sighting of the ghost cow of Hatfield Peverel?

Towards the other end of the old Roman road, now unimaginatively called The Street, lies the nineteenth century coaching inn, The Duke of Wellington. This is the reputed site of a ghostly headless horseman, who haunts the area around the pub and the junction between The Street and Maldon Road. Though not many sightings have been reported recently, I can remember it being spoken

---

3. Hatfield Peverel in old picture postcards. Vol. 1 by Joyce P Fitch
4. The Township of Hatfield Peverel by Teresa. M. Hope, 1930.
5. Hatfield Peverel in old picture postcards. Vol. 2 by Joyce P Fitch

about during my childhood, so was undoubtedly an old village tale.[6]

The ancient custom of Beating the Bounds has been held from time to time, around the parish boundary of Hatfield Peverel. This historic rite was first processed around the village four hundred years ago, when the first 'beat' was perambulated between the 22nd and the 24th of May 1609. For over four centuries the boundary of the parish has been reinforced, commemorated, and ritually reclaimed by this custom. It was revived in 1920 by the Reverend H. G. Harrison, and there is a report in a local newsletter that suggests the custom is still alive and well in the twenty-first century.[7]

During the eleventh century, a college of secular canons was founded in the village by Maud Ingelrica and dedicated to St Mary Magdalene. After Maud's death, at the beginning of the twelfth century it became a priory of Benedictine monks and was rededicated to St Mary the Virgin. The only part of the priory that remains is the nave, which still stands as the parish church of St. Andrew.

It was often rumoured that Maud was the lover of William the Conqueror and bore him an illegitimate son, also named William. The King eventually married her off to one of his knights, Ranulph Peverel. Local lore states that, for her sins, the Devil swore that he would have her soul, whether her body be buried inside or outside the priory's walls. However, she managed to have the old fiend tricked by leaving strict instructions that after her death she was to be interred within the priory wall. During excavations in 1873, a cavity was exposed in the north wall of the nave, and inside was found a stone coffin containing the bodies of a man and woman, and from that day the bones were believed to be those of Maud and Ranulph Peverel.

---

6. Family archive, with thanks to my brother, Jon Langstone for refreshing my memory of this piece of folklore.
7. The Hatfield Peverel Review, issue 228, April 2012, p 3

The priory once housed a reliquary which held a phial, which was believed to hold the holy milk of the Virgin Mary. A bottle was dug up in the 1830s, just to the east of the church that was believed to have been the relic, though has since been lost. Interestingly, and within the same parish, lies the church of All Saints, sited on the banks of the River Chelmer at Ulting. This old sacred place once had a guild of the Blessed Virgin Mary, which was founded in 1477. This Chapel of Our Lady of Ulting, was sited within the churchyard of All Saints, and became a centre of pilgrimage. Medieval documents record gifts of jewellery and crosses, which would have adorned the holy statue and shrine. The guild was dissolved in 1548 and the building was demolished.[8]

In January 1416, Hatfield Peverel Priory agreed to house Northumbrian magician, William Morton as their resident alchemist. He was accompanied by Alan Roys, who is listed in the National Archives as a fifteenth century London creditor. The incumbent prior at Hatfield Peverel, John Bepsay, took Morton in and gave him the accommodation he needed to produce his alchemical elixir. It was agreed that Morton would be allowed to stay for one year, where he proclaimed that he could make gold and silver from whence the king's money could be made.[9]

For the first six months of his stay, Morton worked with the art of fire and experimented with combinations of many ingredients. These were said to have included mercury, charcoal powder, sakeon, vermelion, resalger, vertegrees, sal niter, sal alkale, sawundiner, vitriol, arsenic, and many other substances, most of which, during his later trial, were understandably unknown to the jurors. Alchemy had been outlawed in 1404, by Henry IV, so the clandestine activities of the alchemist at Hatfield Peverel Priory were illegal at the time. His trial was held at nearby

---

8. www.hatfieldpeverelultingchurches.org.uk/all-saints-church-ulting-history
9. The Township of Hatfield Peverel by Teresa. M. Hope, 1930, p 89

Maldon on 31st August 1416. However, Morton was later pardoned by King Henry V, for all treasons, felonies, and trespasses, and was acquitted. It was likely that Prior Bepsay may have previously known Morton, and they had probably conspired in the magic of alchemy previously in their native Northumberland.[10]

In 1542, Henry VIII brought a new law into existence. The act against conjurations, witchcrafts, sorcery, and enchantments. This single act made sure that the village herbalists, wise women, and cunning men could be tried and convicted for their services, and in effect branding them as witches. This was the beginning of a period of active persecution and prosecution, that lasted throughout the rest of his reign and those of Elizabeth I, James I, and Charles I. It may sound strange, but this type of law stayed on the statute books until 1951, although the Witchcraft Act 1735 effectively curtailed most of the witch trials in Britain.

In 1566 Hatfield Peverel found itself and its five hundred or so inhabitants at the centre of a witch trial, where three women were accused of practising sorcery. Agnes Waterhouse, her daughter Joan, and her sister Elizabeth Frances were the family at the centre of the allegations. Agnes and Elizabeth were taught the ancient art of witchcraft by their grandmother, known as Mother Eve, which suggests that there may have been at least four generations of the family practising as folk-magicians, cunning women and herbalists in the parish, across the fifteenth and sixteenth centuries. Mother Eve was probably a cunning woman and would have been practising from around 1450, a time when witches and cunning folk were acknowledged but the practice of was not yet a criminal offence.[11] It is interesting to note that historically, cunning folk were well distributed across Essex, and people would

---

10. The Essex Review 1907, pp 158, 159.

11. Female Power: A study on witchcraft in Elizabethan Essex by Kate J. Cole, p 12

travel miles to consult with them. Over sixty names were recorded as cunning practitioners between 1560 and 1680.[12] The Hatfield Peverel witch family had several familiars between them. The principle ones were a cat called Sathan, a large toad, and a spectacular horned black dog, which had a face like an ape and a short tail. The black dog also possessed a metal chain, which he proudly wore around his neck, and upon the chain a silver whistle was secured.

Sathan the cat was kept busy by Elizabeth. She had inherited the cat from her grandmother Eve, at the age of twelve. Sathan had been with her for sixteen years, aiding Elizabeth in her folk-magic and conjurations. From the lurid accounts of her trial, Sathan was also used in Elizabeth's witchcraft for killing and maiming people, including the death of her own baby and to maim her husband, Christopher, whom it is said she caused to become lame by transforming Sathan into a toad. The toad was then allegedly instructed to jump into one of his boots, which in turn was believed to have caused the lameness.

Elizabeth shared Sathan with her sister Agnes, and again the trial reports that she got the imp to kill her own husband along with one of her own pigs, in return for a drop of her blood and a chicken. Agnes had taught her eighteen-year-old daughter Joan the old craft and ways of the witch, and again the trial evidence suggest that Joan also used the cat Sathan for her own spells. On one occasion Joan enticed Sathan from under her mother's bed. However, the cat suddenly shapeshifted into a large horned dog, with the head of an ape and a silver whistle and chain around its neck.[13] Joan sent the creature to bewitch Agnes Brown as

---

12. Witchcraft in Tudor and Stuart England by Alan Macfarlane.

13. Michael Howard mentions that it is widely believed that a silver whistle was used by a 'master of witches' to summon the coven under his control or to conjure up spirits. See East Anglian Witches and Wizards page 39.

she had refused Joan some food. The horned imp caused some paralysis to Miss Brown and although only a child herself, the evidence was presented.[14]

There is a curious tale about young Agnes Brown, and her bizarre interaction with the horned dog and some churned butter, which was again given in evidence. Agnes Brown seemed to wallow in the limelight of the trial and obviously had an active imagination which was no doubt aided by suggestion and fear. The tale is told something like this:

One day Miss Agnes Brown had been churning butter at the farmstead on the edge of Hatfield Peverel, when she was approached by a strange creature around the size of a dog. It was black in colour and had a grotesque horned head, a short tail and a chain with a silver whistle hanging around its neck. The animal danced around her in a frightening manner, skipping and leaping to and fro, and sitting on the top of a nettle, but Agnes Brown conquered her fear sufficiently to ask what it wanted. The imp replied that it wanted some freshly churned butter. She refused to give any and the beast ran away. However, the hell-dog decided to visit the dairy and opened the door with a key it had secreted in its mouth. It then returned to Agnes Brown stating that it had found some butter and had especially churned it for her.

When little Agnes told her parents about this decidedly peculiar experience, they sought the advice of a priest who suggested that they pray at once. This helped the farming family but had no effect on the horned dog. The beast returned the next day, still carrying the key in its mouth. Agnes invoked the name of Jesus and the animal disappeared. But it was obviously hungry for some butter to put on a piece of bread, as it reappeared later the same day with a bit of bread and asked for butter to be spread upon it. Agnes again refused, saying there wasn't any butter left.

The last appearance of the strange dog-like beast was a few days later, when it again appeared in front of Agnes Brown

---

14. Essex Witches by Glynn H. Morgan

with a knife in its mouth. It urged Agnes to stab herself in the heart. She refused and told him to drop the knife in the name of Jesus, but he said he couldn't as he would not be parted from the knife of his dame. When asked who this dame was, he replied Mother Waterhouse.[15]

They were tried at Chelmsford in July 1566, and Agnes Waterhouse was found guilty and was hanged. Her daughter Joan was found not guilty and released. Elizabeth Francis was sentenced to a year in prison. However, she was later sentenced to be hanged after she was accused of bewitching two other villagers, Mary Cocke and Alice Poole. The village has since held the somewhat eerie reputation of being home to one of the first Essex women to die on a charge of witchcraft. Incidentally, during the early and mid-1980s I used to hang out at The Prince of Orange, which at the time was Chelmsford's most wonderfully notorious pub; where bikers, punks, goths and hippies rubbed shoulders with artists, witches, musicians and visionaries. The pub and its garden became a microcosm of the town's counter-culture, where ideas were spawned, and creativity flowed. Nearby was Waterhouse Lane, which was often rumoured to have been named after the Hatfield Peverel witch family. Primrose Hill to the northern end of Waterhouse Lane, was the site of Chelmsford gallows, where many accused of witchcraft were hanged for their alleged crimes, including Agnes Waterhouse and Elizabeth Frances.

The description of the horned dog sitting on top of a nettle is interesting. This description occurs in another case at Laindon, where a familiar imp does the same and this may indicate the true nature of the Essex witch's familiar as a nature spirit. These mischievous beings are known in folklore as fairies, gnomes, hob-goblins and brownies and this may indicate some sort of localised folkloric survival of the fairy beliefs of the medieval and early modern

---

15. The Township of Hatfield Peverel by Teresa. M. Hope. 1930, p 19

period, where the witch or cunning woman would cultivate a special relationship with these liminal creatures from other realms, to aid and enhance their work. The Essex witch familiars were often presented as a weird world of occult zoology, as seen through the famous illustrations of the time. However, the folkloric shapeshifting of animals, emerges from a rich tradition within recorded folklore from across Britain.[16] Another interesting, if somewhat sporadic tradition also surfaces from the cunning folk of the same period as the witch trials, where they would consult the fairies to aid their magic, and this somewhat supports my theory that at least some of the described familiars of Essex witch history were from the oral traditions of the realms of elemental creatures.[17]

Teresa Hope, writing in 1920s Hatfield Peverel suggests that Agnes Waterhouse genuinely believed in her powers and was the village cunning woman.[18] She also suggests that Mother Eve, who was the grandmother of Agnes Waterhouse and Elizabeth Francis, may have been a witch in the truest sense, practising with others at sabbats and later passing her knowledge to her granddaughters, to keep the old ways alive within the female line of the family. I tend to agree with these sentiments as, reading between the lines in this particular case, there does appear to be a defined family lineage of esoteric knowledge, albeit wrapped up in the garbled political nonsense of the time. So, Hatfield Peverel really was the Witch Village at the centre of eastern Essex, and I have my suspicions that this continued up to, and beyond the time of Teresa Hope. Miss Hope was a member of the Essex Archaeological Society, and she meticulously recorded much of the folklore, archaeology and social history of the parish in the 1920s. Some believe she was

---

16. Call of the Horned Piper by Nigel Aldcroft Jackson, p 40
17. Popular Magic: Cunning-folk in English History by Owen Davies, pp 95, 182, 183, 184
18. The Township of Hatfield Peverel by Teresa. M. Hope. 1930, p 23

also a cunning woman, or at least had some sympathies with the old profession.[19] She lived on the edge of the village at the delightful eighteenth century Crix House, sited close to the beautiful river Ter.

Throughout this book there are references to many other cases of witchcraft of sixteenth and seventeenth century Essex. There is no way of knowing if any of these women were practising witchcraft, due to the nature of their horrendously unfair and unjust treatment. However, the belief in witchcraft was real; and there was, and always still is, the question of whether they were practising as cunning women or herbalists. The answer is not as obvious as you may think, and many of the Essex trials were full of folkloric and esoteric claims and counter claims, which in themselves can often lead to interesting conclusions. It is worth remembering that many of these women were living as widows or spinsters, forced to live on the edge of society with no way of supporting themselves and no right to anything, including property and even the basics such as food. Many of the accused, including Agnes Waterhouse, lived through the turbulent times of the Reformation and it is telling that Agnes could only say her prayers in Latin, which would have been a deciding factor of her guilt at her Elizabethan trial.[20] Devonshire folklorist and historian Tracey Norman has written a brilliant play entitled WITCH and the tale gives a great insight into the historical witchcraft accusations across England and leaves the audience with the conundrum – was she or wasn't she a witch? [21]

---

19. Oral tradition collected from the village by the author during the 1980s.

20. Female Power: A study on witchcraft in Elizabethan Essex by Kate J. Cole, p 13

21. WITCH, an historical play written by Tracey Norman and produced by Circle of Spears Productions. Based on historic records, WITCH has been performed around the United Kingdom for several years and researched through archival evidence of witchcraft trials in Dorset. www.traceynormanswitch.com

part one: tendring

Cross Tenpenny Heath by moonlight, when the shadows are deep between the hedgerows and the waters of Alresford Creek glint beyond the trees. Drop silently into Wivenhoe and stand on the river's brink, where small rowing boats glide over the dark waters of the river, trailing wakes of silver.

Glyn H. Morgan

The large peninsula that forms the bulk of the north-eastern Essex shore is bounded by two main rivers, in the north by the Stour and to the south and west by the Colne. Tendring refers to the old name of the hundred within northeast Essex, and is also a modern district council area. However, I have used the name to refer to the greater peninsula for the purposes of this book. The old hundreds of England were set up to provide varying support for the state, including being able to provide a surplus to support one hundred soldiers, or to refer to an area of one hundred hides, which was supposed to be able to support four families to each hide.

The district contains the most easterly headland in Essex at Walton-on-the-Naze, and the western side of this headland contains a secret archipelago, containing the most easterly inhabited island in Britain. Horsey Island lies in the centre of Hamford Water and can be accessed at low tide via a causeway, which crosses a stretch of water known as the Wade.[22] This is an isolated area of saltings, luminous marshes, and tidal creeks and is a nature reserve of national importance. This mysterious area was the inspiration for Arthur Ransome's *'Swallows and Amazons'* novel *Secret Water*. There is a curious and rare piece of fairy folklore associated with the islands and marshes of Hamford Water. An old tradition dictates that you should put out a bowl of oatmeal for the faeries or brownies at night, to keep them friendly and helpful and to appease the spirits of the saltmarsh.[23] To the east on the Naze promontory rises a tall and gaunt tower, now precariously close to the edge of the crumbling cliffs. When the tower was built it stood at least a quarter mile inland, but over the ensuing centuries erosion has eaten away the edge, moving the coastline westward, and the sentinel now stands less than 50 metres from the precipice. The tower was erected by Trinity House in 1720 to serve as an aid to navigation along the Essex coast. It was designed with the idea that a beacon could be lit on the top, serving as an early form of lighthouse. Tudor maps show that there was a tower of some sort on the Naze since at least the fifteenth century.

It was here at the beginning of the twentieth century that the first of only two known Essex sea serpent sightings was witnessed. One fine morning, Tom Poole, water bailiff and sailor from Brightlingsea was waiting for high tide at Walton Backwater, when a holiday maker, bathing from his boat shouted out that something unusual was swimming towards them. Between their respective boats appeared a creature with a slim neck about four feet long and a head like that of a sheep, but larger. It swam along, turning its head from side to side before it disappeared. It reappeared up tide shortly

---

22. Horsey Island is privately owned, so permission must be sought to explore.
23. Matthew Hopkins: Witch Finder General by Richard Deacon, p 51

afterwards, five hundred yards to the east, where it made off into open sea.[24]

The River Stour forms the boundary between Essex and Suffolk, and historically, the frontier between the old kingdoms of Essex and East Anglia. At its mouth, the river provides both passenger and freight docks of considerable size. The name Stour is a common river name in England, and its origin may lie in the Celtic word *Sturr*, translating as strong, or maybe the Middle English *Stor,* (powerful). Either way the meaning is clear as a strong and powerful waterway delineating the East Saxons old North borderland.

---

24. Last Strong Hold of Sail by Hervey Benham, p 173

1. Manningtree and Harwich

This area is dominated by the dark and despicable deeds of the self-styled witch-finder Matthew Hopkins, who based his reign of terror on the port of Manningtree. The town grew around the wool trade from the fifteenth century and had a thriving shipping trade in corn, timber, and coal until this declined with the coming of the railway. Manningtree also has the distinction of being the smallest town in England, and its sinister past is certainly one of the darkest in the history of witch persecution.

It is easier to begin to get a feel of the utter despair and suspicion during the Manningtree witch-finder period, by

1. Manningtree and Harwich

looking at the political situation of the time. The English civil war was raging across the land, and the area was strongly Puritan and Parliamentarian. Drinking, dancing, sports, and the arts were considered sinful, and theatres were being closed and the feasting and celebration of Christmas forbidden. Archbishop William Laud had been beheaded for his beliefs, and the Protestant Reformation was causing chaos and anxiety. It was within this political mix that pestilence prevailed. There was little employment for the lower classes and the middle classes were on the lookout for scapegoats. The Devil was often blamed for the failure of society, and where disease, death and starvation were rife, superstition could easily be perceived as the enemy. Iconoclasts were everywhere. Defacing shrines, smashing the heads off statues, and destroying sacred relics. The stereotype of the witch was an easy target for all that had seemingly gone wrong with the world. Manningtree, along with neighbouring villages of Mistley and Lawford were about to be 'saved' by Matthew Hopkins and his side-kick, John Stearne.

Hopkins, who self-styled himself as Witchfinder-General, was a young and flamboyant character, who dressed in fine clothes and striking hats. He owned a greyhound, who would most often be at his side as he strolled around the quayside close to the Thorn Inn, a pub that he purchased as the centre of his operations. It all began in March 1645, when Elizabeth Clarke was accused of bewitching a tailor's wife by 'cunning woman Hovye' from nearby Hadleigh, a town on the Suffolk side of the Stour. The tailor's wife had visited Hovye after suffering from lameness and convulsions, and Cunning Hovye had diagnosed the conditions as being inflicted by a curse from her neighbour, Elizabeth Clarke.

Elizabeth was the prime suspect because her mother had been hanged as a witch a few years before. She was questioned by Hopkins and later interrogated by Stearne, who was a renowned psychopath and illegal torturer. She confessed to keeping company with other witches and was found to have three unnatural teats. She was kept under house arrest and 'watched' for familiars. On the third night, she confessed to having indulged in copulation with the devil, who appeared as a normal man. Shortly after this confession, Hopkins and Stearne allegedly witnessed an astonishing procession of bizarre creatures entering the room. A white kitten called Holt, a fat white dog with red spots and stumpy legs, whose name was Jamara, a greyhound with long legs and a horned head of an ox called Vinegar Tom, a black rabbit with the name Sack and Sugar and a pole cat with a grotesque head called Newes, plus four more which were named but not illustrated, called Elemauzer, Pyewacket, Pecke in the Crown and Grizzell Greedigutt. It was noted that Vinegar Tom could also turn into a boy without a head and that other imps would also visit Elizabeth and would transform into men at her bedside before copulation.

It is interesting to note that Elizabeth Clarke was accused by a cunning woman, who no doubt wanted to avert the attention away from her own services. I wonder how many times this happened, but was never recorded? The famous, and much published woodcut of the time features Elizabeth and her familiars, with Hopkins looking on. The other witch is probably Anne West, who was from nearby Lawford and was named as Elizabeth Clarke's witchcraft teacher. [25] Elizabeth's ghost is said to haunt the mudflats of Seafield Bay, sited just over the river on the Suffolk side. Maybe this was an area that Elizabeth and Anne liked to frequent during their life?[26]

Hopkins had some highly questionable methods of investigation, which heavily drew inspiration from the *Daemonologie* of King James, which was directly cited in Hopkins own book, *The Discovery of Witches*. At the time,

---

25. Princes and Peoples: France and the British Isles, 1620-1714: An Anthology of Primary Sources by Margaret Lucille Kekewich

26. www.culture24.org.uk/history-and-heritage/art540471-witchfinder-general-matthew-hopkins-essex

torture was outlawed in England, though it is reported that Hopkins often used techniques such as sleep deprivation to gain confessions from his victims. Sometimes he would cut the arm of the accused with a blunt knife, and if she did not bleed, it was proof that she was a witch. Another of his methods was to 'swim a witch', based on Hopkins own assumption that as witches had renounced baptism, all water would reject them, by making them float. Individual suspects were tied to a chair and immersed into a pond or lake. Those who 'swam' (floated) were guilty. Hopkins and his assistants also looked for the Devil's mark or teat. This was usually a mole, birthmark, or wart. If the suspected witch had no visible marks, invisible ones could be discovered by pricking. Hopkins employed 'witch prickers' to stab the accused with special needles, looking for such marks and it was believed that the witch's familiar would drink the witch's blood from the mark, as a baby drinks milk from the nipple.

Despite rumours that Hopkins himself was swum as a witch, Matthew Hopkins died at his home in Manningtree, on 12th August 1647. He was twenty-six years old. During his career he is believed to have been responsible for the deaths of at least three hundred women. Hopkins was suspected of practicing witchcraft towards the end of his life, and he was accused of acquiring a book containing the names of all the witches in England, which he obtained by means of sorcery. He was buried a few hours after his death in the churchyard of St Mary at Mistley Heath.[27] This medieval church and graveyard is now lost, with a few scant remains scattered between the trees and tangled undergrowth along Heath Road, close to Church Farm.

Nearby lies Mistley pond, where Hopkins 'swam' his witches, and there have been periodic reports of Hopkins' ghost appearing at the pond, shimmering ominously under the light of a full moon. In the neighbouring woods is an ancient oak tree called 'Old Knobbley', thought to be

---

27. Notes & Queries, 1st series, vol. 10, p. 283, 7th Oct 1854

at least eight hundred years old. This wonderfully mature tree has local folklore associated with it, which may link it to the Witchfinder's reign of terror. It is believed that many of his victims used the hollow tree trunk to hide from Hopkins and his fellow psychopaths. The tree was and still is a focal point and would certainly have been used as a meeting place, within the heart of the ancient woodland that once surrounded it. It is interesting to note that Stewart Farrah, writer and prominent twentieth century Alexandrian witch, wrote a script called 'The Witch's Bottle' loosely based on the folklore surrounding 'Old Knobbley' and Mathew Hopkins, for the Thames Television series 'Shadows', which aired in the mid-1970s. The road between Manningtree and Mistley is also home to a ghostly Black and White Shuck, who is believed to appear as an ominous warning of a death in the Norman family.[28] This local family have a large and highly polished black granite Egyptian-style mausoleum in the graveyard of Mistley Towers, and the spectral dog has also been seen wandering around the graves, close to the tomb.[29]

Nearby, at Wrabness, lies an iconic temple-like structure, seemingly celebrating the unusual qualities of the Essex seaboard. It sits like a glowing wayside shrine of saltmarsh alchemy, and it speaks to me as both a memorial and mausoleum to the dark and sinister history of this corner of Essex. Controversial and provocative, Grayson Perry's House for Essex rises from the coastal plain overlooking the Stour estuary, as a giant beacon of gold, red and green. This folly tells the narrative of the life and death of fictional Essex girl Julie May Cope. The outside of the amazing structure is reminiscent of the style and ambience of a medieval Norwegian stave church, yet it is also ultra-modern and brutal. The exterior is covered in green

---

28. The Ghost Book by A. A. MacGregor. Robert Hale, 1955, p. 72
29. www.paranormaldatabase.com/essex/esspages/essex.htm

1. Manningtree and Harwich

ceramic tiles depicting a stylised version of a Sheela-na-Gig, alongside tiles of the Essex coat of arms and the images of hearts and pins. It somehow mixes folk-art with hints of neo-ecclesiastical architecture and is both a celebration of secular womanhood and of the ancient Earth Goddess. Whether loved or loathed, this striking and ornate building brings some exciting and colourful eccentricity to this area of the liminal shore, and I think that it will add an extra and welcome dimension to the Essex coastal folk-narratives of the future.

At the mouth of the Stour lies the port of Harwich, with its busy docks and ferries, connecting Essex to the Hook of Holland. The town once had a hereditary witch family with the name Hanby. Elizabeth Hanby was hanged for witchcraft on 20th April 1601, and she was thought to be the eldest of three generations of witches in the town. The port saw twenty-seven women hang for witchcraft during the seventeenth century. The hangings were always a public spectacle and were centred on the Tudor manor house called The Three Cups. Built next-door to the former medieval chapel of St Nicholas, the house which dates to around 1500 was later converted into a hotel and has been modified over the years, with a Georgian façade added in the eighteenth century. The building has been at the centre of civic life in the town and was used as a court to hold sessions of the peace, where many of the town's accused witches were interviewed during the seventeenth century, and as an interim council chamber during the eighteenth and early nineteenth centuries. The hotel played host to some very famous guests. Queen Elizabeth stayed in August 1561, and in November 1734 the Princess of Orange was forced to spend several days in Harwich because there was insufficient wind for her to sail back to Holland. Local legend states that Admiral Nelson stayed in the hotel several times, and his last visit was in 1801 where it is reputed that he met up with his secret lover, Lady Hamilton and stayed overnight. A ghostly apparition of Lady Hamilton has periodically been seen in the hostelry, possibly seeking the return of Nelson?[30] The inn was finally closed in 1995 and is now a private residence.

There is an interesting glimpse into the town's cultural activities during a regatta, which was held on the 21st of August 1834. The local paper reported that the entertainment and activities included a duck hunt, horse, pony and donkey racing, jumping in sacks, climbing a greasy pole for a leg of mutton and a grinning match, where four men were to grin through horse's collars, and the ugliest face would win a prize. There was also a 'Tea drinking' competition, where the first to drink six cups would win 'one pound of strong tea'.[31]

In 1605, Harwich woman, Mary Hart was charged with bewitching seven pounds of meat and turning it rancid. She was found innocent and released. However, the following year, she was convicted in a session at the Three Cups on a charge of bewitching a sailor and of killing him by sorcery.[32] This time she was found guilty and was hanged. The surname Hart was linked to other witch families in Essex, notably on the Dengie and Rochford peninsulas, further to the south.

The next Harwich witch trial was that of Jane Wiggins and took place in 1634, where she was accused of bewitching an entire ship and its crew. So, how had this happened? Well, as you might expect, Jane was hungry, so she went to the harbour to ask for some fish for her supper. She met up with Anthony Payne, who was the master of a fishing vessel, which was being made ready to sail from Harwich harbour. Jane had previously been known to the crew and was often found hanging around the ship, asking for food which may well have been in payment for her services as a cunning woman. However, Payne was reluctant to give her any more fish, and it was alleged that she cursed the vessel

---

30. www.thethreecups.com/part-5
31. The Essex Standard – Friday 15 August 1834
32. The Harwich Society Journal, No.109, 1997: The Three Cups by Winifred Cooper

1. Manningtree and Harwich

and all the crew. Jane had also been found keeping imps under her bed. These imps took the shape of three large rats with staring eyes and were initially found whilst Jane was out trying to accrue some fuel for her hearth to keep her warm. Her accuser, Thomasine Hedge also had other tales to tell. Apparently, the previous year at Michaelmas, she saw Wiggins carrying two imps in the form of huge rats. They were kept in a box and she left one of them at the house of Edward Maiers, who died four days later. She sent another of her familiars to the home of Margaret Garrett to bewitch her with pains and lameness because she said Margaret wouldn't give her any starch. To aid her in her conjurations, Jane also kept two other familiars that took the shape and likeness of blackbirds, but were reported to have been closer to the size of a chicken. Jane Wiggins was sent to trial before the assizes held at Chelmsford on 26th February 1634. She was eventually found guilty and was subsequently hanged as a witch.[33]

Bridget Weaver seems to have been the last recorded historic Harwich witch. She was tried in 1660 for feeding an evil spirit in the likeness of a bird and for suckling one of Satan's imps.[34] She was initially found guilty and was fined. However, she seems to have survived and was subsequently acquitted, and she promptly disappeared from the history of the town.[35]

An incredible legend of ghostly phenomena and quasi-religious lore has been linked to the Three Cups hotel as witnessed by early twentieth century author, sailor, and artist Donald Maxwell. Although it could probably be described as folkloresque, rather than a traditional tale of the town, and it was undoubtedly embellished by the landlord and staff of the tavern when Maxwell visited, in December 1920.

---

33. Essex Witches by Peter C. Brown
34. Clacton and Harwich and the Essex Sunshine Coast by Terry Palmer, p 45
35. Witch Hunting and Witch Trials by C L'Estrange Ewen, p 253

The tale begins when Maxwell was sailing a small yacht from Lowestoft to Harwich in December 1920. It deals with the patron saint of Harwich, St Nicholas, and some of the folklore associated with him. It is interesting to think about St Nicholas as the 'lord of the sea' and patron of sailors in this context and I think that it is worth repeating the story in its entirety due to Maxwell's wonderfully atmospheric, first-hand experience.

The Legend of the Three Cups

Upon an evening in December, when the wind is in the north-east and when the ocean is grey and the sky leaden, the North Sea is not attractive. When, in addition to these cheerless circumstances, it surrounded me when I was single-handed in a small yacht at night-fall, still many miles from safety, the chances of a comfortable time seemed very remote. I could not boil a kettle and the prospect of lying at anchor until daylight was purgatorial.

I had done a somewhat foolish thing in trying to bring a yacht from Lowestoft to Harwich without any assistance, but as most of the way I was to have a tow by a trawler, and as time was pressing, I thought I would risk it. With a wind like this, I could easily make the Stour when I cast off somewhere between Felixstowe and the Naze.

Everything went according to programme, but after I had let go and made sail several unrehearsed episodes caused delay. The wind had freshened considerably, and I was carrying far too much sail, but being single-handed I shirked taking in a reef. Soon the gaff carried away and I hove-to wallowing in a sea-way until I had made good. This all took time and I feared I might not make the entrance to the river before the tide was heavily against me. Late, however, as it was, I forged ahead over the ebb I could see that I was going to do it, the lights of Harwich heralding a safe anchorage.

It was slow work, wet work and heavy work, wind against tide and a short fierce sea. At last I was in and I took the mud not far from Harwich church upon that bit of shore where the "low-light"

1. Manningtree and Harwich

stands, that curious survival, once a lighthouse, now a shelter. I was in no mood for another night on board, so I stowed everything, put up a riding-light, threw some clothes into a bag and waded ashore, the tide having ebbed sufficiently to allow me to do so. Being the evening of December 5th, the temperature of the water although higher than I had expected to find it, was sufficiently low to make me vow to do no more single-handed winter cruising, whatever the pictorial possibilities might be.

The shore was deserted. It would not be likely that anyone would be about in such cold weather. Against the sky I could see the dim outline of another lighthouse, now dark like the shelter, once the "high-light" which gave a bearing for the entrance, when seen in line with the "low". The gaunt tower of the church loomed up against a rushing mass of clouds that portended snow before the morning.

I sat down in the shelter, put on my shoes and socks and took stock of my position. There were a few lights in the dark mass of houses across the green, and I judged that I was not very far from warm fires and hospitable inns.

As I approached what I thought was the opening to a road or alley, I became aware of a dark figure just in front of me. It was that of an old man in a dress that suggested a pilot. He greeted me and we spoke of the weather and of the chances of snow, and as we walked along together, I asked him where he would advise me to put up for the night.

"The Three Cups," he said, stopping and pointing to a lighted window. "It is next to the church. I will show you the way."

I thanked him and again we walked along together. He was a curious figure and his white beard and venerable demeanour made me think what a good model he would make for St. Peter, the pilot of the Galilean lake, who "shook his mitred locks and stern bespake."

Through a narrow street we entered into a paved court, over which, upon a kind of trellis, there climbed a gigantic clematis. A welcome light streamed out, chequering the flagstones at our feet. Through the window I could see a roaring fire and a glimpse of warmth and comfort that made me very glad I was not still upon the sea. I turned to thank the old man for his courtesy and to invite him to come inside, when I found that he had gone. I went back to the entrance to the courtyard, but no one was in sight. I could have sworn that he had entered the courtyard with me, but I had evidently been mistaken.

I am not superstitious, but I felt there was something strange in the sudden advent of the old man out of the darkness and his equally sudden disappearance. A hot bath, however, and the genial hospitality of mine host of "The Three Cups" soon put the incident out of my head, and I began to realize as I got through a prodigious supper how wet and cold and miserable I must have been.

Although I had often been to the Continent via Harwich in the days before the war and had often been into Harwich on naval occasions during the war, I had never seen the town at all, so before turning in I went for a stroll through the quaint streets and quays of the old town.

It was very dark. One of the two unlighted lighthouses, the tall one, dominated a street like a ghostly sentinel. Out in the river, over towards Parkeston, lay three lights under repair, and there was another alongside the quay by the Train Ferry. Both lighthouses and lightships gave darkness rather than light, and all Harwich seemed to be under a black spell. Its narrow ways were dimly discerned, its windows were for the most part unlighted and where an occasional glimmer shows ghostly images of houses, the shadows were the deeper by contrast and the silence of night was supreme, save for a moaning in the wind across the dark reaches of the Stygian Stour.

I passed three doors, the most curious three doors I should think to be found anywhere and then a place labelled "Naval Yard," though it was a ghostly place not known to the Navy of to-day. A slipway was overgrown with clematis, anchors were buried in weeds and a bell, gaunt and neglected-looking, never summoned any one to work.

Time was when this was a place of ship-building and naval activity, now leased I believe from the Admiralty, who still own it, by a firm for the purpose of repairing lightships and other vessels,

1. Manningtree and Harwich

but the resuscitation of so small a part of the activities of such a place serves to make it more desolate than ever. In the daytime, across a wilderness of decay and grass-grown litter, hammering proceeds and ghostly noises suggesting that a few of the old-time workers have been dug up and are still doomed to do something and to potter about amidst the ruins.

At the corner, on the waterside, standing away from the yard by some fifty feet, is a bulk, and by this, half in the water and half out, is another derelict adding to the desolate look of the foreshore.

The shed on the quay contains a double wheel worked by manpower, for working the crane. It is a very rare survival. As far as I know there are only two examples of this "machine" in England - one which I have sketched in Unknown Kent, at Great Culand Farm, Burham, near Rochester, the other in Carisbrooke Castle. These two are wheels for the purpose of drawing water.

Regaining the light and cheerful fireside of "The Three Cups" I sat and talked with mine host for a while, and he tells me, what I much want to know, what he considers is the origin of the sign and how "The Three Cups" came to be.

The Church of St. Nicholas and "The Three Cups" often, he says, go together. And he tells me that the usual explanation of the sign is that it is a corruption of "The Three Purses," which is one of the most common symbols of St. Nicholas. He maintains that it is held by most that these purses (golden bags tied at the neck) have been turned upside down - hence the present sign.

I take this with a grain of salt, as it seems very strange that this mistake can have been made in so many cases, but I am bound to admit that no one seems to have any other explanation of the association of the three cups with the saint who is no less than our old friend Santa Claus, the patron saint of travellers, sailors, children and dowerless maidens. The purses appeared in this way. Santa Claus or St. Nicholas was a real person, Bishop of Myra, in Asia Minor.

A certain nobleman, it is recorded, had fallen upon evil days, and had become so impoverished that he had no dowry for his three daughters, and it looked as if they would come to dire misfortune. The good bishop hears of their distress, however, and goes secretly to the nobleman's house, placing a purse of gold into an open window. Suitors are immediately forthcoming and one of the daughters marries "well." Again St. Nicholas places another purse of gold in the open window and a second daughter marries. On the occasion, however, of placing the third purse at the window, to enable the third daughter to marry, he is seen and the story of his good works spreads throughout the land. Thus, the three purses became the chief symbol of St. Nicholas.

And so to bed, mine host lighting the way. "You see," he says, "your room contains a portrait of St. Nicholas," and he pointed to a curious old picture not unlike an ikon. "You are in luck to-night for to-morrow is the feast of St. Nicholas. Good night and may the Saint preserve you."

I bade him good night and then when he had gone took a candle and looked again at the picture. The face was familiar, St. Nicholas according to the artist was not at all unlike the old pilot who had shown me the way to "The Three Cups."

I suppose I soon dropped off to sleep. From my bed I could see the part of the overshadowing tower of the Church of St. Nicholas. A thin layer of fine snow was outlining cornices, and the tracery of a window; I noted the chime at half-past ten.

It was three o'clock. I hear the hour strike. Darkness had given place to light. White roofs and glittering gables gleam under the moon riding high in cloudless blue.

The whole town seemed to be awake. There were lights in the windows and lights in the streets. I leaped out of bed and went to the window - the window that looks out upon the church. There was a light upon the roof - a man with a lantern standing upon the parapet looking towards the river and waving it to and fro as if to signal. It was a familiar figure, the old pilot of last night and St. Nicholas, good St. Nicholas, the friend of sailors.

And I saw three ships come sailing in, upon the flood tide, into the Stour and into the harbour of Harwich.

I was soon dressed and running up the street towards the quay. The river, so dark and dead last night, was alive with craft. The lightships were blazing and revolving, the

1. Manningtree and Harwich

lighthouses shining their beams across the water. In every window of every house, lamps were lit and tapers fair, as if to welcome guests of honour as they pass through the streets. And the people looked out of the windows, but all was silent, for a great light came from the harbour where the three ships lay. And there came three Kings and each carried a golden cup, and they went through the streets till they came to the Church of St. Nicholas. And the first of the Kings wore a vesture of white, and the second of the Kings wore a vesture of gold and the third of the Kings wore a vesture of red, and they had crowns upon their heads and carried the golden cups before them. And they stood before the door of the church and entered in.

Now when they knelt before the altar to worship Him, who is the King of Kings, and to share the Sacred Feast, the priest who was before the altar took the golden chalice and with it touched the cups of the Kings. And the three Kings bowed and went forth from the church and into the inn. And in the cup of the first King was poured forth wine to all who should receive it. And the wine of that cup was white as crystal. And in the cup of the second King was poured forth wine to all who should receive it. And the wine of that cup was golden. And then in the cup of the third King was poured forth wine to all who should receive it. And the wine of that cup was red. And the people of the inn and of the town drank of the wine and made merry and rejoiced because the Kings had come to Harwich. And I sought the Pilot and beseeched him that he would interpret to me the mystery of the cups, and he made clear the parable.

"In the cups are the Wine of Life. And that which is white is Truth, and that which is golden is Power, and that which is red is Love. And because the Kings have come to Bethlehem the wine which they carry has become precious and because their cups have touched the sacred Cup upon the altar all wine in the inns of the town and of this land has become sacred to men of good will. And he who drinks of the wine that is white, shall know the Truth. And he who drinks of the wine that is golden, shall know of Power. And he who drinks of

the wine that is red, shall know of Love. For the King has come, that we shall have life, and have it more abundantly."

But these were difficult sayings, and I besought the Pilot that he should tell me how came the Kings of the East to Harwich, for Harwich lies not upon the way to Bethlehem; and why do they come so far? Then the Pilot smiled and said: "Know you not that all places are upon the Way to Bethlehem?"

Then I understood the saying, and I knew who were the Kings. For they that seek shall find, and they that are true men are become priests and kings in the City of God.

The clock struck nine, I awoke and looked out of the window, a cloak of snow was over everything in Harwich. I was soon out and walking down the road towards the harbour. Then I remembered my dream, suddenly, for it had gone from me.

There were the lightships out in the river, a cluster of them dark and forsaken; and there was the tall lighthouse, seen down the street, showing no signs of having shown a light for many a long year, and the low light equally dark and of no account to navigation, looking out upon the water like a blind man who sits beside the highway. A few turns brought me back to the road by the church, and there before me was the scene of my vision of last night, the very place where I had seen the Three Kings, vested in white and gold and red, entering the church. And there - I had not noticed them before - upon the parapet of the hotel were the three cups each with a foaming top of snow.

So now, whoever you may be, when you go to Harwich and see this sign, think of good St. Nicholas, and learn to drink well and wisely of the wine of life.[36]

The town has a history of folkloric practice around the Christmas season, which encouraged the folk-narrative of misrule. First recorded in 1535, the town's youth would congregate in the parish church of St Nicholas, to choose their 'lord', who would be 'crowned' as the Lord of Misrule for the season of Yuletide. Once chosen, he would lead a

---

36. Unknown Essex by Donald Maxwell, 1925, pp 103-117.

1. Manningtree and Harwich

band of noisy musicians and dancers around the streets of the town, encouraging all to leave their homes and make merry.[37]

In 1854, the shipwrights of the town decided to create an event that would both celebrate and commemorate their work, by holding a torch-lit procession in the style of a public demonstration. They called it the Shipwright's Carnival and in the early days it was led by torch bearers and was followed by model ships decorated with lighted candles. These were then followed by the 'guying' men who donned 'Sandwich Boards' which carried slogans and poems which made fun of their bosses. This practice was known as guying, and this eventually gave the event its name of the Harwich Guy Carnival. The event was used to collect money which was shared between naval workers, longshoremen and the poor of the town, and was held on two separate nights at the beginning of November. The second night was also known as Mayor choosing night.[38] Over the following few years, the event very quickly turned into a mix of the shipwright's procession and the more traditional Guy Fawkes parade, and I suspect this was partly due to the time of year that it was held and also the local practice of guying getting mixed up with a penny-for-the-guy. However, it did keep many local and distinct elements, including the Big Heads and the Pithy Pars, which is based on the old Shipwright carnival tradition of carrying a message which makes fun of someone you know and may include a short poem or verse about them. During the 1930s these 'pithy pars' were subsequently published around town on posters and eventually published in the carnival programmes each year.

The Shipwright's carnival continued to expand with bigger, better, and newer traditions being added throughout the rest of the century, and it subsequently became larger and more diverse in its costumes and boat designs. This

---

37. The Stations of the Sun: A History of the Ritual Year in Britain by Ronald Hutton, p 108
38. www.harwichanddovercourt.co.uk/guy-carnival

theme continued well into the twentieth century, barring stoppages for the two world wars. At the procession's height, the Navy yard employees carried six-foot models of fully rigged sailing ships that were illuminated from within by oil lamps, which would have stood out wonderfully within the darkness of a November night. Bonfires were frequently lit at several points throughout the town, often on the foreshore and in the dark narrow streets, and this fiery practise had much in common with many other celebrations around this time of year, particularly the tar barrels at Burnham-on-Crouch. The fiery element of the carnival has continued, and is still prominent today. For many years during the twentieth century, the music was provided by various town bands, including the Parkeston Quay Marine Workshop's Band.

This entire event probably had its origins in the traditions of the secret societies of the Bonfire Boys of the Victorian era, which were mostly populated by young male artisans and labourers from a cross-section of trades. Harwich had its own variant on this theme, made up of the town's young men from the shipwright trade.[39]

Smuggling was rife around the Stour estuary during the eighteenth and nineteenth centuries, and much of the smuggling involved the postal packets based at Harwich. Although these ships were only supposed to carry mail, passengers, and their luggage, many would take on private cargoes. Not all the smuggling vessels unloaded their illicit trade in the mouth of the estuary. Some travelled up-stream as far as Manningtree, where a secret tunnel was used between the quayside and the sixteenth century White Hart Inn. However, the Three Cups Inn was at the heart of the Harwich smuggling operations with a huge cellar and tunnels going off in many different directions, one of which goes under

---

39. *The Stations of the Sun: A History of the Ritual year in Britain* by Ronald Hutton, pp 399 - 400

1. Manningtree and Harwich

Church Street and towards the Guildhall and another heads north-east towards the sea.[40]

One of the most famous of the Harwich smugglers was Bessie Catchpole, who took over the family 'free-trade' business when her husband was killed trying to bring in a haul of tobacco and spirits. She first set foot on the family yawl *'The Sally'* dressed as a man, and she quickly punched a sailor to the ground for laughing at her. She ran the smuggling business for more than two years, keeping suspicion at bay by attending church and having an air of respectability about her, whilst on land, around the town. [41]

The fishing fleet of the town has a long history, and a Trinity House return of 1581 shows that from 1576, the fishing fleets at Harwich and Manningtree had increased by three boats of twenty-five tons. Fishing at Harwich has gone through a series of booms and busts, and during the beginning of the eighteenth century the fleet was down to just three smacks. However, within half a century, fishing was booming again, and as many as five hundred men fished from Harwich, mostly around the Orkneys and the Norwegian coast. Besides trawling for shrimps, the nineteenth century fleet consisted of about twenty bawleys and small smacks, fishing for whelks, which were used as bait for long-line fishing by the larger smacks. By the beginning of the twentieth century the fleet had shrunk once more, concentrating on cod and pink shrimp. The fisherman of Harwich had an old saying that when a pack of white ghost hounds appear in the town, a disaster will befall. These ghost dogs last appeared just before the 1953 North Sea flood.[42] It is interesting to note that these ghostly hounds were white, rather than the more usual supernatural black

---

40. www.thethreecups.com/historical-snippets
41. The Fabled Coast by Sophia Kingshill and Jennifer Westwood, p 133
42. Phantom Dogs in Essex by Ivan Bunn. Essex Landscape Mysteries, No. 2. 1981

dogs of Essex, known as Shucks, of which there are plenty as you head south. However, there is a tantalising clue that the far north-east of Essex once may have had its very own spooky black shuck story. On the banks of the Stour, in the village of Lawford, a marshy area by the river was once known as Shuck Mere Heath, which appears on the 1801 OS map.[43] Maybe this is linked to the black and white shuck of nearby Mistley Towers?

The third Thursday in May every year is the Kitchel throwing ceremony and Mayor Making Day in Harwich. The traditional proceedings include the Mayor and associated Council members processing along Church Street to the Guildhall. Many of the council members wear the traditional robes and black bicorne hats, including the Mayor, who is distinguishable by the Mayoral chain. The leading dignitary also carries a ceremonial staff. Children wait excitedly, outside the Guildhall, where the Mayor stands on the Guildhall balcony, high above. Then in keeping with the ancient Harwich tradition, the newly appointed Mayor, and assisting dignitaries, throw *'kitchels'* to the children below. In excitement, the children hold their hands out to catch the buns, and gesture above to encourage more to be thrown. Kitchels are small, spiced buns, baked locally and the ceremony is unique to Harwich. Held originally for the purpose of spreading goodwill amongst the poor of the town, it has been a local tradition for centuries.[44]

The waterfront still boasts a nineteenth century working pier. Constructed in 1853 Ha'penny Pier is the town's most iconic landmark and is one of a few remaining working wooden piers in England. A ferry still runs from the pier, allowing the structure to retain its original purpose. The pier is also home to a fantastic community arts project

---

43. A Candle in the Dark: An Exploration into the Dark World of the Manningtree Witches 1645 by Jan Williams

44. East Anglian Film Archive. Cat no. 213525. Anglia News: Harwich Mayor Making and 'Kitchel' Throwing Ceremony. 1963 Harwich, Essex

1. Manningtree and Harwich

entitled *'Esturiana: Goddess of Creativity, Harwich and the Estuaries'*. This mosaic, commissioned by the Harwich festival and made by mosaic artist Anne Schwegmann-Fielding was unveiled on the summer solstice 2018, and features a salty sea goddess on the underside of a wooden rowing boat, made from sea-glass and crockery found washed up on the town's beaches. Esturiana has now found her permanent home on Ha'penny Pier, with the assistance of Harwich Haven Authority.

In the neighbouring town of Dovercourt, the local fisherman once believed that it was an ill-omen to have a woman on board their ships, as women were perceived as extremely unlucky at sea, especially on smaller vessels. This fear of sea going female passengers may stem from the folklore of the powerful sea witches who once worked their magic all along the Essex coast. There was once a folktale told in Dovercourt which was entitled *The Four-Eyed Cat*, which introduces us to the mysterious and beautiful sea witch of Dovercourt.

The tale goes something like this:

> *Once upon a time there was a beautiful young lady who lived in Dovercourt, but she was an enchantress who was 'bad at heart' and always knew 'more than a Christian should'. Many of the townsfolk wanted to condemn her as a witch, but her father was a powerful local landowner, so nobody would dare. One day the beautiful sea witch placed a spell on a local fishing boat and its crew. The skipper of the boat was due to be married the following week, but he rejected his bride-to-be for the beautiful and mesmerizing young witch, and was drawn to her through her magical powers. She had beguiled him, and they decided to run away to sea. They secretly departed one moonlit night, and sailed to the old fishing grounds, where they would weigh anchor and live a secluded life away from the town.*
>
> *Meanwhile, the following day a storm had blown up, and the rest of the fishing fleet was lost at sea. Gossip quickly*

spread around the town and soon the entire district was talking about how the skipper of the Dovercourt fleet had a stowed a secret woman on his boat, and how she wanted the rest of the fleet out of the way, so she had whistled up a storm in the fashion of the ways of the sea witches of old. Now all the fishermen of the town were dead, and because of that, a curse was laid on the beautiful sea witch of Dovercourt, and she was magically transformed into a black cat with four eyes, and ever since, her ghostly feline form prowls around after dark, haunting Dovercourt esplanade and Harwich harbour.

Because of this ghostly cat, the fishermen of Harwich and Dovercourt would never cast their nets before dawn, and very importantly they would always throw a portion of their catch back into the sea, as an offering to the 'four-eyed cat'.[45]

The town's parish church also has some strange folklore associated with it. All Saint's church once had the peculiar phenomenon of a talking cross. It spoke so much that it was impossible to get into the church because of the crowds that the discarnate holy voice had attracted, and on many occasions the door could not be shut due to the overcrowding. Although many townsfolk believed the holy rood spoke a confused gabble, and this gave rise to a local rhyme: *And now the rood of Dovercourt did speak, confirming his opinions to be true.*[46]

Heading away from the open sea, towards the west along the river Stour, you immediately enter the part of the Stour valley known as *Constable Country*. The river remains navigable for several miles, and along its lush emerald-green floodplain, beloved so much by the artist John Constable, are stories of ghosts, giants, and dragons.

Dedham has the story of a giant, who left his footprint in a stream called Black Brook. The giant, who is half remembered as the legendary Old King Cole, has a

---

45. The Fabled Coast by Sophia Kingshill and Jennifer Westwood, p 125
46. Dictionary of Phrase and Fable by E. Cobham Brewer. 1898.

1. Manningtree and Harwich

couple of features named after him in the village. Cole's Oak Lane runs along a ridge of higher ground above the Black Brook. In the lane is Cole's Oak House, which is supposedly named after a long-vanished ancient oak, and the entire area is known as Boot's Hole, reminding us of the landscape's folklore and mystery. Close to the house, in the bed of the stream is a huge folkloric footprint that was said to have been made by the giant, during one of his regular excursions from his castle at Colchester.[47]

---

47. Local Curiosities. Lantern magazine No.17, (Spring 1977), p.9.

2. witch ghost coast

Moving away from the Stour Valley back towards the central area of the Tendring peninsula we come to the village of Wix. The village church has two bells, one mounted on a turret, which was always used to call in the faithful, and the other, dating from 1460, is housed in a churchyard cage. This was the funeral bell and was only ever rung at funeral rites.[48] Local folklore tells us that the bell in the cage belonged to the old nunnery, and that the devil had pulled down the bell tower of the nunnery three times. The only way they could keep their bell safe was to house it in a cage to keep the devil out.[49]

---

48. The Essex Village Book by the Federation of Essex Women's Institutes
49. Essex Ghosts and Legends by Pamela Brooks

2. The Witch Ghost Coast

At nearby Kirby-le-Soken, at the head of the creek, lies the black weather boarded Pilot's cottage, more commonly known as the Witch's cottage, maybe telling us something about this coastal wilderness at the back of Walton town's Naze peninsula. The myriad of creeks, secret islands, and wildlife rich saltmarsh here is immense. Grey seals are common in this marshy archipelago, and the witches of the area would have undoubtedly known of the secret inlets and deserted islands where bewitchment and enchantment could take place in isolation. In July 1645, Kirby resident, Mary Coppin, was accused of bewitching Alice Astin and was sent to Chelmsford assizes. The assizes were the forerunner of the crown courts and were in session from the twelfth century until 1972. Despite witness testimonies, Mary was reprieved, but probably died in jail during the following months. In the same year, at neighbouring village of Thorpe-le-Soken, Margaret Moone was accused of suckling her feline familiars, and her daughter, Judith, was apparently known to have invisible familiars, which entered her bed after dark. Another witch from the district was Margaret Grevel, who in 1582, had caused her imps to spoil beer and batches of bread made in the vicinity. Witchcraft was still rife in the village in the mid-nineteenth century, where Goody Gardner practised her marsh-magic. She was once accused of bewitching a flock of geese and to counter the spell one of the geese was roasted alive, and whilst this particularly gruesome piece of counter-witchcraft magic was still active, the locals heard some horrifying screams and shrieks coming from Goody Gardner's cottage. She emerged with huge burns on her body and died shortly afterwards.[50] Walton witch, Margery Grew had a familiar in the shape of a Jay and was accused of bewitchment, raising spirits and murder. She was hanged in July 1645.[51]

---

50. The Dark World of Witches by Eric Maple, p 139
51. Essex Witches by Peter C Brown pp 139, 136, 111

The marshes around Thorpe-le-Soken and Beaumont-cum-Moze are haunted by an eerie luminescent bouncing cloud, which is sometimes seen around Landermere Road and towards the creeks and saltmarshes of Hamford Water. During the 1930s, two teenagers were waiting for a bus, when they saw this ghostly bouncing cloud. They described it as a large misty ball, which quickly bounced down Landermere Road, passing straight through them before continuing down Walton Road, towards the creek at Beaumont Quay. This could be a variation of the folkloric corpse candle, more popularly seen further to the south around the Blackwater Estuary; a type of localised hobgoblin or willow-the-wisp, being the souls of drowned sailors eternally seeking rest.[52]

Beaumont-cum-Moze is interesting, even if just because of the name, which comes from the Old English for *foul pit by a marsh*. The former Roman tidal cut was canalised in the nineteenth century, linking Beaumont Quay with the North Sea, via the islands and salty swamps of Hamford Water. There are the usual tales of smuggling, and of an extensive network of old smugglers tunnels linking Beaumont parish church of St Leonard and St Mary to the nearby saltmarshes and creeks and also to the neighbouring church of Thorpe-le-Soken. So, maybe the ghostly misty ball is the spirit of an old-time smuggler, wildfowler or fisherman from Thorpe or Beaumont, who was drowned in the tidal saltmarsh or lost forever in the murky depths of the North Sea?

Walton-on-the-Naze is a traditional seaside town with a pier and promenade. However, the original medieval village now lies beneath the waves; its old church finally succumbed to coastal erosion in July 1798. On stormy nights local folklore records that you can still hear the ghostly church bells ringing far out at sea. The coast here is still moving back and on the Naze peninsula it is currently eroding

---

52. www.paranormaldatabase.com/essex/esspages/essex.htm

2. The Witch Ghost Coast

around two metres a year. Clacton-on-Sea is the main coastal town in the Tendring district and was developed into a fashionable resort for Londoners in the 1860s. The town has some interesting folklore, customs, and legends. There was once a freshwater pond that held the ghost of a woman and a white horse who would rise from the watery depths during the darkness of night. The pond was sited near the London Road/St. Johns Road roundabout, possibly just to the south-west of the present roundabout.[53] During the seventeenth century, there were many accusations of witchcraft in the area. Joseph Long, the minister of Great Clacton, claimed that local woman, Anne Cooper had confessed to him that she was 'guilty of the sin of witchcraft'. She had confessed to bewitching a colt belonging to William Cottingham of Great Clacton and that she had offered the use of her imp to her daughter Sarah, and she had also sent one of her imps to kill a local girl called Mary. Another witch, Elizabeth Hare, had been accused by Mary Smith of handing over two imps for her own use. Joan Cooper also confessed to having been a witch for twenty years, and to having sent her imps to neighbouring Great Holland to kill a child of Thomas Woodward, as well as two belonging to John Cartwright. Other women accused of sorcery in the area included seventeenth century St Osyth witch, Rebecca Jones, who claimed that she had received her imps from the Devil while working at the house of John Bishop in Great Clacton, and Anne Therston of Great Holland was accused of entertaining evil spirits.[54]

Smuggling was popular during the seventeenth and eighteenth centuries, and Great Clacton was at the centre of operations. The local folklore record recalls that there were once secret tunnels between St. John's church, running to the sixteenth century Ship Inn, and from there to the

---

53. www.hiddenea.com/essexc.htm
54. East Anglia and the Hopkins Trials, 1645-1647: A County Guide by Dr Peter Elmer www.practitioners.exeter.ac.uk

coast. Illicit contraband could have easily been moved in secret along this subterranean route, enabling the villagers of Great Clacton a vital means of survival.[55]

There is an old burial ground near Little Holland Hall, close to the seafront at Holland-on-Sea, which is the site of the ruined medieval parish church and churchyard of Little Holland. This area was once a prosperous port, trading goods across the North Sea from the former harbour at Holland Haven. This port stood on the now lost Gunfleet estuary, and as was the case with so many other harbours from around the coast of Britain, the estuary begin to silt up, resulting in the eventual loss of the estuary and the harbour sometime during the seventeenth century. Consequently, the inhabitants moved away, and the church was abandoned. The ruined church and graveyard are believed to be haunted, and wispy grey figures have been seen drifting around the site after dark. Though popular culture states that they are either phantom monks or ghostly smugglers, it is more likely that they are the ghosts of those who were interred in this ancient graveyard. Interestingly, there is evidence that the graveyard pre-dates the medieval church, and may date to an earlier Anglo-Saxon period. Local folklore suggests that the cemetery marks the site of a tenth century skirmish between the Saxons and a band of Viking raiders.[56]

Nestled close to the centre of the Tendring peninsula lies Great Bentley, which is the reputed site of the largest village green in England. With an area of 17.4 hectares (43 acres). The green always has been a common, for use by the villagers, and despite several planning applications, it remains so to this day. [57] The village has its own dragon legend, which records that a female serpent once lived on Drawswords field. The serpent defied all who would try to dislodge her. They tried many different strategies and

---

55. Local tradition and lore recalled by Clacton resident Deb Langstone
56. www.historicengland.org.uk/listing/the-list/list-entry/1019665
57. The Essex Village Book by the Federation of Essex Women's Institutes

2. The Witch Ghost Coast

eventually tried to lure her away with a vat of beer from the local pub. She loved to drink the beer, but instead of being tempted away, she fell asleep once she had drunk every last drop. Eventually a local hero impaled her on his sword and bore her body in triumph to the village green. However, a spot of venom fell from her fangs on to his foot and he died. It is said that the ghost of the serpent still haunts the village, where odd sightings are still reported, and her occasional hiss is still heard. Rumour has it that she is still looking for a beer.[58] The village has other folklore and traditions, too. The village green, as already stated is thought to be the largest in England. I suspect that due to the central position of the village and green within Tendring, it became a natural meeting place for sports and games. From the eighteenth century onwards, Great Bentley green was used for all sorts of sporting events, including horse racing, quoits, and cricket. The green was also a focal point for fairs and feasts and a maypole was first erected on the site around four hundred years ago. St Swithin's fair was also held on the green, where household goods were sold, and 'cure-alls' administered by the local cunning folk, marsh wizards and charmers. The fair also had entertainment in the form of boxing, roundabouts, and swings. After the harvest had been gathered, the village green would host a 'hiring fair' where people of different trades would parade the emblems of their craft. A crook for a shepherd, a whip for a horseman and a horseshoe for a farrier. Popular village superstitions included telling the bees about a death in the household and local marsh magic instructs that if a tine of a fork accidentally struck into a person, the tine must be greased immediately in order to stop the wound from becoming infected.

A ghostly black dog, called 'Shuck' has been seen periodically throughout the years between Honeypot Corner and Moynes Farm. Smuggling was a very lucrative business

---

58. How Green is our Village. Great Bentley Through the Ages by Carl Morton

in the village during the eighteenth and nineteenth centuries, where goods were brought inland from the lonely creeks under the cover of darkness. The tale of the ghostly black dog would have helped to keep people away and allowed for some movement after dark. A phantom horse and rider story appeared in the East Essex Gazette in May 1964. The terrifying apparition was said to have manifested at Aingers Green along Dial Road.[59]

To the south lies the coastal village of St Osyth. There is a 12th century folk tradition that a dragon once prowled the area. It was described as a dragon of marvellous bigness, which burned buildings as it walked. The legend was repeated in a broadsheet published in 1704. There are lovely carvings on the late fifteenth century gatehouse of St Osyth Priory. The Dragon sits one side with St Michael opposite, decorating the entrance spandrels.

There are many other legends, folk tales, and narratives from St Osyth. The village takes its name from the old story of the holy woman who came to the area in the seventh century. It was in the vicinity that she set up a religious cell. However, she was decapitated during one of the many Danish raids on this part of the coast, and the story tells us that a spring gushed forth from the spot where her head fell. The holy well of St Osyth sits in Nun's Wood, close to Dolphin Pond in the grounds of St Osyth Priory. The well's water has long been believed to have all round healing properties and was collected in the past for cures, charms, and spells. The priory once had the reputation of housing a sacred relic. The religious foundation was fortunate to house the decapitated skull of St Osyth, which was kept in a silver reliquary at the priory. Sadly, like so many other ancient and sacred relics, it disappeared at the dissolution of the monasteries. The priory grounds are also reputed to be haunted by a ghostly monk, who appears in a white robe and carrying a lighted candle, where he wanders around

---

59. Ibid

2. The Witch Ghost Coast

the priory grounds before heading towards the millstream, where he disappears.[60]

Sixteenth century witchcraft features to the fore in the history of St Osyth village. The history of Mother Kemp and her contemporaries is well documented and for the most part is typical of the way sixteenth century witchcraft cases were recorded, with hearings and evidence from all and sundry who had any grievance. However, Ursula Kemp did have a reputation as a cunning woman, nursemaid and midwife in St Osyth before the rumours of more malevolent practice were presented. She was often called on for her services, which included removing spells, helping young mothers, midwifery, and healing. All these practises were very risky in an age of high infant mortality, superstition, and paranoia. One healing charm she is known to have used is one that she was taught by a local cunning woman called Mother Cocke.[61] This particular arthritis charm used a piece of hog dung and a bunch of chervil. These were mixed and then held in the left hand whilst the mix was pricked three times with a knife held in the right hand. The mix was then thrown on the fire. The knife was then used to make three cuts under the kitchen table and was left there until the arthritis went away. Meanwhile, a jug was then filled with ale, three sage leaves and some yellow flowers of the St John's Wort. A sip was drunk early morning and before bed until it was all consumed.[62] The arthritis would then be cured permanently. Ursula used this remedy to cure her first recorded clients, Mr and Mrs Page, who had consulted Kemp to cure their lameness. Ironically, the lameness was believed to have been caused by another witch in the village, and this shows that Ursula Kemp was consulted to provide counter-witchcraft charms and cures as a service to the village. Many other villagers were involved in this business

---

60. Essex Folklore by Sylvia Kent
61. Essex Witches by Glynn H. Morgan, p 25
62. Popular Magic: Cunning-folk in English History by Owen Davies, p 110

of cunning versus sorcery and were subsequently accused of witchcraft. These were Alice Hunt, Alice Newman, Elizabeth Bennet, Margery Sammon, Joan Pechey, Agnes Glascock, Cicely Celles, Anne Swallow, Anis Herd, Joan Turner, Alice Manfield, Margaret Grevell, Mother Ewstace and Mother Barnes. Kemp reported some of them herself during her trial, as did others.

Ursula's downfall seemed to start when she was consulted to help Grace Thurlow's son Davy recover from an illness. Mother Kemp was successful in helping Davy, and Grace later consulted Ursula to help cure her arthritis, and Kemp used the old charm that she had learned from Cunning Cocke, the wise woman she had once known, and from whom she had learned much of her cunning craft. However, Grace Thurlow fell out with Ursula Kemp when she was charged a shilling for her services and refused to pay. Grace then started to make witchcraft accusations against Ursula and was apparently advised to do this by another (unnamed) village wise woman. Kemp also worked with cunning woman Alice Newman, and both were charged with bewitching Edna Starron. The trial at Chelmsford on 29th March 1582 saw fourteen women from St Osyth on a charge of witchcraft in front of local magistrate, Bryan D'Arcy. During the trial most of the women blamed each other or made accusations amid a complicated web of deceit, where the witches' familiars seemed to have been kept remarkably busy with lots of ungodly misdemeanours going on. The familiars included satanic cats, dogs with horns, evil toads, and lambs of Lucifer. The grand finale seems to have been at Michaelmas 1581, where several spirits (familiars) were conjured and raised by various St Osyth witches, and were instructed to take a trip out one dark night to burn down the barn belonging to local farmer Richard Ross.

By the end of the trial, only two of the women were convicted to hang: Ursula Kemp and Elizabeth Bennet.[63]

---

63. Essex Witches by Peter C Brown

2. The Witch Ghost Coast

Of the others, it is not known what happened to them, but there are some interesting descriptions of some of the imps and familiars that were used in their magic. Anis Heard kept rats that had horns and were red and white and looked more like miniature cows, and she also had some blackbirds which assisted her and were housed in a box lined with black and white wool.[64] Margery Sammon had two spirit toads, their names were Tom and Robyn, which she inherited from her mother, who was known as Mother Barnes. Another of the St Osyth witches was Alice Hunt, who was Margery Sammon's sister. Ursula Kemp had also seen one of Elizabeth Bennet's imps, a ferret, lifting a cloth which was lying over a pot.[65] Ursula eventually confessed to have kept four imps of her own. Tyffin and Jack were used to kill, and Pigine and Tyttie to cause lameness and other minor afflictions. Bryan D'Arcy continued to deceive Ursula by saying that he would treat her with clemency if she continued to help him with his inquiries. She was locked up for the night in the village cage and the following morning, D'Arcy continued to question her. It is at this point that Ursula Kemp begins to reveal the identity of the rest of the village cunning women and witches, still believing that she would be set free. From this point D'Arcy was in full-on mania mode, questioning children as young as eight years old, to get the results he both required and desired.[66]

It is impossible to think about all these women of St Osyth without wondering what was really going on here. There is a theory about a Catholic plot at the time of D'Arcy's investigations. Queen Elizabeth's government were getting paranoid and D'Arcy had already investigated a previous case of sorcery, where in 1580, several conjurors had been rounded up in Essex and sent to London to be examined by the Privy Council. Catholic plotters John Lee,

---

64. East Anglian Witches and Wizards by Michael Howard
65. Witchcraft in England by Christina Hole
66. Essex Witches by Peter C Brown, pp 23 - 29

Thomas Glascocke and Nicholas Johnson were thought to have been responsible.[67] Around the same time D'Arcy had investigated a local thirteen-year-old boy named Thomas Lever, who was imprisoned in the county jail in Colchester, accused of being a sorcerer's apprentice to William Randall. Randall was a magician from Ipswich who worked in Essex as an occultist treasure-hunter, who used magic to find buried artefacts. Randall had been one of the conspirators sent to London and was thought to be one of the leading members of a group of magicians who met in Halstead. This group was accused of raising spirits to guide them to lost treasures and other rich pickings. Of course, Lever's mother was terrified for her teenage son, and contacted the Privy Council, whereupon Thomas Lever was released without charge.[68]

In 1921 two skeletons were unearthed in St Osyth by local resident Mr Brooker, who was digging in his garden in Mill Street. The burials were orientated north-south, rather than the more usual east-west. Rumours quickly spread that it was the remains of Ursula and Elizabeth. Local newspapers reported on the finds and told of how the bones were impaled into the ground with iron spikes and chains. The skeletal remains became a paid for side show in an early attempt at encouraging *dark tourism* to the area, and a stream of visitors came to view Ursula Kemp's remains for sixpence a view. One skeleton was well preserved, the other was in an extremely poor condition. Eleven years later the cottage adjoining the grave site mysteriously burned down, and the graves were filled in. Then, in 1963, the famous Museum of Witchcraft based in Boscastle, Cornwall heard that the bones of Ursula Kemp had been exhumed and contacted Mr Brooker's son-in-law. The owner of the Witchcraft Museum, Cecil Williamson, purchased the skeleton, and recalled that when he went to lift the bones, he noticed the

---

67. Witchcraft in England, 1558-1618 by Barbara Rosen, p 103
68. East Anglian Witches and Wizards by Michael Howard, p 43

2. The Witch Ghost Coast

iron spikes or nails that had been driven through her body. Below are the original words written by Cecil Williamson that accompanied her display in the museum.

> *Having been executed as a condemned witch, Ursula Kemp was denied burial by the church in consecrated ground. So, her body was returned from the place of execution to her native village of St. Osyth and buried in common land. While digging for gravel, in 1921, her body was unearthed, identified, and put on public show at the spot where she was found. In 1932, the cottage tea-room adjoining the grave site was burnt down and the grave filled in. In 1963 the museum was asked to take over and remove her remains in order to make way for a sewage scheme. This was done, after first obtaining a ruling from the home office of undertaking. It is of interest to note that when I came to lift the bones, I discovered that iron spikes had been driven through her body in order to hold her down in the grave and so prevent her from haunting the village. Such was the fear of witches in those days. Some of the iron spikes are to be seen beside the coffin.*[69]

But Ursula Kemp's story did not end there. In 1999, Plymouth artist Robert Lenkiewicz purchased the skeleton from Cecil Williamson to add to his already huge collection of artefacts and library of occult books. Lenkiewicz died in 2002 aged 60, and his library, many of his paintings and the remains of Ursula Kemp remained in his St Saviour's studio in Plymouth, whilst the lengthy process of probate was conducted. Eventually, with the permission of The Lenkiewicz Foundation, an archaeological investigation and appraisal of the skeleton was undertaken by Jaqueline McKinley of Wessex Archaeology. Through this investigation much information has come to light.

---

69. A typed interpretation panel on card, written by Cecil Williamson, concerning the story of the burial and remains of Ursula Kemp, a condemned and executed witch. Cecil Williamson Object Label Collection, Museum of Witchcraft & Magic collection, Boscastle, Cornwall.

These discoveries were interesting, though they did not concur with the historic narrative. It is highly likely that the iron spikes were driven into the bones in 1921, when the skeleton was discovered by Mr Brooker. More importantly it is now known that the skeleton was that of a male in his early twenties. Interestingly, his remains have been dated to the same period of the sixteenth century as Ursula Kemp. Did he know Ursula? More importantly why was he buried in un-consecrated ground on a north-south axis. There are rumours of other skulls and bones that were discovered in the 1963 exhumation, including a skull with the head of a spear embedded in it.[70, 71]

The bones that were once thought to be the remains of Ursula Kemp have now been buried in a quiet corner of St Osyth village cemetery by the junction of Clay Lane, just a short walk from the site in Mill Street, where the remains were first discovered by Mr Brooker in 1921. A newspaper report from the *Clacton and Frinton Gazette*, dated 22nd January 2016, finally puts more information in place surrounding the myth and lore of the Ursula Kemp story. Paul Scolding, the grandson of Mr Brooker tells his tale, and shares his memories of the events surrounding the remains and confesses that his grandfather did indeed add the iron nails to the burial, to give more credence to it being the grave of a witch. Paul goes on to say that he was the person who eventually uncovered her before she was sold to the Museum of Witchcraft. He describes the burial place, as he uncovered it in 1963.

There was a very long spine, pure white teeth and nails through the knees and elbows, which turned out to be 18th century. There was a skull beneath Ursula's feet and to the right there was another skeleton.[72]

---

70. Ursula Kemp DVD by John Worland. Fade to Black Television.
71. Letter to This Essex magazine, October 1973 from S. C. Bruce of St Osyth.
72. Clacton and Frinton Gazette. 22nd January 2016.

2. The Witch Ghost Coast

In the centre of the village, in Colchester Road lies The Cage, an historic old village lock up, built of brick with a solid wooden door. It is often cited as an old prison, but in reality, it was a building used to hold suspects whilst they were being questioned or until they could be transported to the courts or be brought in front of a magistrate. The cage would also have been used for holding drunks until they had sobered up. Every village would have had something similar, and further down the coast at Tollesbury, a wooden Cage can still be seen. St Osyth's cage was in use as a holding cell from the sixteenth century to the early twentieth century. Ursula Kemp and her associates would have been held there whilst they were being questioned by Bryan D'Arcy and before they were sent for trial at Chelmsford.

The cage was closed in 1908, and it became a local curiosity until the 1970s, when it was converted into an extension for the neighbouring cottage. You can still see the old wooden door and the brick surround that was once the village cage for St Osyth, preserved as the ground floor house extension. It remains a private dwelling, though a plaque on the external brick wall tells its story. It is reputed to be haunted and a there is a book available about the paranormal phenomena that a recent owner experienced.[73]

---

73. Spirits of the Cage: True Accounts of Living in a Haunted Medieval Prison by Richard Estep and Vanessa Mitchell

3. Colne estuary and oldest town

Just beyond Flag Creek lies the ancient maritime port of Brightlingsea. The town sits on a promontory within the Colne estuary, which was an island until the sixteenth century. The medieval settlement grew from two ancient centres: the thirteenth century All Saints parish church and at the waterfront, where a thriving industrial port had developed, trading oysters, fish, copperas (the manufacturing of ferrous sulphate) and locally made bricks.

The church site has an interesting legend attached to it, called *The Tree from the Tomb*. In 1771 a Harwich man named John Selletto died in Brightlingsea and was buried in a tomb near the main door to All Saints church. John was an atheist, and he cried out on his deathbed:

3. Colne Estuary and Oldest Town

"If there is such a being as God, when I am buried a tree will grow up and break open the stone of my grave".

Over the next two hundred years an elm tree grew from the grave, and eventually began to tilt the tomb over at an angle.[74] Unfortunately, in 1941, the tree was removed, as the tomb had reached a dangerous condition.

Local folklore narratives suggest that a smugglers' tunnel runs from Brightlingsea, under the creek, to St. Osyth and in its heyday, during the eighteenth and nineteenth centuries, this tunnel would have aided and supported the free trading communities along this stretch of coast.

The town has a unique custom which historically links it to the cinque port of Sandwich in Kent. The Cinque Ports were an historic series of coastal towns in Kent and Sussex, originally formed to protect the coast. Some historians have suggested that the ports may have their origins in the old Roman shore forts, built in the fourth century, which were designed to defend the southern and eastern coasts of Roman Britain from the increasing threat of raids from the continent. During the Medieval period, the idea developed further, and some coastal towns in Kent and Sussex became known as Cinque Ports. Through this, the ships and sailors of these towns began to assemble into an early navy, eventually transforming into the Tudor Navy of Henry VIII.

Today the *Confederation of Cinque Ports* continues as a ceremonial institution. Brightlingsea has the unique position in being the only port north of the Thames that still retains its historic links to the organisation. Brightlingsea's *Cinque Port Liberty 'Choosing Day'* is held every year on the first Monday in December. The colourful procession of dignitaries makes its way to All Saints church, with the Brightlingsea Cinque Port banner leading the way. On arrival, the church bells ring out across the town. It is here where a Deputy is chosen for the Mayor of Sandwich. The current ceremony has a

---

74. Notes & Queries' March 23rd, 1929, p.207.

heritage dating back to the mid sixteenth century. Oaths of loyalty are sworn by the new deputy and by any new inhabitants of the town who have been resident for a year and a day. Newcomers then become *'Recognised Inhabitants'*. Ceremonial fees are paid in old money before a short religious service. Whilst *Choosing Day* is held at the beginning of December, another ceremony is held on the waterfront in early summer. *The Brightlingsea Blessing and Reclaiming of the Waters* is another Cinque Port event, but this time it is linked to Ascension Day, so is usually held at the beginning of June. This is a seaport equivalent to *Beating the Bounds*, where the town's waters are reclaimed each year. Cinque Port and Mayoral dignitaries attend along with clergy, the band, and a flotilla of traditional fishing smacks and Thames barges. A blessing is performed on Brightlingsea Hard, and as the vessels leave the quayside, they do so to cheers, horns, bells, and lots of noise. The event is perfectly summed up by their explanatory leaflet:

> *"The processions on foot and by the boats along the creek, and the 'din' on setting off are all part of the ancient tradition of "Beating of the Bounds" or marking boundaries and certain key points of Brightlingsea. The historic event lapsed in the 1950s but was revived in 2014 by the Cinque Port Deputy."*

Just upstream from Brightlingsea, at the head of the Roman River, lies the picturesque village of Fingringhoe. In the centre of the village by the village pond and close to the church is the much-celebrated Fingringhoe Oak. Suggested to be the oldest oak tree in Essex, it is thought to be approximately six-hundred years old. The folk narrative of this ancient tree tells us that a smuggler or pirate was hanged outside the churchyard, and then buried at the nearby crossroads, where an acorn was placed in his mouth. The acorn sprouted and grew from the decaying head of the pirate/smuggler, eventually becoming the beautiful mature tree that can still be seen today. This folklore recalls the

3. Colne Estuary and Oldest Town

ancient symbolism of the green man, whose foliate head can be found in so many churches along the Essex coast, where he can be seen spewing foliage from his mouth, nostrils, eyes, and ears. The tale of the hanged pirate/smuggler was popularised in Baring Gould's famous tale of the Essex coast, *Mehalah*:

> *"On that coast, haunted by smugglers and other lawless characters, a girl might well go armed. By the roadside to Colchester where cross ways met, was growing an oak that had been planted as an acorn in the mouth of a pirate of Rowhedge, not many years before, who had there been hung in chains for men murdered and maids carried off".*

There is a wonderful descriptive account of 1940s farming at Fingringhoe Hall Farm, which is held in the Mersea Museum archives. It was written by former farmhand Daphne Allen, nee Theobald, and it gives a highly detailed account of what farm life was like during that time, including how she worked the horses, tamed the bull, worked in the dairy, and helped with the all-important harvest. From the fantastic written account, we can see that life on the farm was hard and varied. However, one thing that was always looked forward to was the annual harvest supper. Held at the end of the harvest, the feast was held for all the farm workers in the black barn, where they would be served rabbit pie, and afterwards be entertained by the live music of Colonel Furneaux's Regimental Band. Each worker would receive their bonus payment, always left underneath their plates on the great feasting table.[75]

As previously stated, the twelfth century parish church of St Andrew lies close to the old oak tree, and has some interesting dragon carvings. On the spandrels of the south porch are fantastic carvings of St Michael and a marvellously

---

75. www.merseamuseum.org.uk/mmresdetails.php?pid=PH01_DAL&ba=mmpeldon.php

detailed dragon. Inside the church is a statue of another dragon slaying saint, this time St Margaret, who pierces the detailed dragon beneath her feet.

At the village of Great Wigborough, the ghost of a sixteenth century witch haunts the house and grounds of Hyde farmhouse, despite an exorcism.[76] The early Tudor farmhouse lies close to the ancient parish church of St Stephen.

The town of Colchester is often cited as Britain's oldest recorded town, and it certainly has a pre-historic origin and was once capital of the Brythonic Trinovantes kingdom. This old Celtic settlement, which was called Camulodunon, meaning stronghold of Camulos, possibly named after a ram-headed horned deity of the Trinovantes. The remains of an Iron Age defensive site called the Pitchbury Ramparts earthwork north of Colchester between West Bergholt and Great Horkesley, are the principal Iron Age remains of Camulodunon. However, there are also remains of defensive earthworks close to the Lexden barrow and the settlement was protected by rivers on three sides, with the River Colne bounding the site to the north and east, and the Roman River forming the southern boundary. It has been suggested that the Pitchbury ramparts were a seasonal gathering place of the Trinovantes who occupied Camulodunon. On the outskirts of the town lies the late Iron Age Lexden barrow, as mentioned previously. A superb collection of gold, silver and other metalwork remains were excavated here in 1924, alongside remains of pottery. The tumulus is believed to have been the tomb of Addedomaros, leader of the Trinovantes, and contemporary coins have been found to indicate this. Local folklore described the mound as housing hidden treasure, and a belief that it was the burial place of a king in golden armour, with weapons and a gold table.[77] The Trinovantes reappeared in history when they famously participated in Boudica's Iceni revolt against the Roman

---

76. www.paranormaldatabase.com/essex/esspages/essex.htm
77. Folklore of Prehistoric Sites in Britain. Leslie Grinsell

3. Colne Estuary and Oldest Town

Empire in AD 61, where the early Roman town was razed to the ground.

The spot where Colchester now stands was one of the first areas affected by the Roman invasion of Britain led by the Emperor Claudius in AD 43. A military fortress was established here to house Legio XX, and it was occupied for around five years. In AD 49 the legion pulled out and was relocated to support other military strategies. It was at this time that the fortress was reassigned as the first of four *Colonia* to house retired military personnel. During the same period Camulodunon became the centre for the imperial cult of Claudius. A huge temple was built in his name around the time of his death in AD 54. Over the years, excavations have revealed large quantities of luxury items dating from the period of the early Roman Colonia, including fine pottery and jewellery, which suggest that the town had some very wealthy and comfortable residents. Today, Colchester Castle stands on the site of the former temple.[78]

After the revolt by the Britons, spearheaded by the Iceni and supported by the local Trinovantes, the Colonia was destroyed. But Camulodunon, now latinised by the Romans as Camulodunum was completely re-established as a Colonia, and developed over the next three hundred years, eventually developing into a wealthy Roman town, with a Roman circus and two vast theatres, one of which was the largest theatre in Roman Britain.

To the south-east of Colchester, sited on the east bank of the Colne lies Alresford, whose history can be traced back to the Roman occupation. Several villas can be seen marked on the OS map and a local story tells of Emperor Claudius sailing along the Colne from Camulodunum to Alresford Creek to visit one of the villas. During the eighteenth and nineteenth centuries, Alresford Creek was used extensively by Thames Barges for the transport of goods to and from London, and Thorrington Mill still sits proudly at the head

---

78. www.colchesterheritage.co.uk/roman-colchester

of the creek, standing testament to the heyday of the east coast sailing barges.

The town's folklore contains the narrative of the "Colchester legend", which claims that King Coel was a ruler of Colchester and was the father of the town's patron, Saint Helena. The legend originated from a folk etymology indicating that the legendary figure of Coel was once thought to have been the town's namesake. Over the centuries, folklore has suggested that he was responsible for some of the ancient buildings in Colchester. There was once a large public well dating back to Roman times, which is still in existence under the pavement at the junction of High Street, Head Street and North Hill named "King Coel's Pump", the Balkerne Gate on the ancient town walls was known as "King Coel's Castle" and the remains of the Temple of Claudius over which Colchester Castle was built was known as King Coel's Palace; and in addition, on the edge of the town you will find the remains of a Roman quarry called 'King Coel's Kitchen.[79] As previously mentioned, Coel is remembered as a folkloric giant in Dedham, which lies around 10 miles to the north of Colchester. The folklore continues with the life of Saint Helena, and tradition records that she built her own *Chapel of St Helen* which lies in St Helen's Lane, and local lore often sites that either King Coel or St Helen built the town's Roman walls. It is interesting to note that most prestigious medieval Colchester fraternity, with influence across the entire town, was the guild of St Helen. This guild was founded on the esoteric traditions that Helen had remarkably close associations with the borough. As daughter of legendary King Coel, she was born in Colchester and had married Constantinus. Soon after this Helen gave birth to a son, who would become the future emperor Constantine. The fifteenth century fraternity was responsible for the upkeep of regular spoken mass in the ancient chapel of St Helen near the castle. Sometime during 1407, St Helen's

---

79. The Colchester Archaeologist, Issue No.14, 2001, p.17, 26.

3. Colne Estuary and Oldest Town

Guild had moved to a second chapel on the south side of Crouch Street. This probably belonged to the Church of the Crouched or Crutched Friars, a thirteenth century friary and hospital, which stood approximately where the Tesco Express store now stands. Whilst at this site, the guild spent money on repairing the town walls. Although this chapel was in a state of disrepair, it was more visible than the smaller chapel of St Helens, plus it had something far more valuable. The chapel housed some of St Helena's sacred relics. These took the form of some bones of St Helen and some of the ancient and holy wood of the True Cross which she was believed to have discovered in Jerusalem. This would have been the real reason for their abandonment of the original chapel, which was thought to have been built by Helena herself and her followers. The Fraternal Guild members would have been aware that a few years previous, the relics had been discovered and stolen. Thieves had broken into the chapel and removed the golden reliquary containing them. Three miles out of town, seeing that they were likely to be caught red-handed, they had thrown the reliquary into a deep pond. But the relics had refused to sink, and the reliquary had remained floating in the water sufficiently for the pursuers to recover it. Encouraged by this miracle, in 1402, the chapel's patrons had obtained *a grant of indulgence to pilgrims* from the archbishop of Canterbury, and this encouraged more to visit the shrine of St Helena and her golden reliquary containing her bones and pieces of the True Cross. Then, in 1407 the chapel had been assigned to a newly reorganised fraternity and guild of St Helen, licensed to maintain a chantry of five chaplains and to support thirteen poor people through their holy shrine.

This reconstructed guild was responsible for creating the town's coat of arms, which is still in use today. The symbolism is a folkloric glyph of the town's ancient lore and legend, and contains elements of the True Cross and three nails, which Helena discovered, along with three crowns, linked in legend to the Magi or Three Wise

Men, whose legendary remains were also rediscovered by Helena. The town charter states: Sancta Elana nata fuit in Colcestria. Mater Constani fuit et Sanctam Crucem invenit Elana (St. Helen was born in Colchester. Helen was the mother of Constantine and she found the Holy Cross).[80] The medieval town would have remembered their saint on her feast day and the chapel would have been central to the celebrations and worship. It is likely that the reliquary would have been paraded around the town by guild members, being taken to key places sacred to the cult of Helena, including the town walls, her holy well and the ancient chapel that she was believed to have constructed. The early fifteenth century townsfolk would have taken pride in the way the cult of its homegrown spiritual guardian had flourished and prospered, and the new coat of arms told this story perfectly.[81]

It is interesting to note that the esoteric and sacred cult of the three crowns forms part of the greater folklore of neighbouring East Anglia, and also across rest of the island of Britain. There are stories of three buried crowns along the Suffolk coast, and further north, legends of crowns hidden in the vast lakes of Cumbria.[82] Taking a wider folkloric context, the three crowns also represent the sacred islands of Lindisfarne, Iona, and Glastonbury.[83]

Colchester town centre has its very own St George and dragon carvings. Situated on one of the few surviving fifteenth century buildings which is now the Red Lion Hotel. The oldest archway is decorated with St George

---

80. Essex Borough Arms and the traditional Arms of Essex and the Arms of Chelmsford Diocese by W. Gurney Benham, Benham and Company. Colchester, 1916.

81. Colchester in the Early Fifteenth Century by Richard Britnell Dur.ac.uk

82. Under Three Crowns by A. J. Forrest, 1961, p 134. (And written up as fiction in 'A Warning to the Curious' by M R James)

83. Spirit Chaser: The Quest for Bega by Alex Langstone

3. Colne Estuary and Oldest Town

and the Dragon and two male figures which could possibly represent merchants.

The church of St Nicholas once stood on the high street. Demolished in 1955, this church was once at the centre of the boy bishop custom dating back to the fifteenth century. These were elected on the feast of St Nicholas, December 6th, and held the 'mock' office until Holy Innocents on December 28th. The candidate was chosen from the town school and from the choirboys. On election day they processed around the parish before the chosen boy took up his 'duties' in the church. Dressed in his mitre and robes and brandishing his crozier, he would carry out 'duties' inside the church over the Christmas period. One account, reported by the headmaster of the school, from December 1422, records that the boy bishop was attacked and dragged from the highway and left lying in a pool of mud.

A few years later, in 1429, the church was at the centre of a charge of heresy. William Chiveling was accused, found guilty and condemned. He was imprisoned in the Moot Hall and a few days later, on November 4th, he was publicly burned at the stake at Balkerne Gate.

All that is left of the church of St Nicholas is a small part of the churchyard, now a small garden containing tombstones to the rear of St Nicholas House.

The town holds an annual historic Oyster feast every Autumn, which includes the opening of the fisheries and the grand feast, now held on two separate dates. The formalities take place with the town Mayor and official dignitaries at the helm, taking the form of a civic custom dating back to 1846. Attendance is by invitation only and as it is a popular event; a public lottery is held each year so that locals get a chance to participate alongside the invited guests. The Colchester oyster fishery dates from the Roman occupation and a much later royal charter was granted to Colchester in 1189, by Richard I. There was much dispute over the centuries between Colchester and Brightlingsea over the oyster beds fishing rights in the Pyefleet Channel.

The origins of the oyster feast can be found in the St Dennis Fair, which began in 1318 and was held on October 9th each year. This was an end of harvest gathering, where items were purchased to see folk through the harshness of Winter.[84] The opening of the fisheries ceremony is held on the first Friday of September and the oyster feast is held on the last Friday of October. The opening ceremony is performed on a Thames barge in the Pyefleet channel, where the first *'Colchester native'* (Ostrea edulis) oyster is consumed. At the end of October, the oyster feast is held in the Moot Hall.

In his article, *A Case of Nineteenth Century Witchcraft at Easthorpe*, Essex historian G W Martin brought to life a local case of suspected witchcraft versus cunning man folk magic. This short article, published in local magazine, *The Essex Countryside*, August 1966 edition gives a great starting point to explore this piece of localised social history and to place it in a wider context of the cunning man and marsh wizard traditions of Essex witch country.

During the summer of 1858 rumours were rife of witchcraft in the village of Easthorpe, which lies to the south-west of the ancient town and historic port of Colchester. It all started when Emma Brazier complained that she had been bewitched by local resident Mrs Mole. The Braziers, a local farming family, also accused Mrs Mole of laying spells on their livestock. Remarkably, this caused one of their pigs to climb to the top of a cherry tree for a feast of cherries. They called in Mr Burrell, to deal with the bewitchment.[85] He was known around the area as 'The Wizard of the North', which sounds very grand. However, he was unable to counter the sorcery, despite using all of his counter-witchcraft skills, so eventually they called on services from further afield, and James 'Cunning' Murrell

---

84. Just how old is the Oyster Feast? by Andrew Phillips. Essex County Standard of 7th October 2005 www.camulos.com/oyster.htm

85. Essex County Standard, Wednesday 22 September 1858

3. Colne Estuary and Oldest Town

travelled up from Hadleigh to put an end to the old witch arts of Mrs Mole, with one of his famous witch bottles.[86] It is recorded that he charged three shillings and sixpence for his services. Murrell's witch bottles were legendary, and it was rumoured that he could summon any witch through their use. However, it appeared that Mrs Mole survived his visit, as a few weeks later the rector had to put her under his protection. He also proclaimed that Emma Brazier was insane and had tried to have her admitted to the union house. James Murrell was again called to help, and by the time he arrived, a large crowd had gathered outside Witch Mole's house. The police eventually stepped in and Emma Brazier was arrested and detained.

The 'Wizard of the North' sounds like an interesting character, but who was he? *Cunning Burrell* was possibly William Burrells, who is listed as the parish clerk in the 1862 records from the village. However, the original account of this case states that he was from Copford. The rector of St Mary's at this time was Rev. George Cranley Bowles and he had an assistant the Rev. Amos William Pitcher, who was the parish curate.

There is an interesting side story to all of this, which as far as I am aware, has not been recorded elsewhere. A few weeks later the rector was also suspected of practising the magical arts and was seen with other clergy acting suspiciously. Rumours spread that he was practising cunning craft to rid the village of the influence of witchery once and for all. It may be that he had some extra help with this; they would have certainly known William Burrells. It is also interesting that the reverend had protected Witch Mole during the earlier incident.

It is fascinating that St Mary's clergy were accused of practising folk-magic and counter witchcraft charms, as they would have been aware of an old artefact that was kept at the church. This took the form and shape of a

---

86. The Ipswich Journal, Saturday 25 September 1858

spectacular Sheela-na-gig carving and local tradition records that you can counter any witchcraft in a parish by gathering twelve local clergy of like minds together. It is certainly not an isolated case, as many other priests and vicars of the time, from across Britain, were up to the same magical shenanigans, including demon exorcisms, ghost-laying and counter-witchcraft folk-magic.[87]

It is intriguing to ponder as to whether Bowles had taken much notice of the Sheela-na-gig. He would have undoubtedly been aware of its protective and deflective qualities and it is tempting to think that he may have been the person responsible for removing the carving from the church and placing it in the garden of the rectory, as is locally recorded, for some esoteric or folkloric reason? Maybe he was utilising the power of the statue to repel negativity and to help to foster his own witch-finding and banishing techniques. The folklore surrounding many Sheela carvings suggests that they were often referred to as the 'Hag' or the 'Idol' or were given names. The carvings were regarded with great superstition and held in the utmost respect. The Easthorpe Sheela has the name ELUI carved to the right-hand side of her body, and there is much academic speculation as to what this means. I suggest that it is simply her name, as why else would it have been put there? However, I would like to suggest an alternative theory.

The ancient British goddess Elen may hold clues to rediscovering the true nature of the Easthorpe Sheela. It has been noted before that St Helen seems to have an affinity with Sheela-na-gigs.[88] In Yorkshire we have three examples, with one of the oldest Sheela carvings at St Helena's church in Austerfield, and another at St Helen's church, Bilton in Ainsty.[89] The third is a Sheela in private possession at

---

87. A History of Anglican Exorcism: Deliverance and Demonology in Church Ritual by Francis Young. 2018
88. Robin Hood: The Green Lord of the Wildwood by John Matthews
89. The Sheela Na Gig Project: www.sheelanagig.org/wordpress/bilton-in-ainsty

3. Colne Estuary and Oldest Town

Helliford, just a few miles from St Helen's well, Eshton; and in Derbyshire, there is another Sheela-na-gig at St Helen's church in Darley Dale.

Whilst the name ELUI remains obscure, the word could possibly read as ELIN, and this would make more sense. The character of Elen (Elin) is portrayed as a mythical road builder in the Mabinogion and is seen by many as a guardian goddess of Britain.[90] As St Helen she is patron saint of archaeology and importantly for this study, the patron of Colchester, where she features in the town's folklore and culture.[91] It is tempting to suggest that the Easthorpe Sheela was named Elin or Elen, after a long forgotten pre-historic goddess of the Trinovantes, who was later remembered in the Mabinogion tale - The Dream of Macsen Wledig, and in Christian hagiography as St Helen, finder of the true cross and the three crowns of the Magi.

Many Sheela-na-gigs across Britain and Ireland were believed to have powers of healing and the ability to deflect the 'evil eye', and this is probably linked back to the protective cult of local goddesses and other spirits of place.[92]

The Easthorpe Sheela currently resides in Colchester Castle Museum. She stands around 20 cm tall and is carved from clunch, a form of gritty grey chalk. The softer qualities of clunch made it popular for decorative use and it is a popular building material in west Norfolk and Cambridgeshire. It can be seen inside Ely cathedral, where it has been used extensively for decorative purposes. This stone is not local to north-east Essex, which may suggest that the carving originally came from elsewhere. The figure was kept above the south doorway of St Mary's in an alcove, a favoured spot for Sheela-na-gig carvings, seemingly placed

---

90. Finding Elen: The Quest for Elen of the Ways edited by Caroline Wise. Eala Press, 2015. P 57
91. Ibid. P 160
92. Sheela na gig: The Dark Goddess of Sacred Power by Starr Good

in churches, along with other grotesques as protective charms against the devil and other supernatural advances. As already mentioned, she also served time as an ornament in the rectory garden rockery.[93] She was finally removed from the church in the early 20th century, possibly during the 1910 restoration, as it was felt that the carving wasn't suitable for church decoration. The Sheela has been dated to the 12th century by Colchester castle museum, so she has been around for some time.

Opposite the church is Little Badcocks Farm, a 17th century timber framed farmhouse. It also has an old protective charm against the practice of malevolent magic. Above the fireplace is a daisy wheel apotropaic charm, put there to protect against witchcraft and the evil eye.[94] Also known as a hexafoil, these are one of the most recognisable protective marks and are often found in historic houses above fireplaces and by stairwells and entrances.

The appearance of James 'Cunning' Murrell of Hadleigh in this witch hunt is typical, if not likely, as Murrell would have been an old man of 73 at this time. However, Murrell was known to have travelled across Essex, Suffolk and Kent to administer his witch destroying magic. He was rumoured to only travel at night, and always carried a whalebone umbrella and a basket into which he gathered herbs. He often wore iron goggles and a bobbed tailcoat topped off with a hard hat. In his own district of south-eastern Essex, he was known as 'The Devil's Master', a title that he seemed to like, and it certainly helped to keep him aloof from the people that he served. He would often have detailed discussions with the local vicar, Rev Thomas Espin, and he was known to have said that Murrell knew the Bible inside out, and certainly had a better knowledge of the holy book

---

93. The Sheela-na-gig project website: www.sheelanagig.org/wordpress/easthorpe

94. Magical House Protection: The Archaeology of Counter-Witchcraft by Brian Hoggard. 2019

than the good reverend. Murrell's reputation, however, was strong amongst the working folk and from the description of his arrival in Easthorpe, some fifty miles north of his home territory would certainly testify to this. To quote G W Martin's article, written in 1966:

> *Meanwhile the news of the expected arrival of Murrell spread over a wide area, and at the appointed hour of his arrival 200 people had gathered near to the old lady's cottage. Drunkenness and riotous behaviour were characteristics of the meeting, and the rector was obliged to stand guard at the cottage door.*

So, in summary, we have a recorded account of a witch hunt through village hysteria and folk-magic cunning. An actual name of a supposed marsh wizard who called himself 'the wizard of the north', and I assume that being a reference to the north of Essex, as opposed to the south of the county, which was very much under the magical control of 'the devil's master' James 'Cunning' Murrell. Much of this evidence was first reported in the local papers of the time, and has since been reproduced across a few publications, having first resurfaced in the Essex Countryside magazine in 1966. None of these accounts name any of the clergy or have speculated on the identity of 'the wizard of the north'. I have tried to give some depth to the account by researching some of the locals of the time, and I feel that we finally have a few more clues on the social history behind this episode. I am also surprised that the Easthorpe Sheela-na-gig has never been linked into this tale, despite her glaring presence throughout, as an open secret, just waiting to be added into this brilliant account of 19th century folk-magic, witchcraft and cunning-clergy.

Inside the parish church of St. Michael and All Angels in nearby Copford, lies the remains of an interesting and incredibly rare twelfth century church fresco. Framing the beautiful sacred art, which richly decorates the apse above the altar, is the chancel arch. This is also richly decorated with patterns and bands, and central to the design are the twelve signs of the zodiac, which terminate each side of the arch, above the capital, with a rising sun and opposite, a crescent moon. It is incredibly unusual to have the complete zodiac depicted in any church, and this is the only one currently known of in England.[95]

The church also has some unusual folklore connected with the north doorway, which is known as the Devil's door. There is a local tradition that an invading Dane was caught trying to plunder the church. As a punishment, he was flayed, and his skin placed over the door. In the early eighteenth century some fragments of what was thought to be parchment were discovered under the hinges, which were part of the original door. When the 'parchment' was analysed in the early twentieth century it was found to be human skin. This grizzly church-lore is also linked to Canewdon church further to the south.[96]

In 1996 archaeologists started a dig at Stanway on a site that was going to eventually disappear under a rapidly advancing gravel pit. Little did the archaeological world know that this site would reveal a hitherto unrecognised form of high-status burial practice from two thousand years ago in late Iron Age Britain.[97] This location was first discovered in 1932 from aerial photography and showed five ditched enclosures, with three of them laid out in a line. The earliest enclosure was dated as a farmstead from the third or second century BC and would have contained round houses and animal pens. The remaining enclosures were subsequently identified as wooden chambered burial sites, one of which was later called the warrior grave, as the grave goods indicated, and another cremation of a possible scribe

---

95. www.copfordchurch.org.uk/wall-paintings
96. Old Wives' Tales by Eric Maple, p 72
97. The Colchester Archaeologist, issue 10 1996/7: Your move Doctor! The gaming board and other discoveries from Stanway

or clerk, as an inkpot was found among the grave goods.[98] The three burial enclosures that form an alignment opposite to the farmstead have been dated to circa AD 50. However, from a folkloric perspective, the reason that this dig is so interesting is because of what was found in burial enclosure number five, and importantly how it was interpreted. This was the grave of a high-status Briton, and the archaeologists from the dig concluded that he was highly likely to have been a druid, surgeon, and healer.

Burial practices of this and earlier periods involved much ritual and ceremony and the grave goods associated with *The Druid of Camulodunon* are impressive and ritualistic, and included fine tableware, many brooches, glass bowls, and amphora. However, there were also some unique finds, one of which was a wooden gaming board with blue and white glass counters. Laid on top of the game board were the cremated remains of the druid's body. His or her surgical tools were laid in next, along with a collection of strange metal rods and rings, which are believed to be tools of divination, two brooches and a bead made from Jet. Further finds included a copper alloy strainer bowl (a type of early tea pot) with traces of artemisia pollen. Artemisia or Mugwort was used in the preparation of herbal remedies and is still widely used in herbal medicine today. Mugwort also has psychoactive properties and has been traditionally used in folk-magic to aid divination.[99]

In conclusion, this late Iron Age British druid, healer and surgeon lived during the first half of the first century AD and died circa AD 50. Living in a land still dominated by the British Celtic tribes of the Trinovantes and Catuvellauni, he or she would have been an important person of high ranking within society and would have witnessed the beginnings of the Roman invasion and the

---

98. The Colchester Archaeologist, issue 6 1992/3: Warrior Burial
99. The Druid Plant Oracle by Philip and Stephanie Car-Gomm, p 83

Romanisation of their way of life. The words of the local archaeological trust perfectly sum this up:

> *"It is hard to avoid the conclusion that he belonged to the stratum of late Iron Age society that comprised druids, diviners and healers. It is conceivable that this grave was the final resting place of a British druid."* Colchester Archaeological Trust

Lying within the southern suburbs of Colchester lies Berechurch. It is in this locality where a local legend is recorded, known as the ghostly horseman in the sky, which seems to have its modern origins in 1980, when a family witnessed a flying horseman at full gallop in the sky above Berechurch Hall Road. They described him as looking like a first world war soldier, sitting upright on horseback. It is interesting to note that a subsequent report suggested that this area was used for breaking-in horses to be later used by the army during the 1914 – 1918 conflict.[100]

A Bronze Age cauldron was discovered at Sheepen Hill in Colchester in 1932. The artefact is the earliest recorded bronze cauldron found in Britain. Made from riveted bronze plates with cast bronze ring handles, the cooking pot dates from around 1100 BC. It was found buried on its side in a pit on the Hilly Fields at Sheepen, and is believed to have been placed there at some point between 1275 BC and 1140 BC, as a ritual offering. The cauldron is now held by Colchester Castle Museum.

During the seventeenth century, the coastal marshes of Essex were renowned for sheep farming, where wool was the main crop. However, almost as a by-product, the sheep were milked and a hard cheese was produced, with a strong taste and a thick rind. It kept well through the long winter months, making it a staple food for survival. The ewes were milked in small marshland huts known as 'wicks', and several places along the coast still recall this through place-name

---

100. Memories of an Essex Ghosthunter by Wesley Downes, pp 9, 10

3. Colne Estuary and Oldest Town

etymology. The word wick stems from the Old English word wic meaning dairy farm. In the Tendring peninsula we have Jaywick as a good example of this.

The same settlement has become known in modern folklore narratives, as a place where fairy folk can be seen. In 1982 two schoolgirls reported seeing two small elf-like figures around a metre in height playing in the school grounds. They were described as looking like little old men with long white beards and pointed hats. They were discovered digging a hole in the playing fields and were later referred to as the *Gnomes of Jaywick*.

A similar account was reported at Boxted, to the west of Manningtree, along the Stour Valley. In 1993 a villager awoke in the middle of the night to see six gnome-like figures dancing clockwise in a circle around a shining hexagonal crystal. The gnomes were around thirty centimetres in height, and each had a long white beard and was dressed in green and brown clothing. A pet cat was trying to pounce on the elementals, but they were moving much too fast for it to be able to catch them.[101] There is another account of contemporary fairy lore at Colchester, where during the 1960s, a resident of Victoria Road witnessed a group of fairies dancing around an old tree trunk.[102]

---

101. East Anglian Witches and Wizards by Michael Howard, p 180
102. www.paranormaldatabase.com/essex/esspages/essedata.php

part two: Blackwater

It is enchanting and enchanted country. On a brisk June morning the great heaped white clouds go sweeping across the wide skies, and the peewits wheel below them; a summer afternoon finds the floodtide rippling and searching among the marshes shimmering with that most exquisite of carpets, the mauve-tinted sea-lavender; at evening the descending sun casts a spell over the moisture-laden waters and sends land merging into sea and bathes it all with rose, pearl and gold; on a bitter winter's night the wild swans strain low over the creaking ice-floes, lit in weird ghostly spasms and the ragged clouds race across the moon.

Hervey Benham

The Blackwater estuary is a vast expanse of tidal power, and is a shoreline littered with the ghosts of my ancestors. Here is a strand where the clandestine places of land and sea merge; punctuated with mysterious, secretive, and isolated islands. Osea, Mersea, Ramsey and Northey; Cobmarsh, Pewet and the Ray all sit on the water here, some now more accessible than others; due to land drainage and tidal flux. Here the highest tides bring overspill and nervous excitement that the old alluvial marshes are once more, creeping landwards. The red ochre sails of traditional barges once plied their trade upon this waterway, which links land, river, and sea to generations of cultural traditions and interesting lore. This magnificent estuary, recognised as a *Ramsar Wetland of International Importance* site, lies at the very heart of the estuarial Essex shore. It was here, on this eastern coast that in pre-Roman times the Celtic tribe of the Trinovantes held sway. Collaborators of Boudica and the Iceni, there isn't much now to show they were here, but the ghosts of this lost British tribe survive deep within the land and on the tides.

The Romans sailed the estuary, and were followed by Saxons and Vikings. The famous Battle of Maldon was fought on the marshy causewayed shore, between Northey Island and the mainland, and a statue of the defeated Saxon, Byrhtnoth, stands at the harbour entrance at Maldon, reminding us of his historic defeat at the hands of the savagely brilliant Viking army. The phantoms of these early medieval soldiers haunt the Maldon shoreline and the ethereal islands of Northey and Osea are still inhabited with the ghostly tenth century battle cries of the struggle between Saxon and Viking.

4. mysterious isle

Mersea Island sits at the confluence of the Colne and Blackwater estuaries. The island oozes mystery and enchantment, ghosts rise from the mudflats like vapours escaping the marsh gas and time and space blend past and future on her secret shores. The isle seeps folklore from every atom, and its exquisite siting, central to the twin estuarine alchemical conflux, all adds to the mix. The island's name comes from the Old English word *meresig*, meaning "island of the pool", and may have the same Old English root as

4. Mysterious Isle

the Scottish lowland word *merse*, meaning low level fertile ground by a river or shore.

The island attracts things strange, and the wide tidal expanse lends itself to moonlit nights, and tales of supernatural encounters, where the uncanny meets the profane. This is a landscape of the old-time wildfowlers, the hunter-gatherers of nineteenth and early twentieth-century rural necessity. Where folk hunted on these lonely marshes, tales of spookiness seemed to follow.

Crossing the causeway, known as the Strood, is the only way to the island, unless you have a boat, or catch a seasonal ferry from Brightlingsea. To the south-west of the Strood crossing, amid the salty creek, lies the lonely and haunted Ray Island, where the sharp tang of salt stings the lip and the uncanny laughing cry of the Shelduck can be heard, said by local fisherman to be the ghostly sound of dead sailors.

During the 1920s, wildfowler Ivan Pullen once camped on Ray Island. It was a full moon, and a cloudless sky and Ivan had settled down in his tent to wait for first light, when the Widgeon, Mallard and Redshank would make flight. It was shortly before high water, and the bright moonlight enabled a clear view from one side of the island to the other. The old track across the saltings had disappeared under the rising tide and all was still. Ivan was just turning over to go to sleep when he heard footsteps from the direction of the track across the mire. The 'squish-squish' of booted footfall across the saltmarsh, was getting closer to the tent, and before Ivan had the chance to unlace the tent flap, the footsteps were going through the tent and across to the other side of the island, where the moonlight was reflecting across the sedimentary plain towards the briny creek. The ground shook as the footsteps passed, and Ivan grabbed his gun and flew out of his tent. He expected to see some fellow wildfowlers, but there was no-one around. He was alone on the small island, though he had heard the footsteps of others. He took fright and packed his tent, and as soon as the tide receded sufficiently, he waded across the muddy creek to the mainland.[103]

This mysterious isle holds many other intriguing mysteries and is also a haven for wildlife. The island stands at the wild edge of the Essex shore, far away from the hustle of the urban centres. Red Squirrel roam wild here, undisturbed by the larger grey variety, which have been kept at bay by the surrounding sea; and the skies are ruled by the Marsh Harrier, king of the raptors on the island. The many creeks on the island's muddy shore tell tales of the past. Where smuggling and pirating were rife, ghosts can always be found. In 2005 some mystery bones were discovered by a walker on East Mersea beach. The Police report said that the bones were too old to merit an investigation, and archaeologists deemed they were too new to be of historic interest. The bones were of a male, and it is thought that he died sometime during the latter part of the nineteenth century. Rumours began to spread that the remains of a Mersea smuggler had been unearthed. However, despite the romance surrounding the story, it is unlikely that we will ever know the truth as to why his bones were found on the beach. He was laid to rest in the churchyard at East Mersea parish church.[104]

In 1996, at Cooper's Beach, East Mersea, a set of seventeen monstrous footprints was discovered on the sea wall. Each print measured 15 cm across, and each showed signs of extended claws. Maybe a ghostly black shuck had put in an unexpected appearance, and for once left some sort of physical evidence?[105]

The Romano-British barrow, lying along the edge of East Mersea Road, is possibly the last remaining of a pair of barrows that once existed on the island.[106] It sits just beyond

---

103. Essex Ghosts by James Wentworth Day
104. Mistral. Journal of the Mersea Island Society, 2005. p 15
105. www.paranormaldatabase.com/essex/esspages/essex.htm
106. The neglected Mersea Island Barrow by Leslie B. Haines. Essex Countryside magazine, 1969.

the seaward end of the causeway, rising from the road and covered with trees. When excavated, the cremated remains of a man aged between thirty-five and forty years old was found inside. Presumably, he would have been an important Roman, living in a luxurious villa on the Island. Evidence shows he was likely to have suffered from stiffness and spinal pain, due to a disease of the joints.[107]

It is probable that his body was burned on a pyre close to the site of the barrow, and once cooled some remains were put into a green glass jar, along with some pine resin and frankincense.[108] The jar would likely have been sealed before burial, and it is easy to imagine an arcane and sacred burial ritual with frankincense burning and words spoken, as the green bottle was sealed and interred in the central chamber of the tumulus, which was likely built by native Britons of the Trinovantes tribe, whose culture had thoroughly embraced round barrow building since the Bronze Age.

As may be expected, some folklore has become attached to the old barrow. It is reputed to be haunted by the ghosts of two Viking brothers, who are doomed to fight each night for the love of the same woman,[109] and one of Mersea Island's most famous ghosts, that of a Roman Centurion, who walks the Strood causeway on certain nights. It was long thought he may have been sent to guard the burial site, as the incumbent must have been an especially important person for such a lavish tomb. Some say it was Sabine Baring Gould who first brought the folk-narrative of the ghostly Centurion on the Strood to a wider audience, and the spectre was particularly active around the autumn equinox, often appearing on the nights between the 20th and 23rd of September each

---

107. The Mersea Barrow Bones: experts confirm 'unique find' by Sue Howlett. Mersea Courier 17 June 2013

108. Ibid

109. Likely a fiction by Sabine Baring Gould, in his novel Mehalah the barrow is called Grimhoe

year.[110] However, there is no evidence for this, and it was Mrs Jane Pullen, landlady of the Peldon Rose between 1881 and 1935, who seems to have first spoken about the ghostly tradition. She heard the ghost one moonlit night, whilst walking home from Mersea to Peldon. She reported that the footsteps came down off the Roman barrow and across the Strood, where she met two other local residents, who could also hear the clanking, marching footsteps.[111] All three witnesses assumed it was a Roman soldier, which would suggest that the tradition was already established.[112]

Churchyard folklore can be fascinating, and in the graveyard at East Mersea parish church, there is a burial covered with an iron cage. One story tells us that this is the grave of an island witch called Sarah Wrench, and she was buried on the north side of the church with a cage over her tomb to keep her witch-ghost from rising. However, other rumours suggest that she either had a child out of wedlock, and died whilst giving birth, or she was a victim of suicide. The cage is probably a mort-safe, a device used to prevent grave robbers. But there would have been no reason to place this on her grave at the time she died as the Anatomy Act of 1832 had stalled the need for grave robbing, allowing medical schools to get legal supplies of body parts from the workhouses. Whatever the case, Sarah Wrench died noticeably young; she was fifteen years old, and consumption caused her demise. Although buried on the north side of the church, there appears to be little evidence that she was a witch, and local research reveals little of interest for the folklorist.[113]

---

110. The Supernatural Coast by Peter Haining, p 137

111. Essex Ghosts by James Wentworth Day

112. Memoirs of Mrs Isabella Rosa Dawson 1880-1972. www.merseamuseum.org.uk

113. Sarah Wrench, died 6 May 1848, buried East Mersea. merseamuseum.org.uk

4. Mysterious Isle

There was a saying in many of the old farms on the island – *"poverty in the stable, poverty in the house"*.[114] Pre-industrialisation meant that the horses were the most important asset on any farm, and before the second world war most farms were still horse-powered. Many stables would have secured protection charms, such as a holey stone (hag stone) on a thread, which was hung over the horse's back at night to prevent sorcery, illness, and nightmares. The holey stone or hag stone is a flint stone with a natural hole through it. These can be found on many Essex beaches, and would certainly have been utilised in folk magic protection on the farm and in the home.

A ghostly yacht was once witnessed from Monkey beach, on the waterfront at West Mersea. This curiously named sandy beach sits peacefully between mudflats and saltmarsh. It was here, where a local man once spotted a wrecked yacht just off the coast with the small crew shouting for help. The man tried to save the sailors, but he lost consciousness during the rescue attempt. He later awoke on the beach, where he discovered to his dismay, that there was no evidence that either the boat or crew had ever existed.[115]

---

114. A recording of Arthur Wapling, reflecting on the changes he has seen in farming on Mersea Island during his lifetime. sounds.bl.uk/Accents-and-dialects/Survey-of-English-dialects/021M-C0908X0020XX-0100V1

115. www.paranormaldatabase.com/essex/esspages/essex.htm

5. Devil haunted marshes

The village of Peldon lies at the mainland end of the Strood, and the Rose Inn was once a smugglers' haunt. There was a pond by the pub with a false bottom, where a brick well had been built.[116] It was here where the Mersea smugglers would hide their contraband until they received the 'all clear' to distribute along to Tiptree Heath and eventually to market.

The custom of eating goose at Michaelmas persisted in Peldon at least up to the end of the Victorian era. Michaelmas Day celebrates St Michael and All Angels and falls on 29th September. It was once part of the ritual year, and was celebrated as such in most parts of the country. Cooking a goose to celebrate the day was a custom from the Middle Ages, and according to local folklore, eating one on St Michael's day would bring financial luck for the coming year. Peldon folk had the saying - *Eat a Goose on Michaelmas Day, want not for money all the year.*[117]

---

116. East Anglian Magazine Vol 20 1960-61 p534; Smuggling on the Blackwater by Roger Frith
117. The Peldon Vulture. Mersea Museum / Peldon History Project

5. Devil Haunted Marshes

Immediately to the south of Mersea lies Cobmarsh Island, and to the west lies the Salcott channel, which leads inland to the Creekside village of Salcott. This was once a hub of eighteenth-century smugglers, as barges could be sailed right to the head of the creek. It was here that the illicit cargoes were unloaded and, in a similar manner to the Peldon smugglers, were thrown into a pond. Again, as at Peldon, it had a false wooden bottom, which could be drained to retrieve the goods once it was safe to do so. Many of the old houses facing Salcott creek were lookouts for the illicit traders and hurricane lamps were put into top windows to warn that it was not safe to land.[118]

Further west lays the moated site of Devil's Wood. This site is linked to the folklore of the Devil and Barn Hall. This traditional old Essex folk horror narrative is a classic example of diabolical devil lore, with layers of interesting themes to explore. The basic folk legend goes something like this -

> *One day, a local squire decided to build Barn Hall in what was known as Devil's Wood. Soon after the builders had begun to dig the foundations on the small island in the centre of the wood, strange occurrences had begun. It was hoped that by building the new hall at this spot would forever thwart the Devil's sabbaticals from gathering in their traditional meeting place. Each morning, when the builders returned, they found the trenches they had dug had been filled in. This went on for a few days, so in desperation, the squire ordered that a guard be put on duty during the night, to find out what was happening. On the first night the guard heard someone approaching.*
>
> *"Who goes there!" he shouted. "I, Satan and my hounds," was the reply.*
>
> *The guard replied, "This place is protected by God and me." The Devil and his hell hounds turned and fled. On the second*

---
118. East Anglian Film Archive. www.eafa.org.uk/catalogue/694

night the Devil once more appeared. Again, the guardsman inquired as to who was there, and again Old Nick revealed himself and his pack of demon dogs. Only this time the guard made the mistake of declaring that only he was protecting the site, and not God. On hearing this, the Devil picked up a piece of building timber and declared "Wherever this timber falls, you shall build Barn Hall". The Dark Lord threw the timber high into night sky, and it twisted and turned over and over until it landed a mile or so to the west. The demon hounds then surrounded the guardsman, preventing any escape. The Devil turned upon him, and with the hounds baying, ripped out his heart. The Devil then vowed that he would have the man's soul whether he was buried inside the church or out. It was eventually decided that he should be buried within the church wall. There are those who say, that if you look closely, you can make out the Evil One's claw marks on the walls of All Saints parish church, where he tried in vain to search out his soul.

In the north wall of the church at Tolleshunt Knights you can still see an effigy of a knight holding his heart. The Devil's hounds, incidentally, are said to haunt the nearby marshes on stormy nights, and the folklore of the Tolleshunt Knights Devil may indicate that we have recovered some lost wild hunt lore of the Essex coast, where the Devil and his demon hounds chase across the sky and into the grainy swamps of Salcott Creek. Here, under the light of the full moon and glistening stars, they continue to haunt the marshes and collect the lost souls of long dead bargees and fishermen of the past.

The beam, which the Devil threw up the hill was incorporated into the cellar of Barn Hall, which can apparently still be seen today. However, it would be an unwise to attempt to view it, as the Devil placed a curse on the beam, so that anyone who dared to enter the cellar would receive his deadly spell. Barn Hall was built

5. Devil Haunted Marshes

at the beginning of the sixteenth century, so the tale can probably be traced back to this time, if not earlier.

The fields surrounding Devil's Wood are believed to be haunted by strange beings. An account from the 1980s gives us a clue as to how the area can cause panic through its eerie reputation and unusual atmosphere.[119] The harvest had been completed, and the farmer was keen to get the field ploughed before the weather broke. He asked his son to plough the field into the evening, and the young farmer ended up using the powerful floodlights on the tractor to get the job finished. As the darkness of night fell across the land, the tractor driver began to glimpse movement along the edge of the field. At first, he thought that he was seeing a fox on her twilight hunt, but as he continued to plough his furrows, he began to feel very uneasy. He was convinced that he was being watched and he kept seeing and hearing movement close to his tractor. A large dark shape then cut across his path, and in a panic, he stalled the tractor. As he tried to restart the engine, he became aware that something unseen and malevolent was trying to open the tractor door; he turned the key again, now frantic to escape. The engine spluttered into life, and he headed off at full speed across the ploughed field. The tractor was bouncing around dangerously, but the young farmer wanted to get away from the terrifying dark field as soon as he could. He eventually reached the road and he headed home. The field was sold soon after this incident, and folk are still wary of driving past it at night.

To the north-east, the Devil haunts the marshy promontory between Pyfleet Channel and South Geedon Creek. There was once an old weather-boarded shepherd's cottage called 'Found Out' on the edge of the marsh. It sat by an old pond at the end of the old cart track from Langenhoe Hall Farm. The old cottage arrived at its unusual name through a strange old folk tale.

---

119. Supernatural England by Betty Puttick p 88

When the Lord God made the world, this was the last place He found out – and the owd Davvil was a-living here then.[120]

This little shard of marshy land to the north of Mersea Island is the Devil's country, and another story concerning the 'Owd Davvil' has him joining the twelve strong mowing gang as the thirteenth stranger called Hoppin' Tom. This was originally recounted by marshman, adder-catcher, bull-tamer and poacher, Ted Allen, and was told something like this -

Once, long ago, a gang of twelve men was sent to mow Langenhoe Marsh, and very soon after they began work, a mysterious stranger surreptitiously joined them. The men were soon feeling irritated, as he mowed faster than any of them, and as a result, he earned much more money. Then one chap spied that he had cloven hooves and knew at once that he must be the Devil. Subsequently, the mowing gang formed a plan, and they had thrown down a load of iron bars in the long grass overnight. The following morning, 'the Owd Davvil' mowed through the iron with ease, it was like they were made of butter. But later when he came to draw his pay, the farmer spied his hooves, and exclaimed "You're the Davvil called Hoppin' Tom, and I won't pay you" and the Devil let out 'a shrik like an owl and flew off in a sheet o' flame'. As Tom flew off, he threw his drinking bowl into the field, and that's why we still call the small pond the 'Davvil's Drink Bowl' to this day. We never saw Hoppin Tom again after that; well not us, anyway.[121]

Hidden within this old folk tale, we may have a folkloric echo that leads us into the secretive world of traditional marsh-magic, where twelve members met with the leader of their clan, to make the witchy number of thirteen. Perhaps it was on the very cusp of Langenhoe Marsh,

---

120. In Search of Ghosts by James Wentworth Day, p 149
121. Essex Ghosts by James Wentworth Day, p 25

5. Devil Haunted Marshes

that the leader of this mysterious group was once known as *"the Owd Davvil called Hoppin' Tom"*.

The plough and sail village of Tollesbury lies on the northern bank of the Blackwater estuary and is almost completely surrounded by salt marsh, reed beds, creeks, fleets and saltings. This area is a truly wild part of the Essex shore, with little development, and is home to a huge variety of wildlife. Although once extinct, this part of the coast is now, once again, the domain of Marsh Harriers and Short-Eared Owls. At the end of the nineteenth century there were close on one hundred fishing smacks operating from Tollesbury Fleet, and oyster fishing was the main industry. The village has always been reliant on both the sea and the lands fringing the salt marsh for agriculture.

The *festival of the gooseberry pie* was an old Tollesbury tradition, which was held around the feast of St Peter, who was patron protector of fishermen. At the beginning of the nineteenth century coal was imported from Tyneside; and pots, pans, and dishes from Sunderland. These would arrive on the quay by *Billy Boys*, which was a Ketch rigged trading barge; and the Sunderland earthenware pans became the fashionable dish for creating huge gooseberry pies for the festival. There was much rivalry amongst the villagers to see who could bake the best and biggest gooseberry pie. However, the pans were too large for the small cottage ovens, so they had to be sent out to the village bakehouse ovens.

The day before the festival, the pies were trundled in carts and barrows to the bakeries. The following morning, the pies would be baked to a beautiful golden finish, and when the crust was broken, the succulent blood red gooseberries were revealed in all their mouth-watering glory. The area of the old village green, now known as the square, would have been at the centre of the celebrations, and in the past, there were six taverns in the village with two on the green. The scene was overlooked by St Mary's church; and between the churchyard and the historic fourteenth century Roebuck House, stands the weather-boarded village lock-up. Also known as The Cage, the small building dates from the seventeenth century, and would have held anyone participating in drunken or riotous behaviour, or those awaiting passage to the local assizes.

The gooseberry pie festival is still held, and is hosted each year by the local sailing club. These days it is customary for other sailing clubs in the locality to take part in the celebrations, and to race their boats to Woodrolfe Creek, laden with their own gooseberry pies, to partake in a festival of dancing and pie eating.[122]

The old wind-blasted woods on the edge of the saltmarsh around Tollesbury are said to be 'devil ridden' and have been rumoured to have attracted the ghosts of many local witches and others practising the old folkways and magical arts. Related to this is the local ghost-lore of a phantom druid, who manifests once a month under the light of the full moon. During this time, he appears in all his ceremonial regalia in the woods on the edge of the mire.[123]

These ancient saltings on the north shore of the Blackwater estuary are also home to the ghostly Black Shuck or Phantom Seadog. One tale tells us that William Fell, marshman and gamekeeper, was travelling home one dark night from Peldon. His horse and trap was trundling along the Wigborough Road towards Tolleshunt D'Arcy when a huge black dog as big as a calf, and with eyes like bike lamps mysteriously appeared and followed the trap right up to Guisnes Court.[124] Another tale tells us that on a frosty and moonlit January night at the stroke

---

122. Tollesbury Gooseberry Pie Fair by Douglas J. Gurton. www.merseamuseum.org.uk

123. The Supernatural Coast by Peter Haining, p 11

124. Phantoms, Legends, Customs and Superstitions of the Sea by Raymond Lamont Brown, p 150

of midnight, a local girl was cycling from Salcott to Tollesbury to fetch the midwife. There was one spot along the road that she always hated, by the lane to Gorwell Hall, known locally as Jordan's Green. This isolated spot had always been feared and disliked, as it is where a man was once buried with a stake through his heart, giving rise to all sorts of gossip, including that of a vampire.[125] It was at this spooky spot, where the cyclist saw a large black dog, its head level with her handlebars, and whose body was as at least as big as her bicycle. The dog was reported to have a black coat which looked unkempt, and a huge tongue which looked like velvet. It kept pace with the girl until she reached Seabrooks Lane when it disappeared. The girl eventually reached the midwife, and on her way back, the dog again appeared at the junction with Gorwell Hall Lane, where it appeared so large that she could barely cycle around it.[126] Gorwell Hall Lane is also the spot where a mysterious ghostly white lady can sometimes be seen.

Belief in witches and magic was still rife up to the beginning of the first world war, and the following accounts are from the early part of the twentieth century.

A local counter witchcraft charm was practised in and around Tollesbury, called branding the witch. This involved cutting a piece of your own toenail and placing it with a lock of hair from the person who had cursed you. These were both thrown into a fire. Immediately afterwards, you should place a poker into the fire, and allow it to get red hot. It was then slowly withdrawn from the flames, and as you did so, this would brand the witch and break the spell. The cursing culprit could then be identified, as he or she would show burn marks on their bodies.

Another counter witchcraft charm was used when someone had been 'overlooked' by a witch. You should

---

125. In Search of Ghosts by James Wentworth Day, p 151
126. Haunted Britain by Antony D Hippisley Coxe, p 103

light the copper and get the water almost to the boil. Set the 'overlooked' or 'cursed' person down by the water, and place one of their legs into it. You should get the person to keep the leg in as long as they could bear it. Then put them to bed. The following day the person was healed. However, the witch would be suffering with a scalded leg, so was identified.

Tollesbury folk had yet another way of identifying a witch. It was believed that if you saw a mouse and a cat eating from the same dish, the owner was a witch. Mice were favoured creatures of the Essex marsh wizards and witches, who kept them as familiars to help make magic. One Tollesbury sea witch was suspected of bewitching her son's oyster smack. Each time he dredged for oysters, he would overshoot the spot. Unfortunately, there are no records of any names in this piece of sea-witch-lore. There was also a gypsy witch who travelled around the village, and at least two others who lived in the village, who had reputations as cunning folk, and were consulted about things strange and uncanny and children were warned not to look at the cottage where one of them lived.[127]

The parish church of St Mary the Virgin sits upon the highest point in the village and parts of the building date from the eleventh century. The ancient churchyard is haunted by the ghost of a white rabbit which is reported to appear and run around the graves on some of the darkest nights of the year.[128]

In nearby Tolleshunt D'Arcy, there is a record of a 1960s Black Shuck sighting. A cyclist reported being attacked by a large black dog at dusk, whilst travelling down the coast road, towards Goldhanger. He apparently leapt off his bike to scare the animal, and it promptly vanished before his eyes.[129]

---

127. Ghosts and Witches by James Wentworth Day, p 167
128. Ibid, p 168
129. https://www.paranormaldatabase.com/essex

5. Devil Haunted Marshes

A May Pole has stood in the centre of Tolleshunt D'Arcy since the nineteenth century, with two hawthorn trees planted at its base. The pole has been repaired a few times since it was first erected and local physician Dr John Salter donated the two trees in November 1896. It is not known if villagers ever actually danced around the maypole or even gathered around it, but there was once a tradition of active 'birchers' in Tolleshunt D'Arcy.[130] This would involve groups heading out on May Eve to gather different wood and plants to make offerings at the homes of many villagers. They would silently hunt around the parish for the plants and tree cuttings they needed and would leave different types outside each house. Lime (prime), pear (dear) and wicken, [a local term for rowan] (chicken) were laid on the chosen property's threshold. There were also the more abusive ones of nut (slut) and briar (liar). Nettles and thistles were reserved for the worse offenders, and the young men of the parish would try to throw branches of May (hawthorn) through the open windows of any maidens they wanted to attract. The comings and goings between the village and parish woods would have continued throughout the night, and has many common themes of other May Eve celebrations and customs from across England.

Historically, the area immediately between the estuaries of the Blackwater and the Colne lay two of the smaller historic coastal hundreds of Essex. To the north of the Dengie shore was the old Thurstable Hundred and beyond the Tollesbury marshes lay Winstree Hundred.

At the centre of Thurstable, lies an ancient earthen tumulus or barrow, which although has never been excavated, has a curious piece of folklore associated with it. The tumulus has been classified by Historic England as a Bronze Age bowl barrow, and is still in good condition.[131] It was once believed to have been the location of 'Thunor's Stapol', which marked

---

130. In the land of the Tolles by Keith Lovell, p 7
131. https://historicengland.org.uk/listing/the-list/list-entry/1009449

The Liminal Shore

the very centre of the hundred.[132] The name Thurstable may give us an origin for this story.[133] Thurstable derives from Old English, Þunor (Thor or Thunor) and stapol (a post or a pillar).[134] The barrow lies two hundred metres to the South-West of Tolleshunt Major's twelfth century parish church. Dedicated to St Nicholas, the site has grand views across to the Blackwater Estuary, and with the ancient barrow so close, it is easy to see why our distant ancestors would have chosen the site for a potentially important burial.

---

132. The Essex Hundred-Moots. An attempt to identify their Meeting-Places by Miller Christy. Transaction of the Essex Archaeological Society Vol XVIII, Part III. 1926

133. East Saxon Heritage, an Essex Gazetteer by Stephen Pewsey and Andrew Brooks, p 80

134. The Place Names of Essex by P. H. Reaney, page 302. 1935.

6. Ancient Port of Maldon

The lower reaches of the River Chelmer between the ancient county town of Chelmsford and the Saxon port of Maldon are largely unspoiled, with water meadows and floodplains. The Chelmer and Blackwater rivers converge at Maldon, to form the wide estuary, though both courses of these rivers were significantly altered during the creation of the Chelmer and Blackwater Navigation, which opened in 1797, and in effect created a new port at Colliers Reach, where a sea lock connected the Navigation with the tidal Blackwater Estuary. The area around the sea lock soon sprung new dwellings and commercial buildings, befitting a commercial harbour, and by 1799 a hamlet had been built and the area became known as Heybridge Basin. The hamlet soon got the reputation of garnering a spirit of independence, and rumours spread to the neighbouring towns and villages that the basin was not a place for outsiders. Despite the port welcoming sailors from all over the world, the more local 'outsiders' were not so welcome, and 'Basiners' were known to chase folk from neighbouring Maldon across the marshes with knives, often threatening to kill them. The Basin was also known as *'Cannibal Island'*, and this stems from a local folktale which is still told today:

> *There was once so much gossip of evil events and terrifying devilry which were believed to be taking place in Heybridge Basin, that the good Christian folk of Maldon decided to send a missionary. However, a few weeks later nothing had been heard of the "man of God", so a search and rescue party was dispatched. A full and meticulous enquiry ensued, but only his leather boots were eventually found amongst a pile of kitchen waste. With the rest of his body and clothing seemingly lost, and no further lines of enquiry to be taken, the rescuers returned to Maldon empty-handed. Rumours quickly spread that the 'Basiners' had cooked the missionary's body, serving him up as a local delicacy to both the visiting merchant-sailors and Basiners alike, in the unruly dockside tavern. Two hundred years later a bi-centennial party was held in the Old Ship Inn, where 'Basiners' celebrated with a birthday cake covered in the cleric's bones, boots, and dog collar.*

There was once a tiny and mysterious old fisherman's cottage which stood on the seaward side of the sea wall, not far from the entrance to the sea-lock. This once housed a pipe smoking elderly lady, who lived there alone. Known in the village as an eccentric, she was feared by some as a witch and would offer cures to those that needed them. Once during a storm at high tide, the sea broke through and engulfed the surrounding water meadows. The old cottage became cut off by the flood and the old lady had to be rescued. She was found sitting on the reverse of her kitchen table, floating serenely on the flood tide, puffing away on her clay pipe, and smiling, casually remarking that she knew one of the Basiners would turn up sometime to collect her. [135]

---

135. This Essex, January 1974, p 45

6. Ancient Port of Maldon

To the north-west of Heybridge Basin lies the historic settlement of Heybridge. This town has the honour of holding onto the remnants of a custom called Rush Bearing, which was preserved at the parish church of St Andrew by the Freshwater family. This local family bequeathed a sum for weekly alms of food and clothing to the poor of the parish, and ten shillings was also donated to the annual Rush Bearing ceremony, held on Whit Sunday, where the church was decorated with rushes and maple boughs.[136]

Lying on the southern bank of the Chelmer, close to Maldon, lies the historic Beeleigh Abbey. Originally home to the Premonstratensians or White Canons, and built in 1189, it now largely consists of a sixteenth century farmhouse.

During the 1980s I corresponded with the owner of the abbey about the contemporary folklore of the site. She told me that a large quantity of human remains had been discovered in the garden pond during the 1950s, and that she had once had a strange experience whilst sleeping in the haunted bedroom; and subsequently believed she had been bitten by a vampire.

The 'haunted bedroom' story was first reported in This Essex magazine in 1974, where it was claimed that owner, Christina Foyle had a disturbing experience in a sinister bedroom in one of the oldest parts of the abbey, where two puncture wounds appeared on her body, whilst the room was shaking and vibrating with poltergeist activity. This particular room is reputed to be haunted by the ghost of Sir John Gate, courtier and soldier to King Henry VIII and Edward VI. He was beheaded on 22nd August 1553 at Tower Hill, London for being one of the primary participants in the plot to establish Lady Jane Grey on the English throne. Gate was from an ancient Essex family harking back to the early fourteenth century and, in 1540, Henry granted Beeleigh Abbey and its land to Sir John, which substantially increased

---

136. www.joinmychurch.com/churches/St-Andrew-Maldon-Essex-United-Kingdom/134757

his land and property held in Essex. Sir John also haunts the grounds of the Abbey, and his annual ghostly walk takes place on the 22nd of August, where his shimmering apparition is said to walk both the gardens and the riverside.

From an account by occult author and ghost-hunter Peter Underwood, in his 1975 book The Vampire's Bedside Companion, it seems that Christina Foyle had also recounted her 'vampire experience' to him, as he told the story in the above-mentioned book. The tale goes something like this:

> *Christina Foyle had slept in the room a few months before Underwood's visit, and she had decided to sleep in the room because it had not been slept in for at least fifty years due to its eerie reputation. All was quiet until around three o' clock in the morning when she was awoken suddenly as the entire room had begun to vibrate, the bed was moving, and a water jug spilled over. Once the seemingly paranormal phenomena subsided, she was horrified to discover two tooth marks on her shoulder and another on a finger.*[137]

During my own correspondence with Christina Foyle about the strange occurrences at the abbey, she confessed that she felt that she had been bitten by a vampire and would never sleep in that room again.[138]

Mrs Foyle also told me that her father had once discovered the remains of an old tunnel in the rose garden, and local legend suggested that it went through to the busy quays at Fullbridge.[139] Other disturbances have been witnessed in the abbey over the years. Mysterious bangs, crashes and breathing noises have been heard, bed covers have been moved and a four-poster bed is haunted by an invisible ghost at slumber.[140]

---

137. The Vampire's Bedside Companion by Peter Underwood
138. Personal correspondence between the author and Mrs Christina Foyle
139. Ibid
140. Beeleigh Abbey by Christopher Foyle

6. Ancient Port of Maldon

The Abbey once held a sacred and venerated relic. The heart of St Roger was brought to Beeleigh shortly after Bishop Roger Niger died. Roger was born in Maldon and was elected Bishop of London in 1228. He was buried in St Paul's Cathedral on 2nd October 1241, during a solar eclipse. His heart was returned to his birthplace and interred in Beeleigh Abbey. It is thought that the shrine containing his heart was situated in the crossing between the Lady chapel and the Jesus chapel in the abbey church. Beeleigh Abbey became a pilgrimage site, and in 1289, pilgrims included Edward I and Queen Eleanor. Interestingly, during archaeological excavations during the first decade of the twenty-first century, a fragment of a stone carving was found. Around six centimetres in height, it depicts two cupped hands holding a heart. Could this have been part of a larger statue that formed the shrine of St Roger's heart?[141]

There is some curious folklore concerning a sixteenth century Beeleigh Abbey treasure hunt by witchcraft. In 1591, local men, Edmund Hunt and George Oder, were before Maldon Borough Court on charges of witchcraft. This was in connection with their project to seek the legend of buried treasure at Beeleigh Abbey. They had probably heard talk that the monks had buried something within the grounds when the abbey was dissolved in 1536. They consulted Maldon cunning man, Thomas Collyne, who suggested that they took a piece of the abbey's earth to John Dee, in London, in the hope that he could help them to find the treasure and maybe assist them into obtaining a licence to dig for it.[142] Hunt also procured a parchment with magical drawings on it,[143] which he had obtained from Cunning Collyne.[144] It is

---

141. Ibid
142. Masculinity and Male Witchcraft in Old and New England 1593-1680 by E. J. Kent
143. Maldon – a History by Charles Phillip
144. Essex Boys by Karen Bowman

highly likely that Thomas Collyne knew John Dee already as he had consulted with him previously in 1578 on a political matter.[145] It is not known if any treasure was ever found, but rumours and hearsay still persist to this day.

Twenty years before the Doctor Dee/Cunning Collyne occult treasure hunt was being discussed in the town, Alice Chaundler and her daughter Ellen Smith were accused of practising witchcraft. Alice was accused several times of bewitching people to death in Maldon, for which she was executed in 1574, after appearing before an inquisition at the Moot Hall. After her death, her husband John Chaundler went to visit Alice's daughter to demand repayment of some money she had lent her. Ellen refused to give him money, and they had a falling out. The result of this disagreement was deemed to be that John was unable to keep any food down, and he died of starvation. Ellen Smith had a son, and one day he was turned away by neighbour John Eastwood, whilst begging for alms. That evening the Eastwood family witnessed a rat running up their chimney, shortly afterwards a toad fell back down. They captured the toad with the fire tongs, and thrust it into the fiery hearth, which caused the flames to burn bright blue and to burn out very quickly. This was said to have caused Ellen Smith great pain, and Ellen even visited the Eastwood household to enquire about their health, maybe fearing that they had been practising counter-witchcraft charms. In a later confession, it was revealed that Ellen had kept three familiar spirits, each within its own spirit house. 'Greate Dicke' was contained in a wicker basket, 'Little Dicke' in a leather bottle and 'Willet' contained in a wool pack. One may wonder if one of these was a toad, and whether the others may have been a rat and a white mouse, as was so common for the marsh witches of the Essex coast? It is interesting that another girl had succumbed to Ellen's *death by witchcraft* and on her death bed, she screamed out 'away with the witch' and immediately after, an imp like

---

145. Arch Conjurer of England: John Dee by Glynn Parry

6. Ancient Port of Maldon

a black dog was seen standing by the door.[146] Ellen Smith was hanged for witchcraft in April 1579. Her story was immortalised in the contemporary pamphlet *A Detection of Damnable drifties practized by three witches arraigned at Chelmifford in Essex.*

George Gifford was a sixteenth century puritan minister and witch hunter who lived in Maldon. He was a firm believer in witchcraft and cunning men and women, but was seen as a bit of a moderate in how they were discovered, tending to stay away from the mass hysteria, and looking for actual evidence and taking more care with prosecutions. However, he was none-the-less, still a prosecutor of suspected witches. He had many of his papers published and his two most famous are about witchcraft; *A discourse of the subtill practises of deuilles by witches and sorcerers* (1587) and *A Dialogue Concerning Witches and Witchcrafts* (1593), for which he is best known. In 1584 he joined a synod of nonconformist Essex ministers and publicly refused to adhere to the established church. In the year 1580, around the same time that Gifford arrived in the town, Humfrey Poles, a conjuror practising in Maldon was ordered by the Privy Council to be apprehended. Gifford would have been aware of his case for sure, as he would have also known about the Beeleigh Abbey treasure hunt by witchcraft, and would most definitely have known the Maldon Cunning Man, Thomas Collyne, as aside from his cunning man duties, he was also involved in law enforcement around the town.[147] Gifford appeared at the hearing of another Maldon witch, Margaret Wiseman, who had also been accused of practising witchery in both West Mersea and Bradwell-on-Sea. Unfortunately, there are no records to show what happened to her.[148] Gifford was

---

146. The Dark World of Witches by Eric Maple, p 49
147. Arch Conjurer of England by Glynn Parry
148. The Damned Art: Essays in the Literature of Witchcraft, 1977. 'A Tudor Anthropologist: George Gifford's Discourse and Dialogue' by Alan Macfarlane. P 144

outspoken in his community, and had this to say about the sixteenth century Essex cunning man traditions:

> *With his charm of words, he can catch rats and best snakes, take away the pain of the toothache, with pair of shears and sieve find a thief. Many other pretty knakes he glorieth in, as if he attained great wisdom. The cult is devilish, when anything is done the Devil worketh it, he is the instructor of the enchanter.*

This is an interesting view, as although negative, it shows the powers that the cunning folk had across communities during the sixteenth century and onwards right up to the early twentieth century. Gifford did, however, hold the powers of the cunning man in awe. He gave several examples of how the work of the cunning folk of Essex helped to find a communion cup, the curing of a sick child and the saving of bewitched cream.[149] Gifford also spoke of a local woman who feared the faerie folk of the marshes. To keep them away she wore a charm bag around her neck. This held a fragment of parchment which contained a verse from the Gospel of St John.[150] This is not only an interesting piece of localised folk magic, but also gives us a brief glimpse into the fairy lore of the Essex coast, most of which has been lost over time. Though it has been said that the Maldon saltmarsh is thought to be the home of various marsh-sprites, including many hobgoblins, faeries and brownies, and they can be seen walking on the saltmarsh at twilight.[151] So the above charm is probably a Maldon enchant against the faeries of the muddy creeks and the tangy tide-marshes that dominate the town. However, there was, and probably still is a better way to appease the faeries and even get them on your side. There is a tradition of putting a bowl of oatmeal out for

---

149. Witchcraft prosecutions in Essex 1560 – 1680 a sociological analysis by A. D. J. Macfarlane, p 163
150. Witches and Wizards of East Anglia by Michael Howard, p 136
151. Essex Ghosts and Legends by Pamela Brooks, p 86

A traditional cottage in Canewdon. Once the home of 'Granny' Garner, the last of the historic cunning women of the village.

Below: An Egyptian style mausoleum in the graveyard at Mistley Towers is haunted by a black and white shuck, who is seen as a portent of death.

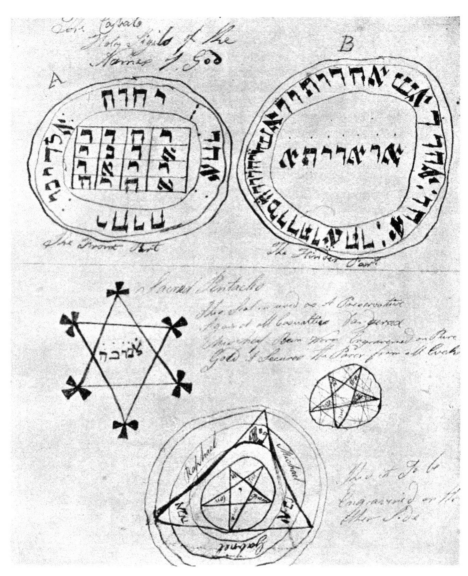

An example of Cunning Murrell's sigils from his notebook. Published in 'A Wizard of Yesterday' by Arthur Morrison. Strand Magazine, Volume XX, July – December 1900

Ashingdon church. Reputed to be the site of the battle of Assendune, and later, a site of miracles and garveyard hauntings.

Below: At the burial site of Matthew Hopkins, amidst the scant remains of fallen masonry, where the medieval church of Mistley once stood I found this haunting face looming from a long dead tree trunk

Bateman's Tower at the historic Cinque Port of Brightlingsea. On the distant horizon is Langenhoe marsh, where the Owd Davvill called 'Hoppin' Tom' haunts the desolate marshes.

Below: Battlesbridge Harbour, where the ghost of the 'Hopping Witch' can sometimes be glimpsed at dusk.

Beeleigh Abbey Refectory. 1920 postcard. The Abbey has many old ghosts. It is also home to a 1970s account of a sinister Vampire.

Below: Bradwell-on-Sea, where St Cedd landed in 654 AD and built his 7th century chapel on the liminal shore.

Bronze Age Barrow at Tolleshunt Major. The folklore of this site connnects it to local deity Thunor and it sits at the sacred centre of the old Thurstable hundred, named after the old god of thunder himself.

Below: Burnham-on-Crouch, where the anarchistic Tar Barrells once blazed through the town.

Canewdon church, notorious for its folklore of the village witches, forever linked to the fate of the tower.

Below: Canewdon village sign, sits by the crossroads as you enter the village from the west. It is here where a witch is believed to be buried with a stake through her heart.

Colchester Castle, built on the site of the Roman temple of Claudius, which was famously sacked by Boudicca and her army. Later history inlcludes the diabolical imprisonment of many accused of witchcraft.

Below: Esturiana, Goddess of the Essex shore, by Anne Schwegmann-Fielding sited on Ha'Penny Pier, Harwich.

Fingringhoe Oak. This oak is said to have grown from an acorn placed in the mouth of a pirate who was hanged and buried at this spot.

Grayson Perry's 'House for Essex' sits above the estuary at Wrabness. For me it evokes the ambience of a wayside shrine, remembering all those who were put to death by Matthew Hopkins during his psychotic witch hunt.

Below: Hadleigh castle. One of Cunning Murrell's old haunts, where he studied the stars, collected herbs and collaborated with smugglers.

Hadleigh church. It is here at the eastern end of the churchyard where Cunning Murrell is buried in an unmarked grave.

Below: Harwich harbour, where historic acts of sorcery, sea witchery and smuggling add to the atmosphere.

Harwich high lighthouse, now long disused, still sits gaunt and sinister on the edge of St Helen's Green.

Hythe Quay, Maldon. The home port of some of the last remaining historic Thames Barges.

Below: Lexden Barrow, the royal tomb of King Addedomaros, leader of the Trinovantes.

Maypole at Tolleshunt D'Arcy.

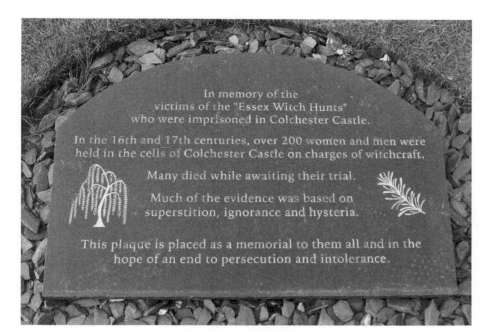

Memorial at Colchester Castle.

Mistley Pond, where Hopkins swum his witches.

Northey Island causeway, where the 'Slaughter Wolves' battled with Byrthnoth's army.

North Fambridge, where Mr and Mrs Hart were swum as witches.

Old Knobbley captured in 2013. This 800 year old oak can be found in the village of Mistley. Photo credit Morag Embleton and www.oldknobbley.com.

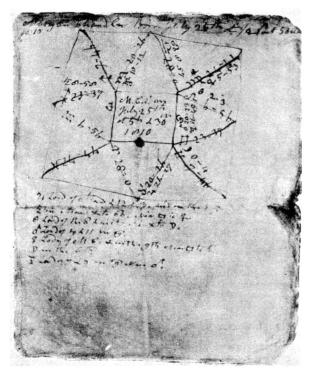

One of Cunning Murrell's horoscopes from his personal notebook, published in 'A Wizard of Yesterday' by Arthur Morrison. Strand Magazine, Volume XX, July – December 1900

Postcard from 1920 showing Beeleigh Abbey, where during the sixteenth century a group of Maldon cunning men went in search of treasure.

The site of James Murrell's cottage in Endway, Hadleigh. Modern offices now sit where the terrace of weatherboarded cottages once housed The Devil's Master. Murrell's cottage (nearest the church) can be seen below on an old postcard. Courtesy of Hadleigh & Thundersley Community Archive.

St Andrew's 12th century Priory church, Hatfield Peverel. Once a place of miracles, enchantment and alchemy.

Below: St Helen's chapel, Colchester. Site of the medieval Guild of St Helen and a source of 'The Colchester Legend'

St Mary's church Easthorpe. Once the home of the Easthorpe Sheela-na-Gig and the centre of 19th century witchcraft and cunning.

Below: St Osyth Cage, where village cunning woman Ursula Kemp was held before trial.

Thames Barge leaving on the flood tide. Hyth Quay, Maldon.

Below: The 7th century 'Anglo-Celtic' church by the salt marsh at Bradwell-on-Sea where the Black Shuck stalks on balmy summer nights and the ghostly thunder of hooves can be heard after dark.

The ancient oaks at Mundon, lying close to the salty shore. Folklore records that the trees are remnants of an ancient Druid grove.

Below: The author standing on the top of Naze Tower. This 18th century navigation mark stands 26 metres above the Naze overlooking the eerie Walton Backwaters, home to a rare sighting of a Sea Serpent. Pic Jon Langstone.

Above: The Elizabethan ferrymans cottages, where Dick Hyams, one of the last of the old ferryman at Hullbridge lived. He also practised as a marsh wizard and chimney conjurer.

Left: The famous and somewhat controversial photograph said to depict George Pickingill, the last Wizard of Canewdon

The Ferry Boat Inn at North Fambridge is haunted by the spirit of Old Witch Hart.

Below: The haunted and eerie Mistley Towers lie at the heart of Matthew Hopkins' territory, where he held his witchfinding reign of terror.

The haunted and eerie Mistley Towers lie at the heart of Matthew Hopkins' territory, where he held his witchfinding reign of terror.

Below: The high and low lights at Dovercourt, which once guided shipping safely into port. It was along this coast where the town's sea witch haunts the salty strand, appearing as a mysterious four eyed cat.

Above: The high and low lights at Dovercourt, which once guided shipping safely into port. It was along this coast where the town's sea witch haunts the salty strand, appearing as a mysterious four eyed cat.

Left: The Horned Cat on the south side of Canewdon parish church.

The Liminal Shore at The Naze, Walton. Here the cliffs are crumbling at speed, around 50cm a year.

Below: The Romano-British barrow is a central monument within the folklore of Mersea Island

The saltmarsh on Maldon's hinterland is haunted by Hobgoblins, Brownies and other marsh sprites, inlcluding one called Rollicking Bill.

Below: The sign on the side of the notorious 'Cage' in St Osyth.

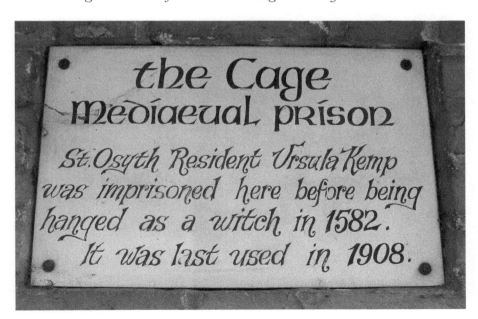

The Three Cups, once central to the civic life of Harwich. Historically a popular hostelry, it was also used as a court to convict many of the towns women on charges of witchcraft.

Thundersley graveyard, where a spooky game was once re-enacted to raise the spirit of the oldest grave in the boneyard.

Thundersley hilltop church, possibly built on a pagan site of the Grove of Thunor.

Tollesbury marshes, where a ghostly druid haunts and the black shuck runs.

Below: Walter Linnett's haunted cottage sits on the mysterious lip of the saltmarsh at Bradwell. The traditional wildfowlers home, built in 1798, is now a bird hide.

6. Ancient Port of Maldon

the faeries, hobgoblins and brownies at night, and such customs have been maintained until quite recently around the remote salty creeks and on the lip of the mudflats of the Blackwater estuary.[1] One of these strange saltmarsh elementals is known as Rollicking Bill, and it is reputed that he can be seen skipping and dancing over Maldon's marshy foreshore at twilight.[2]

Maldon's Hythe Quay is home to a small fleet of traditional Thames Barges. However, if you were able to travel back in time, around one hundred and fifty years ago, you may have experienced a fleet of over two thousand barges plying their trade up and down the coasts of Essex, Suffolk and Kent, moving goods to and from ports large and small. These barges were once the lifeblood of Maldon's prosperity, facilitating trade of straw, bricks, manure, grain, and horse feed with London. Needing only two crewmen and a lucky ship's cat to sail, the flat-bottomed hull enabled the vessels to navigate the winding, shallow creeks of the Essex coast with ease.[3] The last remaining barges at Maldon go a long way to help keep alive the traditions of the Essex bargemen and of the sea, where these majestic barges were once sailed with an innate instinct gained from the generations that preceded the art. It was often perceived that the craft of sailing these vessels was with the bargemen from birth, and was inexplicably and silently passed from generation to generation.

Sailing both out at sea, and deep within the tidal saltmarsh, the dark muddy sails would have once been a familiar sight, billowing along the spit-way and into the shallow farm creeks; docking alongside wooden jetties, which serviced the requirements of both farmer and miller. Life was hard working these boats, and when in port, the various two-

---

1. Matthew Hopkins: Witch Finder General by Richard Deacon, p 51
2. www.paranormaldatabase.com/essex/esspages/essex.htm
3. Documentary: The Essex coast, from the Thames estuary to Harwich Harbour. eafa.org.uk/catalogue/229

man crews, both skip and the mate, would gather to hold a *'tarpaulin muster'*. These temporary markets were set up to gain some beer money, and the bargees would try and sell whatever they had in their pockets or stashed in their bunks. All these items would be slung on the hatchway, forming a makeshift bargemen's bazaar. If they mustered enough to visit the pub, they would take their mouth organs and fiddles, and after the first drink, would play for the rest of the evening's session in exchange for beer.[4]

Just along the harbour on the Bath Wall, an unofficial guild of fishermen held 'The Tin Shed Parliament'. This was made up of successive generations of indigenous Maldon fishing families mostly living in the area around St Mary's fisherman's church, North Street and the Hythe. Their fleet of fishing smacks were moored along the nearby quays, and when the tide was out, they held court. Also known as The Bath Wall Parliament, there were always at least two members sitting, keeping time by the tide rather than the clock, both day and night. Speaking in the centuries old East Essex dialect, they would debate the traditional ways of oyster-dredging, punt-gunning, winkle-pailing and net fishing. This old fishing parliament fell into decline during the early 1960s, and the old tin shed, and wooden bench are no more. An informative plaque now marks the site of this largely forgotten piece of fishing heritage and seafaring culture.[5]

Salt making is another of the town's historic industries, and as with all good things on the Essex shore, it begins with a folktale:

> *It all started two millennia ago, when Casius Petrox, a Roman Commander, was posted to the Blackwater Estuary. He soon found that he didn't like the marsh fog, nor the*

---

4. Barging Down the River; a documentary by Dennis Rookard. youtube.com/watch?v=7VPAC4C9gmo&t=11s

5. The Bath Wall (or Tin Shed) "Parliament" plaque, sited close the Marine Lake, Maldon

damp and cold easterlies that blew across the saltmarshes. He quickly came up with a solution, and discovered a remedy that he particularly liked was hot bath in local sea water. He found that this greatly helped relieve his suffering, and one day his foot soldiers got a bit overzealous with heating the briny water, and instead of a steaming bath of water, they produced a tub full of sea salt crystals. Salt was a prized product in those days, and was highly sought, so Petrox abandoned soldiering and became a salt maker.[6]

There is still evidence of ancient salt making on the coast around the Blackwater in the form of the so-called red hills. These important sites of industrial archaeology date back to the Bronze Age, and were at their height of productivity in the Iron Age and throughout the Roman occupation. The 'hills' are made of broken fragments of fired clay from hearths and evaporation pans, which give the mounds their red colouration, alongside ash, charcoal, and unfired clay. These sites were used for heating the brine, enabling the sea salt to be harvested and used as a valuable commodity for trade and most importantly for the preservation of food. The sea salt industry still flourishes in Maldon, and since 1882, the Osbourne family have been producing the famous Maldon Sea salt from their premises close to Hythe Quay.

Alongside Maldon's maritime past, there is also a rich legacy of farming; and in 1995, local historians Ken Stubbings and Mike Watson re-introduced the town's Plough Monday traditions and celebrations. This old calendar custom has a long history in the eastern counties of England. An entry re-discovered in St Andrew's parish church records, in neighbouring Heybridge, mentions 'the guarding of the white plough' in 1522, where one shilling and threepence was given to the church, to guard the plough prior to Plough Monday. This gives a certain provenance to Maldon's revived Plough Monday traditions, and has

---

6. www.maldonsalt.co.uk/about-maldon-salt/the-history-of-salt

inspired Maldonians to continue the modern observance, for the last twenty-five years.

Plough Monday is traditionally held on the first Monday after Epiphany, (6th January). Today, the Molly Dancers lead a procession from Hythe Quay up through the town ending at All Saints. The dancing procession is led by a mock lord and lady and right at the front, the white plough. All dancers are disguised with blackened faces, tatter jackets and cross-dressing. This disguise was a particularly important part of the Plough Monday of old, as the event allowed a way for the farm workers to beg for alms by dancing and playing music in the streets. If money was donated, then all was well, but if nothing were gifted, the plough would be dragged through the gardens and across the lanes and fields of the gentry, as a rebellious punishment.

So, the origins of Plough Monday lie in a menacing, topsy-turvey message of organised begging, much needed by the workers of the fields. These days a local brewery produces a special ale for the occasion. The Ploughboys Ale is a stout with added port, which helps to keep out the cold on a dark January night. The day previous is known as Plough Sunday, where the white plough is brought into the quayside church of St Mary to be blessed and looked after until the following day. This blessing represents the beginning of the farming year and carries the hopes of the community for a plentiful harvest. So, on Plough Monday, the plough can either bring a blessing or a curse, depending on whether alms were given to the musicians and dancers, or not.[7]

Other interesting lore from the town includes a small plaque, known as the *Maldon Martyr Stone*, set into the wall of the old iron works, sited close to Fullbridge Quays. This records the horrifying account of one of Maldon's most grizzly events. During the reign of Queen Mary, Catholicism had returned as the state religion, and anyone found guilty of

---

7. www.youtube.com/watch?v=FkVv9ivSuJA Plough Monday at Maldon, a film by Paul Desmond

heresy against the Catholic church was likely to be burned at the stake. On 28th March 1555, Stephen Knight was burned alive. Knight had previously spent time in Newgate Prison in London with other Essex martyrs, before being sent back to Maldon to be publicly executed as a stark and fiery warning to other potential Maldon heretics.[8]

The Maldon Mud Race has become a popular annual tradition along the promenade. The event has its beginnings in 1973 when a local pub regular was challenged to serve a meal on the muddy foreshore dressed in a dinner jacket. The event then evolved into a 'drinking game' which saw dozens of thirsty folk racing across the river at low tide, to a waiting barrel of beer. Here the participants, lagged in salty mud, could grab a beer before the return journey, which often became a muddy crawl. The modern 'mud race' event has become a regular annual charity bash, with money going to worthy causes.

It is a sad tale, but Maldon is also known for having the fattest man in history as one of its former residents. This accolade belongs to Maldon grocer and candle maker Edward Bright known as the 'fat man of Maldon'. Born in the town in 1721, he was a post boy in his youth riding daily to Chelmsford. In 1750, at the end of his short twenty-nine years of life, he weighed in at 44 stone (279kg) and it was believed that he was the fattest man in England. He lived and traded from a house on Maldon's High Street, opposite the historic site of St Peter's church and is buried at nearby All Saints. He is remembered as an honest and affable trader and a loyal and tender father. A bronze statue, showing seven men within his coat is sited just off the high street, close to where he once lived, somewhat perpetuating the 'sideshow freakishness' that he possessed during his life. The folklore states that the last time his waistcoat was sent to the tailors to be adjusted, local tailor Edward Codd wagered a bet whilst drinking in one of the town's many hostelries. He

---

8. Book of Martyrs by John Foxe

gambled with fellow drinker, Mr Hance, stating that seven hundred men could be contained inside Bright's waistcoat. He won his bet when seven men from the *Dengie Hundred* were buttoned in with ease.

Out where the estuary widens, sits Northey Island, mysteriously bound to the mainland by an ancient tidal causeway. It is here where the famous battle of Maldon was fought between Byrhtnoth, Ealdorman of Essex and an invading Viking force led by Olaf Tryggvason. We can perhaps, glean something of the battle from the remains of the Anglo-Saxon poem entitled *The Battle of Maldon*. Originally written in Old English, there are several online translations, which allow us to gain an insight into this historic battle.

> *Then the slaughter-wolves waded—caring not for the water—*
> *the Viking army, westward across the Pante,*
> *across the bright waters, carrying their board-shields,*
> *sailing-men to the shore, bearing yellow linden.*
> *There they stood ready against the ferocious one,*
> *Byrhtnoth and his warriors. He ordered them*
> *to form a shield-wall with their shields and for the army*
> *to hold fast against their foes. Then was the fighting near,*
> *glory in battle. The time was coming*
> *that fated men must fall there.*

The passage above gives us a chilling glimpse of what Byrhtnoth and his army were up against. The Viking army berserkers were an elite force of bodyguards employed to intimidate. These 'slaughter-wolves' or 'were-wolves' were often believed to have supernatural powers, and some believed them to be true were-wolves, descending from the Wulfing bloodline. All very intriguing from the perspective of Essex folklore, and somehow fitting on this liminal shore.[9]

---

9. Hunting Werewolves by Graeme Davis, p 55

6. Ancient Port of Maldon

Byrhtnoth was killed in action on the 11th of August 991, aged 60. His name is composed of the Old English beorht (bright) and noð (courage). He is the subject of various memorials around Maldon; a stained-glass window in St Mary's, a small statue on the external south wall of All Saints, and a statue that guards the entrance to the harbour, facing across the estuary to the causewayed battle site, between Northey Island and the mainland.

Further along the estuary lies Osea Island, connected to the mainland via a long causeway from Decoy Point at Mill Beach. This island is now privately owned but has the eerie tradition that it was the final resting place of many of Byrthnoth's troops, which were killed on nearby Northey Island causeway during the Battle of Maldon.[10] A little further along the broad estuarine tidal shore, towards the south-east, lies Ramsey Island. However, its marshes were drained at the end of the nineteenth century and Ramsey Creek was dammed where it met the estuary, so its true island status has been temporarily stripped away.

Marsh Samphire (or glasswort) was traditionally harvested all along the Essex coast, and particularly at Goldhanger and Maldon, where its quality was once seen as exceptional.[11] This terraqueous fleshy plant loves to grow in the muddy hinterland of the saltmarsh. It is deliciously edible and according to local superstition, was best harvested on midsummer's day, as this ensures the succulent stems have not become too woody. The plant's name comes from the French *sampiere*, a corruption of "Saint Pierre" (Saint Peter) who is the patron of fisherman and whose feast is held on the 29th of June. Being so close to midsummer, and on the feast of the fisherman's patron, this date was another particularly auspicious time to collect the plant.

There was once a group of twenty-five mysterious tumuli close to the foreshore, between Mill Beach and Goldhanger.

---

10. Islands of Essex by Ian Yearsley, p 67
11. Folklore of Essex by Sylvia Kent

Local tradition tells that this was the barrow cemetery of the fallen Saxon and Viking soldiers of the Battle of Maldon, whilst another old tale thought that they were the barrows of the Trinovantes. However, excavations from the early twentieth century did not reveal any burials or artefacts. The excavation and the close proximity to the tideline has meant that today, nothing remains of these enigmatic tumuli. The area has been known as Barrow Marsh or Barrow Hills since 1574, and remains a perplexing mystery, and one which may never be solved. A windmill once stood nearby, known as Barrowhill Mill. It was erected in 1703 and later rebuilt in 1831, after it was destroyed by a savage storm.

The isolated creeks and marshes on the shores of Goldhanger were ideal for the eighteenth-century smugglers. The marshes were thought to be unhealthy, so there were very few large houses near the creeks. Villagers have heard tales that have been handed down across the years, of their forebears turning a deaf ear to strange noises after dark and during the dead of night. Often farmers would find their horses lathered on the morning inspection, with a keg of brandy left in the porch. The Goldhanger smugglers had a depot at Chapel Farm and the wheels of the carts were bound with sacking to conceal the noise and horses' hooves were clothed to hide the footprints. This often gave rise to tales of ghost horses and carts, and the smugglers actively spread these rumours to keep folk at bay. The Chequers, the only hostelry listed in Goldhanger in 1769, may have played a part, and goods were often stored for a time in the cellars behind the alehouse.[12]

The fifteenth century Chequers Inn lies next door to the ancient parish church of St Peter, and there is a time-honoured folkloric visual connection between the Inn and the fifteenth century church tower, as a chequers pattern can clearly be seen about halfway up the western face of the tower. Village folklore also recalls that in 1599,

---

12. Goldhanger - An Estuary Village by Maura Benham

6. Ancient Port of Maldon

a Goldhanger witch was excommunicated by church authorities. Unfortunately, nothing is remembered about her or her craft, but we can speculate that the retention of this long-forgotten folk-practitioner has returned to us in an echo of folk-memory, maybe telling us that she once served the village as a cunning-woman.

part three: Dengie

What old tragedy, one wonders, lies behind the story of the Headless Horror of the Sea Wall, told by generation after generation of country folk who live by the Rivers Crouch and Blackwater.

Eric Maple

As the mist rolls inwards, covering layers of history, I find myself standing on the edge, overlooking the temporal and mysterious shoreline of the Marsh Wizards and Sea Witches of the Dengie. Their eerie conjurations and incantations cut through the thick atmospheres of the past. Folklore spawns on the frill of this land, and an unexpected glimpse of a ghost barge with its russet sails, silently propelling it along a hidden creek at dawn, send my spine a-tingling. These old wooden barges, suddenly appearing like pallid ghost-ships sailing across the land, can induce shivers and goose bumps, and it is surprising that there aren't more phantom ship tales on this lonely coast.[13]

There is something irresistibly fascinating about the waterside of the Dengie peninsula. Its long eastern strand is made from a buffer of saltmarsh that separates terra firma from the wild North Sea. The northern shore snakes along the broad glistening sea of the Blackwater Estuary, often thought to be haunted by para-dimensional creatures, ships and people that are of another time. The Dengie's southern lip lies along the long tidal shores of the Crouch, where the river witches practised their craft of enchantment along its length, from Burnham to Battlesbridge and across its breadth from Creeksea to Wallasea.

Inland, the Dengie moves westwards from the lonely flat expanses of reclaimed saltmarsh towards isolated hilltop churches, and a soft pastoral rolling landscape. Interesting villages sparsely populate this place, and rumours that witches and wizards still practice here, echo across both the lowland mire and shallow valleys. One of the high points is the hilltop church at St Lawrence, which sits on an ancient beacon hill, overlooking the remnants of Ramsey Island, now sadly drained, and joined to the mainland. Age-old charms and cures were still relevant here well into the twentieth century, where marshmen still wore eel-skin garters to insure against rheumatism and snake-skin hatbands were worn to keep headaches away.[14]

On the western approaches to the district lies the highest hill in eastern Essex. The summit of Danbury rises 111 metres (367 feet) above the landscape. A settlement was first established on the hilltop during the early Iron Age, where a hill fort was hewn from the summit. This would have been a settlement of the British tribe of the Trinovantes, and within the single ditch and bank would

---

13. Rural England by H Rider Haggard
14. Tracking down the witches of Essex by Eric Maple, This Essex magazine, July 1973

have been a village of thatched round houses. The fort is roughly oval, but extraordinarily little now remains to be seen of the earthworks. This would have been a great spot to settle in the Iron Age, sited on high ground, at the very western extremity of the Dengie promontory between the Rivers Blackwater and Crouch. The site now encloses the mainly fourteenth century church of St John the Baptist and its surrounding graveyard. The remaining ramparts are hidden in the hedgerows and an aerial view shows the rough shape of the fort lined by the perimeter of the church yard and allotments. The hillfort would have been reused by the Romans, and then by the Saxon tribe of the Dæningas, as they began to settle in the fifth century. Both the village and the Dengie peninsula names are derived from this Saxon tribal name.

Here the Devil leads the folk narrative around the ramparts of the Iron Age hill fort. A story is still told of a great electrical storm that hit the hilltop in May 1402, and of the Devil that caused it.

Way back in the history of the parish church of Danbury comes this tale of devilment and sorcery. It all began one May evening during Evensong. The year was 1402, and the Old Devil was still regularly active on the ancient pagan hilltop of Danbury. This evening though, he decided to make an appearance in the church disguised as a grey friar. The congregation first knew something was amiss, when his dark horns were seen protruding from under his hooded cloak, and his eyes flashed red with diabolic delight. Before anyone could even think about what was happening, he leapt up onto the altar, outrageously revealing his outstretched wings and shining red eyes for all to see. Then as the Devil raised his dark wings to the roof, a great lightning strike hit the church with a terrific explosion, tearing the roof and part of the chancel to pieces. The Devil made his way to the church door, laughing, and running through the worshipper's legs. As the congregation watched in horror, he began a demonic dance with his cloven hooves tapping sharply on the flag stones below. A tumultuous wind and deafening claps of thunder ripped through the damaged building and lashed at the hilltop, the likes of which had never been witnessed before.

One parishioner fell ill afterwards, and his legs, which were brushed by the Devil became blackened with disease. Once outside the mischievous old Devil flew up on the gale and stole the fifth bell from the tower. His demonic outline was seen flying across the village, illuminated by the electric charges of the lightning, which was now firing out across the land. The bell was dropped in what became known as Bell Hill Wood, and the tale concludes by stating that a crater can still be seen in the wood, where the heavy bell hit the ground.[15]

The church dedication of St John the Baptist is an interesting one. In Cornwall, the fires of St John's Eve are still lit, to celebrate his feast. It is possible that the church dedication on the highest hill in East Essex reveals an age-old secret that the old midsummer's eve fire tradition was once held in Danbury. Local author and historian Mary Hopkirk wrote a bit about this in her 1945 book about the village, in which she states that:

> *The Britons chose hilltops for their ceremonial bonfires, and this seems a likely site. These fires, which were connected with sun worship at midsummer, lingered into Christian times and were taken over by the missionaries, who could not abolish them, as bonfires to celebrate St John's Eve, (which falls at midsummer).*[16]

Danbury was also home to both witches and cunning folk. In 1560, John Smythe, beer brewer, common wizard, and enchanter, was accused of bewitching John Grant

---

15. For a more detailed look at the interesting esoteric history of Danbury see: The Knights of Danbury by Andrew Collins
16. Danbury: Historical Notes and Records of the Village of Danbury by Mary Hopkirk, p 63

and Bridget Pecocke, who then languished for a period of between three weeks and three months, before they died. He also appeared before the courts for stealing sheep and bewitching cattle.[17] Another suspected witch practising in the same century was Mother Stookes, and in the early part of the seventeenth century, Susan Spillman. It was during the same century, that Danbury became known as the residence of Cunning Barnard. In 1641, Thomas Fuller from Layer Marney, travelled to Danbury to seek the assistance of Cunning Barnard in connection with some stolen property from Layer Marney Towers. Fuller was coachman at the Towers during the time of the theft, and it is probable that he was trying to clear his name, and wanted Cunning Barnard to seek the stolen property through his secretive powers of wizardry.[18]

Just a little further to the west of Danbury comes one of the few remaining tales of the 'little people' in Essex. The tale comes from the eighteenth-century manor house known as Springfield Place, which still stands on the edge of the historic Springfield village green, close to the church and just to the north of the old wharves and quays beyond Springfield Lock, where the Chelmer and Blackwater navigation connects to the coast. The area is now a suburb of the sprawling county town, but somehow still manages to retain a sense of otherness and mystery despite its urban nature.

During the second-world-war the house was used as a hostel for girls and it was during this time that a strange tale was told of two girls who complained that a sinister little elf had touched their faces whilst they slept. The bedroom was subsequently kept locked after this was reported, but shortly after a 'hideous little dwarf' was seen in the bedroom. This tale was reported in the local press and as a result, a letter

---

17. The Penny Farthing - The Maldon Museums Association Newsletter. Issue 43, Winter 2005: Which was a Witch article.
18. Witchcraft Persecutions in Essex 1560 – 1680 by Alan Macfarlane

Part Three: Dengie

was sent from Mary Petrie, whose family had once lived at the house for several generations. She quickly confirmed that the house was known for weird sightings of unusual creatures and in particular, the Blue Room was known for its 'Funny Man'. One night the mother of an infant awoke in the bedroom, after her child had cried out due to teething troubles. The child kept repeating 'funny man, funny man' and as the mother looked around the room, she caught a glimpse of a small dwarf-like creature with his back to the fire. She retreated under the bedclothes, and a few moments later, the apparition had gone.[19] This strange elemental also haunts the nearby churchyard and has been witnessed periodically since the mid-nineteenth century.[20]

---

19. Haunted Britain by Antony Hippisley Coxe, p 107
20. www.paranormaldatabase.com/essex/esspages/essex.htm

7. sea secrets

Odd stories still feature in this marshy domain of Dengie. On December 24th in the year 1640, comes an eerie and perplexing piece of time-slip folklore involving a traditional sailing barge that was trying to return to port in a thick sea mist in the Blackwater estuary. This salty old tale, which was still told in the district until at least the mid-1980s, goes something like this:

> The barge *Elizabeth* came slowly sailing through the mist on its way home to Maldon. It was carrying a cargo of lime and wood, and the sailors were anxious to get home, as sailing from Burnham had been slow. On approaching the mouth of the River Blackwater, and with the tide now quickly receding, the wooden barge became stuck on the mud, due to the thickening sea-fog and lack of any wind.

7. Sea Secrets

"Where are we?" asked Amos, who although a seasoned bargeman, was becoming anxious.

"Somewhere off Sales Point on the Dengie Flat, I expect," replied a sombre skipper. The barge creaked and groaned on the thick bank of oozing mud. Darkness was falling across the sea, as the foggy December night began to draw in around them. The hours would pass slowly for the two-man crew, as they waited anxiously for the tide to turn.

"Curse the weather," said John Gilden, who although the skipper with many years' experience at sea was becoming worried at their predicament.

"They will be waiting for me at the Hythe," said Amos his mate. The barge creaked in the cool breeze. "They say these marshes are haunted, yer know."

"I know," replied John, as he again tried to peer through the thick sea-mist.

"Did you hear that?" said John.

"Hear what?" cried Amos, shrinking into the shadows below the dark sails.

"I heard a buzzing noise," replied the skipper.
Both men sat in silence, waiting, and listening, hardly daring to breathe. Then suddenly the boat started to move. "Thank God for that; the tide is turning!"

With both men excited at the prospect of getting back to the warmth and beer in the Jolly Sailor they didn't hear the buzzing sound had returned. Then Amos heard a strange noise coming from the stern. Both men froze in horror as it dawned on them that they were not alone. John was the first to investigate. He made his way along the deck, and as he peered over the side into the water, he saw a body. He grabbed a boat hook and fished it out. As it flopped on deck, he noticed that it had a strange human form, with terrifying large round blue eyes, and a strange muttering came from its mouth which neither men could understand. The grotesque figure then raised an arm and proceeded to rip the skin from its head.

Both men took a few paces backwards towards the cabin. They were shocked and concerned by the monstrously odd *creature that they had pulled from the estuary. However, the wind suddenly got up, and both men were keen to catch the tide homewards. They quickly forgot the strangely grotesque and unholy merman that lay aboard their vessel and a short while later they heard a splash, and on looking at the water's surface they could just make out the strange aquatic being swimming away towards the ship's dinghy. Then, before the crew could stop it, the creature had untied the dinghy and was rowing away into the darkness.*

John was relieved, and not long after Amos sighted the beacon fire pot, glowing from the top of St Mary's tower, this guided them safely towards Maldon's Hythe Quay and as they slid alongside, they were grateful to be back at their home port and away from their somewhat uncanny estuarine experience…

An historical footnote from three hundred years later, helps to explain what occurred on that dark and foggy night in the Winter of 1640.

Vigilant Farmer Makes a Capture. Christmas Day, 1940. Thomas Harper, a farmer of the Dengie marshes near Maldon, captured a German pilot on Christmas morning. The pilot, still clad in his flying suit, was found asleep in a small dinghy stuck in the mud. He spoke no English and was taken to the farmer's house where he had Christmas dinner with the family before being taken away by the police. It is assumed that he had ditched into the sea and had stolen the dinghy to try and escape. The dinghy bore the name "Elizabeth" but no vessel in the region is registered as such.[21]

Just a couple of miles to the south of Maldon, as you enter the Dengie peninsula, lies the village of Mundon. The old and disused parish church of St Mary sits between

---

21. Ash magazine, number 5, autumn 1989. "Timeslip on the Marsh" sent in by reader Barbara Harris of Heybridge, Essex. Folk-narrative as told in the local area with alleged, but unfounded backstory which is professed to have been printed in the Daily Mirror 30 December 1940

7. Sea Secrets

the village and Mundon Creek. Here you can witness an ancient oak grove, reputed to be nine hundred years old, and which is believed to be the site of an even older druidic sacred enclosure. Nearer to the truth maybe is that the oaks were planted for the medieval shipbuilding industry. Either way, although now dead, the petrified corpses of the ancient oaks still stand today as an unusual and otherworldly monument to the past.

The Devil's handprint at Steeple is an old legend, featuring the former site of Stansgate Abbey, now Stansgate Farm. Stansgate Abbey was a Cluniac monastery founded in 1112, on the marshy southern shore of the River Blackwater, lying on a promontory between the islands of Osea and Ramsey. It was here that the monks once farmed the abbey grounds, and one day a lone cleric was ploughing furrows in a field next to the abbey. The work was hard going, and the ground sodden with wetness seeping in from the saltmarsh. He stumbled and cried out in anguish, cursing that if Satan would do his work for him, the Devil could claim his soul. Shortly afterwards the clouds thickened in the sky and The Owd Davvil himself suddenly appeared and took the plough. The farmer was shocked and awed by his presence and quickly retreated to the safety of the abbey, at once in fear of his mortal soul. The Devil pursued him and made a grab for him by the arched doorway. However, the farmer managed to retreat into the church just in time, and the marks of The Owd Davvil's hand were left in the stonework forever after.

After dissolution in 1525 the church was used as a barn, and the last of the abbey ruins had all been demolished by 1922. The old field is still called the Devil's Marsh, and it is believed that it wasn't ploughed again until 1946 for fear that the fiend would re-appear.[22] As often is

---

22. The Place-names of Steeple by James Kemble. www.essex.ac.uk/history/esah/essexplacenames

the case, a variant of this tale states that the Devil was cornered inside the abbey church and locked in. But when the monks returned with their Abbot, they found only his claw-marks, as he had escaped through one of the high windows.[23]

In 1566, the village of Steeple had its very own marsh wizard named Cunning Hawes, who was accused by the Rector of Creeksea of being a soothsayer and diviner and of keeping familiars to aid his work. The same rector also accused another villager named as Mr Richmond of being a diviner.[24]

On the marshes at Dengie village comes a tale of a ghostly supernatural party, that was witnessed at an old farmhouse at Court Farm. One dark winter's night, whilst waiting for some friends, a man noticed a party occurring in a nearby farmhouse, with guests apparently dressed as Victorians. After a while, the man got bored waiting for his friends, and instead decided to head to the farmhouse. As he approached, he could clearly see through the windows that a celebration was in full swing. He noticed a fiddler stood in one corner, playing a tune, but no sound could be heard. When the man knocked on the door, the scene completely vanished, and the farm became dark, unkempt, and lifeless. Whilst investigating the strange paranormal manifestations the following day, he was told that the farmhouse had been empty for years and was derelict.[25]

The mystical traditions of the Essex saltmarsh has long given us the folkloric tales of the Corpse Candles. These marshland lights would appear just above the high-water mark, and they are said to represent the souls of those drowned at sea. These lights continue to haunt the

---

23. A Ghost Hunter's Guide to Essex by Jessie K. Payne

24. Witchcraft Prosecutions in Essex: 1560 – 1680 by Alan Macfarlane, p 372

25. paranormaldatabase.com/essex/esspages/essedata.php?pageNum_paradata=6&totalRows_paradata=425

saltmarsh until the bodies of the deceased have been given a proper burial, and this belief still holds good on the lonelier parts of the Essex coast where saltmarsh, creek and swamp still hold sway.[26]

---

26. Ghosts and Witches by James Wentworth Day, p 166

8. the Lonely places of marsh-mystery

The riverside village of Bradwell-juxta-Mare sits at the furthest extremity of the Blackwater estuary. Here the past and present meld betwixt the strange white cladding of the decommissioned nuclear power station and the haunted remains of the ancient Roman road, which leads to the Othona shore, where Cedd intoned his mystic Nature prayers at his seventh century chapel, built by himself and his followers, who arrived from the holy isle of Lindisfarne to convert the pagan East Saxons. Today, the ancient chapel stands sentinel on the shoreline, constructed from the remains of the Roman Shorefort of Othona. It is here, out on the periphery, where the Cowslip, Samphire and Blackthorn grow, that the incorporeal spirits of place allow for liminal experience.

The indigenous spiritual atmosphere of the chapel has been kept alive by the nearby Othona Community, who live simply in a purpose-built centre, which lies just out of sight, between the chapel and the estuary. The community was founded by Norman Motley, who had his spiritual roots in the 1930s East End of London. He served as curate at the vast Hawksmoor church of Christchurch at Spitalfields, where charity was administered to the cosmopolitan slums around the famous fruit market. Upon the outbreak of war, Motley joined the RAF as a chaplain, and it was through his war experiences that he first thought about alternative ways to live and serve. Then during September 1945, he and a friend from the RAF, Leslie Stubbings visited Iona to meet George Macleod, the founder of the Iona community. The three men spent the night by the Sound of Mull and were all stunned by the news of a day earlier which described the dropping of the first atomic bomb on Japan. They all felt that a new age had been born, one which filled men and women with unimaginable horror. After the visit to Iona, Macleod tried to persuade Motley to rebuild Glastonbury as a community to both rival and reflect Iona and Lindisfarne. Motley subsequently visited Glastonbury, but his vision was not of rebuilding, but of creating something new and different. His ideal was that any community he created must be willing to accept all comers and be completely inclusive. A place of retreat was envisaged, where folk could come and contemplate, discover, and leave feeling fresh and renewed for the return to their daily lives. The centre of the Celtic Christian tradition of Lindisfarne on Holy Island was contemplated as a place for the community, but it was Motley's wife, Violet who had often mentioned a chapel in the marshes, which led to their March 1946 visit to St Peter's-on-the-Wall on the remote Essex shore. There had been synchronicities that had gently pushed them to Bradwell: unconnected folk had mentioned the site, plus a newspaper article suddenly appeared along with a photo of the then ruined chapel. The numinous power of the old chapel built by the hands of Cedd and his followers, who had of course sailed down from Lindisfarne in the mid seventh century, had taken hold of Norman and Violet Motley. They both felt that they had returned home. They subsequently gained permission from Chelmsford Cathedral to hold services there and got permission from the Army to use some garrison huts which had been abandoned in a field close to the chapel. They moved into the beginnings of their newly named Othona community in July 1946,[27] and I feel that over the last sixty-four years, they have played their part in helping to keep alive the hallowed ambience and sacred remoteness of this wetland expanse, on the

---

27. Much Ado About Something: A History of the Othona Community by Norman Motley

8. The Lonely Places of Marsh-Mystery

verge of the land, continuing to work in the shadow of St Cedd, fourteen hundred years after he first set foot on this mysterious bluff by the Blackwater estuary.

The ghost-lore of the area is fascinating. At the top of this list should be Walter Linnett's cottage, a small traditional weatherboard cottage which sits on the saltmarsh side of the sea wall, close to, but hidden from the old chapel by a dense thicket of stunted trees and coastal shrubs. Built into the ghostly outlines of the old Roman fort, this rare example of a traditional marshman's cottage was originally constructed during the Napoleonic wars, and may have housed the operators for the important semaphore signal station.[28] Linnett moved into the cottage in the late 1870s and began to raise a family from a living of wild fowling and fishing. Eight children were raised in this small and very cramped cottage and many rumours abound that the young children went to their beds made from boxes which were placed in cupboards.

The small cottage is soaked in the spectral activity of its former occupant. On many occasions sleeping residents have woken in the bedroom to find a figure standing over them or seen a face peering through the windows. In most cases the description appears to fit Walter Linnett, who in his lifetime hated visitors.[29] Linnett's Cottage is now used as a bird hide and is jointly managed by Essex Birdwatching Society and Essex Wildlife Trust.

The land around the ancient chapel is haunted by a rich and diverse range of spirit visitations. An invisible ghostly galloping horse and rider can sometimes be heard on moonlit nights, travelling along the sea wall from Weymarks beach, past the chapel before the sound fades as it travels south. The hoofbeats are reported to be loud and distinctive and have frequently woken folk from their slumber, including a camper at the Othona Community,

---

28. www.historicengland.org.uk/listing/the-list/list-entry/1146868
29. Essex Ghosts by James Wentworth Day, pp 30 - 33

who reported hearing the ghostly hoofbeats in June 1967. He also spoke of some ghostly legends that are connected to the chapel. A ghostly glowing light is sometimes seen from within the chapel. However, on entering the light is nowhere to be seen. Dim shadowy figures can also sometimes be seen in the chapel at night, and although the building is calm, friendly, and welcoming by day, a malevolent presence has been felt in the ancient structure after dark. The chapel was once at the centre of local smuggling operations, and maybe some of the eighteenth century free-traders still haunt the ancient building. On the sea wall beside the chapel a ghostly Roman centurion keeps guard at his post at the site of the old shore fort. Sometimes he appears at dusk, and at other times under the light of the full moon.[30]

As was reported by the Othona Community member in the 1960s, the old chapel still has a general air of tranquillity and ancient sanctity surrounding it, but at night the atmosphere can change suddenly, and a heavy feeling of dread and fear has been reported. I have encountered this myself on more than one occasion during night-time visits to the site, where I have witnessed the phenomenon of the ghostly light from within the chapel, and have also seen faint ghostly shapes both within and around the outside of the chapel.

Further snippets of Bradwell ghost lore suggest that ghosts can only be seen between midnight and *'brekkaday'*, and you cannot speak to them unless you are spoken to first. They will often whisper in your ear, but this could also be a guardian angel or a devil, so according to Bradwell lore, you should beware. Also, those born at midnight had the power of second sight and were particularly gifted at seeing ghosts.[31]

A large spectral black dog with a shaggy coat and shining eyes haunts the Othona shoreline and the Bradwell Marshes.

---

30. Ibid, pp 35, 36
31. The Realm of Ghosts by Eric Maple, p 188

8. The Lonely Places of Marsh-Mystery

Sighted as recently as 2002 by a man and his son, who were out 'lamping' for foxes on the saltmarsh. Along with a rifle and a torch, they were heading along the coast path on the top of the sea wall when an exceptionally large 'wolf-like' black dog emerged from the bushes. It had a shaggy coat and huge paws and crossed the footpath in front of them. They both later described the dog as much bigger than a deerhound. [32] They both described the peculiar way that the dog paid no interest in them at all, not even an acknowledging sniff or bark. They also described how farmers out combining at night during the harvest had also seen it. When they told others in the village, they admitted that it was known locally as 'Old Shuck'. According to one report, it seems that the Bradwell Old Shuck is particularly associated with the grain harvest, as all reported sightings have been seen around late summer.[33]

Bradwell-on-Sea had its own marsh witch. Her name was Diddy Horn, and she lived on the edge of the village at the beginning of the twentieth century. She was once caught bewitching a churn of butter, and the remedy was to thrust a red-hot poker into the milk, upon which Diddy came running out of her cottage screaming, and called out 'to stop burning the butter'. After this Diddy Horn was never seen again, though I suspect she retreated to her liminal ways as herb-doctor and cunning woman of the village.[34]

The ghost-lore and marsh-witchery of the Dengie can be summed up perfectly by one of Bradwell-on-Sea's former residents, Mrs Argent, who once stated that:

> *"The power of the witch is born in them. There's a bit of the devil about them, you see. Witches always had white mice. They*

---

32. East Anglian Witches and Wizards by Michael Howard, p 177
33. www.hiddenea.com/shuckland/dubiouscases.htm
34. The Witches of Dengie by Eric Maple. Folklore vol 73, no. 3 Autumn 1962

would sit and talk to them. The time to see ghosts and witches is breakaday, but only when the witches are ghosts...'[35]

Bradwell village had several reported cases of witchcraft during the sixteenth century. Margaret Lyttelberie was accused of bewitching two villagers, Elizabeth Motte, and Joan Osborne, causing them to become ill. At her hearing at Witham assizes on 27th of July 1584, Margaret pleaded not guilty. However, she was found to be guilty of causing illness by bewitchment and was imprisoned for one year. There were other suspected cases around the same time and in 1577, Joan Litelberie was accused of being a witch, along with Margery Sowman. In 1591, Mother Saunder was also suspected of witchcraft and she fled the village as a result.

In June of the same year, Margaret Wiseman of Bradwell, was accused of sorcery by Timothy Wardell of Maldon. She denied that she was a witch and, as there was no evidence forthcoming, she was released without charge. However, the village tongues wagged and soon Mother Wiseman was back in the spotlight as someone had seen a broom sweeping the witch's house alone, unaided and without the hands of any human. Again, she found herself in front of the magistrate. But in a strange twist of fortune, her former accuser, Timothy Wardell defended her saying that he had never seen a broom sweep in her house aided by witchcraft or any other magic. The testimony gave Margaret her second reprieve, but this failed to quieten down the rumours and gossip of her being a witch, and the envious prospect of having an automated broom around the house.[36]

Looking out towards Pewet Island, the Green Man pub sits by the shore at Bradwell Creek and historically has always been popular with the local marshmen and bargees. In the early years of the twentieth century, the landlord at the time always kept a large cauldron of hot potatoes

---

35. Ibid
36. Essex Witches by Glyn H. Morgan pp 59 - 60

8. The Lonely Places of Marsh-Mystery

hanging on a large hook over the ancient inglenook fireplace, as a warming ready meal for the crews as they sailed in on the flood tide. [37]

At nearby Mayland, comes the legend of a glowing supernatural lady who majestically rides a white horse across the starry night sky. But village folklore states that she could only be seen if you viewed the sky through the branches of a particular tree. Unfortunately, despite the veneration of this tree, it was felled by a farmer, and ever since, the ghostly horse and shimmering rider of the starry-sky have not been seen. In the vicinity there is also the ghost of a headless calf, who haunts the lonely and desolate marshes around Mayland Creek; and this traditional tale was still told in the latter part of the twentieth century, to ensure children were home before dark. Another piece of ghost lore suggests that you should always beware of the *Headless Horror of the Sea Wall*, who stalks the coast after dark, seeking all who are lost on the briny edge of the Dengie.

The picturesque village of Tillingham lies close to the coast, separated from the sea by the desolate and beautiful Tillingham Marshes. The Devil haunts a crossroads in the village, and once had a grudge against a local farm worker, and warned him that he would be waiting for him at the crossroads. During this devilish meeting, onlookers were astounded to see the farm worker fighting an invisible foe, and as he fled, he was pursued by the sound of the Devil's hooves. Another tale of the Devil at Tillingham sees him pursuing a local greengrocer whose soul had been mortgaged to him. One day, the fiend discovered the greengrocer selling turnips from his barrow on the green by the church. Terrified by his sudden macabre manifestation, the greengrocer fled inside the church, and the Devil pursued him but was unable to enter the sacred interior. In frustration the evil-one kicked a hole in the church wall and destroyed the greengrocer's barrow and

---

37. The Romance of Essex Inns by Glyn H. Morgan, p 66

turnips.[38] The Devil can be discovered lurking in many an old boneyard across this district, and the oldest churchyards in the Dengie had a tradition that the most ancient grave was the burial place of the Devil, and by running around it seven times you could hear him rattling his chains.

One of the strangest Essex folklore tales hails from Tillingham, and dates to 1652. Local girl, Mary Adams, was a member of the pantheistic, anarchistic, and heretical Christian sect called *The Ranters*. This sect was regarded by the government as a threat to social order and members often appeared in public without clothing and rejected civil and religious laws. Neighbours noticed that Mary was pregnant and when challenged she announced that she was the Virgin Mary and that she had miraculously conceived the child of the Holy Spirit. She denied that Christ had manifested as flesh, and that she would bring forth the saviour of the world. The local minister Reverend Hadley ordered that she be arrested. Mary was imprisoned until after the birth of her child, and the child was born on the ninth day of her labour. However, the child was stillborn and was described as an ugly misshapen monster with no hands or feet but with claws like a toad. Immediately after the birth, Mary's body became covered with blotches and boils and within a few days her health had deteriorated so badly that she committed suicide by stabbing herself with a borrowed knife.[39]

Many customs were once common across the Dengie marshes. In the 1950s Tillingham you would be told to break a lapwing's egg into a cup of tea, if you were feeling unwell; and at Woodham Walter, the village wise-woman could cure burns by making the sign of the cross over the burn and muttering an incomprehensible incantation.[40]

---

38. The Witches of Dengie by Eric Maple. Folklore vol 73, no. 3 Autumn 1962
39. The Ranters Monster by George Horton. London, 1652.
40. Essex. Its Forest, Folk and Folklore by Charlotte Craven Mason. 1928

8. The Lonely Places of Marsh-Mystery

Warts would be cured by rubbing the affected area of skin with a piece of chalk, after which, a chalk mark was drawn inside the chimney, and as the mark faded, so would the wart.[41]

On May Day morning, the villagers at Purleigh would sing in the May from the top of the tower of All Saints church, overlooking the surrounding landscape.[42] Purleigh was also home to a witch named Isabel Whyte, who was accused of killing farm animals in March 1600. The following animals, belonging to Thomas Ward, were believed to have been struck down dead by enchantment. The two cows, a ram and nine pigs were found dead on the farm, and of course witchcraft was immediately suspected. Isabel was accused of bewitching the animals and causing them to die. Luckily, she was found to be innocent, and was acquitted of all charges.[43]

The more inland districts of the Dengie were, and still are, populated with arable farms, and here we find some folklore that persisted around the harvest, up until the beginning of World-War-Two.

The last load of corn that was brought in was always the most important one. These were called 'the rakings' and they were gathered by as many men who could work the field with huge rakes, most often collecting as much that would fill a wagon or two. Once collected, some of the men would sit atop the wagon on the rakings, holding up a large bough, which had been cut from a nearby oak tree. This may have been done in some sort of remembrance of the sacred oak tree of the druids, with the bough being seen as symbolic of important feasts such as harvest, being held within the mighty oak groves of old, much like the one that remains at Mundon.

---

41. The Witches of Dengie by Eric Maple. Folklore vol 73, no. 3 Autumn 1962
42. Essex. Its Forest, Folk and Folklore by Charlotte Craven Mason. 1928
43. www.essex-family-history.co.uk/witches.html

The Liminal Shore

As the wagons left the fields in convoy, harvest horns were blown, and some now-long-forgotten songs were sung. These harvest horns were made of bullock horns, and were kept in pride-of-place at the farmhouse, for their ceremonial end-of-harvest use each year. Once all collected in, the farm hands would be paid their 'largess', which signified the last of the harvest pay, and probably the last pay of the farming year for most.[44]

---

44. Essex. Its Forest, Folk and Folklore by Charlotte Craven Mason. 1928, pp 127, 128

9. hart family and the curren

The centre of all folk-magic practice on the Dengie was the town of Latchingdon, where many generations of Hart family witches lived alongside members of the mysterious cunning folk clan known as *The Curren*. This institution was first mentioned by Eric Maple in his paper on the *Witches of Dengie*, where he stated that the name was an older term for the Dengie cunning tradition, but was *'no longer remembered'*.

The Hart family were, by far, the most notorious witches to reside in the district and records exist stretching back to the sixteenth century. Many villages in the area have folklore relating to witches from the Harts, and one common theme was that you could always spot them by the look of power in their eyes, and most tales of the family include the story of the stolen church bell from Latchingdon.

The sixteenth century Mistress Hart suffered from a particularly nasty aversion to church bells. She was especially annoyed by the bells at Latchingdon church. One night she removed the bells from the church tower and took them to Burnham where she attempted to take them to Canewdon on the opposite side of the river. Instead of a boat she used a barrel and used a feather for an oar. Not surprisingly, neither she nor the bells made the crossing. Legend has it that on stormy nights the bells can be heard tolling from under the River Crouch and Mistress Hart still haunts the southern bank of the river, between Canewdon and the ancient ferry crossing at South Fambridge. She has also been seen on the northern bank of the river at the Old Ferry House, (now the Ferry Boat Inn) where she silently haunts the area by gently drifting around the lonely marshes, manifesting under the light of the moon and stars. Village lore also records that Mistress Hart sometimes appears as a more scary ghost, without her head. Interestingly, one particular manifestation saw the glowing spectre of the old witch floating by the fireplace of the inn.[45]

There are folkloric rumours that another witch of the Hart family clan lived at North Fambridge and she and her husband were so disliked by the villagers, that they were taken to the river where they were tied to a boat and dragged behind it. Mr Hart sunk and nearly drowned but Witch Hart floated. This was taken to be a sign that Witch Hart was guilty as it was believed that witches could not drown.[46]

Towards the end of the nineteenth century, the last in line of the historic Hart witch family lived at Deadaway Bridge. The bridge spans a tiny threshold waterway which empties into the nearby Mayland Creek, and marks the brink between the parishes of Latchingdon and Mundon. Harriet Hart was not liked by the villagers and she was renowned for

---

45. The Witches of Dengie by Eric Maple. Folklore vol 73, no. 3 Autumn 1962. The Ferry Boat inn stands where the Ferry house.
46. www.essex-family-history.co.uk/witches.htm

9. Hart Family and the Curren

causing storms, blighting crops, and bewitching pigs. On one occasion the entire village came together to light a cleansing ritual bonfire as a counter witchcraft act to break her powers. Harriet had the gift of being able to fly across the district at night on a hurdle, which seems to be the favoured magical and folkloric vehicle of Essex sea-witchery. She had a legion of imps in the shape of white mice and she would use her imps to bewitch cartwheels, and the only way of removing the conjuration was to lash the wheels with the horse whip, or by calling one of *The Curren*, who would use one of their walking sticks to the same effect. She also stole a bell from Latchingdon church, a family trait, and sailed it across to Wallasea Island where another witch called Mother Redcap lived, and the two ladies planned a collaboration to use the church bell as part of their folk-magic rituals.

Rumour had it that Harriet kept her many imps hidden in her cottage, which was sited close to Deadaway Bridge. One night a man was riding past, when he met a vast army of small animals with fiery red eyes. He lashed his horse and escaped, although to his dying day he claimed that the creatures were Mistress Hart's imps on their way to cause mischief.

Despite her harsh reputation, Harriet did have a sense of humour and did also help people as a Cunning Woman. There is a record of an incident where she worked some love magic and saved a young girl from meeting a *wrong-un*, and on the same night encouraging the benevolent meeting of a better suitor, and through this beneficial enchantment, Mr Rutherford became the happiest man around.[47]

On her death bed, Harriet Hart did try to confer her powers to her grandson through the traditional rite of *passing on her imps*. After he had visited his dying gran, he left the cottage on horseback, but as he began his journey, a hoard of white mice scurried across the garden and tried to follow him. He forced the horse to gallop and

---

47. The Witches of Dengie by Eric Maple. Folklore vol 73, no. 3 Autumn 1962

escaped the infestation of imps, and through this act, broke the spell of lineage and the imps died at Harriet Hart's side.[48]

As previously stated, the Dengie Hundred had its share of cunning men and women, who at some time in the past were known as *The Curren*. They had the reputation of beneficial marsh wizardry and all the connections of respectability. They attended church or chapel on Sundays and for the most part practised their art curious and ague healing without too many problems. Most of *The Dengie Curren*, like their darker counterparts, seemed to centre on Latchingdon. These marsh wizards and cunning men had the power to stop farm machinery with their eyes. 'Silly Bill' Spearman was one such wizard, and it was believed he was descended from one of the old Essex gypsy families. Another cunning man was known as Buzzy of Latchingdon, who also served as a policeman in the district. On one occasion a villager tried to follow one of the *Latchingdon Curren* home but was thwarted by a bit of Curren folk-magic whereby a cart load of turnips became enchanted, animated, and charged with chasing him away. Maybe these Curren marsh-wizards had some knowledge of psychedelics, too?

It was believed that the source of the power of the witch, wizard or cunning practitioner was in the act of *'cooking a rat'*. Eric Maple remarked *'Whether this was in the literal sense, or not, it has not been made clear'*. Though I think this term is more to do with these creatures that were kept as the familiar spirits of the wizard or witch. In other words, these *'rats'* were the folk memories of the fairy folk or genius loci of the farmland, salt-marsh and sea; and I suspect that the term *'cooking a rat'* may have meant something a bit more abstract, as in charging a spell or invoking a charm, or even seeking out and tapping into the powerful and sacred spots along the coast, saltmarsh and farmland of eastern Essex.

---

48. Ibid

9. Hart Family and the Curren

Another Latchingdon counter witchcraft charm that was used by *The Curren* was to do some *'hustling'*. This meant thrashing any object that was believed to house the mischievous spirit of the witch or imp with a stick, and I think that this and other folk memories of these sticks that *The Curren*, and other Essex cunning folk used proves without doubt that these were more than mere walking sticks. It was also the custom across both the Dengie and Rochford Hundreds to always leave the tallest thistle in the field standing, as this was known as the Devil's thistle. The old lore of the marsh wizards also decrees that their walking stick should always be made from these tallest thistles, and only members of *The Curren* should pick them.[49] There is a curious description of the Devil as he apparently manifested on one of the dark lanes leading to the nearby marshes. He was described as at least seven-foot-high, with one cloven hoof and one ordinary one. His ears were described as like rhubarb leaves, and when the Devil flapped them, the turbulence they created would blow you over and hold you down. This devilish apparition was also reported to offer anyone who witnessed him, some food. This was always bread and crab apple, and you were forced to accept it, or the old Devil would stamp his cloven foot upon you.

It appears that the Dengie cunning men were not always trusted to be good enough at their craft, and although the Dengie folk feared the reputation of the witches and wizards to the south of the river, there were occasions when the '*Old Man Witch*' George Pickingill of Canewdon was consulted. On one occasion two farm labourers from Dengie village decided to make their way to the Fambridge ferry and cross the water to visit Pickingill in his old decrepit cottage at Canewdon. As they set off one of them commented "I wonder if the old bugger is at home". On arriving at their

---

49. Author's archival collection of East Essex Witch-lore, and also alluded to in The Dark World of Witches by Eric Maple, p 161.

destination, they heard the sounds of a window being opened, and Old George shoved his head out and shouted, "Yes the old bugger is at home". It is interesting to note that Old George himself made use of a blackthorn walking stick, and we will discuss more about this later, as we head south of the Crouch.

The famous yachting town of Burnham-on-Crouch lies on the southern shore of the Dengie peninsula, and has many stories to tell of smuggling, witchcraft, and ghosts. The river from whence the town has its origins rises in a pond hidden in Wilderness Wood on the edge of the village of Little Burstead. It then flows due east for around 25 miles until it reaches the North Sea between Holliwell Point and Foulness Point and is navigable for seventeen miles between Battlesbridge and the sea.

Burnham town once had the anarchistic folk tradition of fiery tar barrels, which were rolled around the town on 5th November. Today the town celebrates its carnival at this time, but the carnival's origins lie in the traditions of fire in the streets, merry making and general mayhem and misrule. The tradition was first reported in 1856, when John Harris, a Burnham labourer was charged with rolling a blazing tar barrel through the street and setting fire to hay on the highway. The custom appears to evolve from this date with a male and female effigy being burned, and visitors to the spectacle would arrive 'bedizened', meaning that they would dress up in gaudy and outlandish clothes. The flaming barrels would be rolled through the streets using sticks and wooden hoops. Over the years the event grew and by the 1890s a group of youths known as the *'Ropeyard Gang'* were rolling the blazing barrels through Burnham high street each November, supported by local businesses. At the festival's height, a torchlit procession, masked revellers and the town band joined the festivities. However, some residents started to petition the local constabulary to get the event stopped. During the first decade of the twentieth century, incidents were gradually toned down and the beginnings of

9. Hart Family and the Curren

the modern carnival began to take shape.[50] However, the spectacle of the tar barrels, flaming torches, the ropeyard gang and the bedizened revellers evokes a spectacle that would have been worthy of the liminal shore, and I would have loved to have witnessed it.

Smuggling was rife in Burnham during the nineteenth century, and to help combat the smugglers, the hulk of a ship named *Kangaroo* was moored where the Royal Corinthian Yacht Club is now sited. This ship was used to house the families of local Coast Guards to keep the free traders of the Crouch at bay. On the opposite bank of the river, Charles Darwin's ship *Beagle* once served a similar purpose, and the remains of Darwin's ship still lies buried under the mud of the Crouch's major tributary, the River Roach, within the Paglesham mudflats.

An old cobbler and cunning man from Burnham once told of a local way to heal warts. The Burnham wart charm was often used, and is described thus:

> *Rub a piece of chalk on the wart and then use chalk to draw a mark within the chimney inside the home of the person affected. Then as the chalk mark faded the wart would disappear.*

This is almost identical to the previously mentioned wart charm which was used by the wise woman of Woodham Walter. It is interesting that this was passed on from a cobbler, as this profession does seem to crop up when researching cunning men of the Essex coast.

Lying on the river between Bridgemarsh Island and Burnham is the ancient village of Creeksea. One of the major buildings here is Creeksea Place, an Elizabethan mansion. The grounds are haunted by the ghost of a large white stallion, which can be seen on dark nights, thundering around the gardens, with mane and tail flying. Nearby at Tinker's Hole, deep within a devil haunted wood, lived the

---

50. www.essex-family-history.co.uk/carnival.htm

witch called Fanny Bird. One night during a storm, she was out in the woods by the creek in a bid to invoke the elemental powers of the Old Horned One. During the rite, a bolt of lightning struck her arm and caught fire. However, she did not die, and apart from a withered arm, lived to tell the tale. She was accused of many things including bewitching farm machinery, controlling the weather, performing rituals to summon the Devil and on her death bed, she tried to pass on her powers by handing her imps to her daughter. However, though the daughter was very much like her mother, she refused to take them. Her husband Thomas Bird was a marsh-wizard and practised as a cunning man. He had a particular penchant for practising weather magic. He liked to raise storms and like his wife he was also struck by lightning. He was hit on the leg and forever afterwards had a limp. For years after these events, they could easily be spotted as Fanny had a withered arm, and Thomas had a limp. However, they both had the reputation as powerful weather workers, and Thomas was often called on by local farmers, fisherman and sailors to adjust the weather accordingly for the maximisation of each profession.[51]

Tinker's Hole is also home to the shimmering ghost of a gypsy girl. She appears dressed in a long and flowing white dress at Hellfire Corner. The ghost-lore surrounding her has the glowing spectral visitation haunting once every month, during the darkness of the new moon. For it was here during the early nineteenth century that she was knocked down and killed by a coach and four horses as it thundered along the road, trying to reach Burnham before the tide turned.[52] Another woman rumoured to be a witch lived in Ostend Street, Burnham. Mary Cockley (nee Sadler) had the reputation of ill wishing and was feared in the town because of this. Mary came from a Burnham fishing family called Sadler and was born in 1826. She

---

51. Essex Witches by Glynn H. Morgan, p 53
52. www.burnham.info/visitors/q-i/ghost-stories

9. Hart Family and the Curren

married Tollesbury coal porter, William Cockley, in 1848, and they subsequently had eight children. William died in 1878 and Mary remained a widow for another twenty-seven years. She died in Creeksea in 1905, aged 81. Eric Maple mentions her in his paper on the witches of Dengie, and he recorded a recollection from one local man, Mr Playle. As a boy, he refused to run an errand for Mary and was threatened with:

'You'll come home wetter than when you set out'

Mr Playle still refused to run any errands for Mary that day, and off he went. However, he fell into a pond the same day and almost drowned, and on his return home Witch Cockley laughed and jeered as he walked past her cottage. Playle's mother was so enraged by this that she struck Mary with a house flannel. After this, Mr Playle's mother became extremely ill, and rumours spread that Mary had cursed her. It seems that the Playle family lived next door to Mary Cockley, in Ostend Street.[53] Also, of interest here is a mention of Mary Cockley and the Burnham Guy Fawkes tar barrels tradition. Local paper The Essex Newsman reported on the tar barrels in their 12th November 1881 edition:

> *Not for several years past has the celebration of the fifth of November in this district been of so demonstrative a character as on Saturday last. At Burnham at intervals during the day the juveniles mustered in strong force, some of them being grotesquely bedizened. In the evening, a large number of persons assembled in the High-street, where a large bon fire was lighted, and several tar barrels were rolled about the street. There was also an extensive display of fireworks. Some attempts were made to interfere with the proceedings but without effect, and notwithstanding the*

---

53. www.deadfamilies.com/Z3-Others/PDF-Files/Book-MaryCockley-Alleged-Witch-Of-Essex-0704-2019-01.pdf

efforts of Police constable Piper to prevent it, an outhouse on the premises occupied by a widow named Cockley was beaten down by a number of men in disguise, and carried away to the fire, where it was consumed.

So, was Mary Cockley a witch, and did she practice folk-magic and sorcery? With only one or possibly two instances reported by her neighbours, the Playle family, it seems that we will never really know for sure. Though as she was a widow for many years, she probably earned a reputation due to the culture of the day, and maybe she gained an income from herbs, charms, and midwifery as so many other widows did at the time.

At the other end of the tidal Crouch lies the creekside village of Battlesbridge, where tidal lock gates keep the river navigable and the harbour in use. The village has some interesting folklore, the first of which concerns the celebration of St Agnes Eve, which was once widely observed across the county. The lore states that on January 20th each year you should sit by a windowsill at Midnight and stare out into the dark night. As you gaze into the darkness a figure will materialise. The vision will represent the person most likely to influence the sitter's life during the next twelve-month period.

Sometime during the late nineteenth century, a Battlesbridge girl decided that she should observe the St Agnes Eve custom and sat at her window overlooking the river by the quay. She was anxious to see her future husband, and on the celebrated night, a ghostly image of a man appeared and handed her a knife wrapped in brown paper. He then vanished, leaving only the faint starlight, which gently illuminated the high tide lapping against the harbour wall.

A few months later a man arrived in the Crouch-side village, he gained a property there and married the girl. Shortly after their marriage, the man opened a kitchen drawer and discovered the knife that she had been given. With his in-laws as witnesses, he turned to his wife and said, *"you are the*

9. Hart Family and the Curren

woman who forced me to come here one cold January night, it really did happen, though I thought it was a dream!" He unwrapped the knife and promptly stabbed his wife with it. [54]

The village also has a ghost who haunts the riverside. This is the eerie spirit of the former village witch of Battlesbridge, known as the hopping witch, who put fear into the hearts of all who saw her. The cottage where she lived was always given a wide berth and if anyone should enter, they never came out again.

Just a short distance upstream lies the mysterious village of Runwell, where a strange mix of devil-lore, churchyard ghosts and holy well customs make for an interesting excursion.

The parish church of St Mary has a plethora of ghosts, including the ghost of a priest, a headless horseman, a spectral lady and the Devil, who will appear if you run around the church anti-clockwise nine times at midnight. Inside the church on the back of the door can be found the Devil's claw mark, and a curious piece of folklore explains this in some detail.

One day during the sixteenth century the rector of St Mary's at Runwell became ill and took to his bed. A provisional replacement priest was found called Rainauldus, who was a bit of a maverick, who believed in the occult and practised his own esoteric form of Christianity. One morning shortly after he had taken up his temporary position, he was taking communion at the altar, when he noticed that the Devil was trying to manifest from within his mouth. Within minutes he had exhaled the beast, and

---

54. This was originally collected by 'Jop Summers', and was recorded in the article An Essex Hedgetrimmer's Ghostbook by Raymond Lamont-Brown. This Essex, March 1974. This article was later republished in 'The Best of Essex: An Anthology of Memory Articles and Photographs' compiled by E. V. Scott. Despite contacting author Raymond Lamont-Brown, I am still unable to discover who 'Jop Summers' really was, and I still eagerly await the promised reply and explanation from Mr Lamont-Brown.

the Devil was chasing him around the church, much to the horror of the parishioners. With the fiend gaining strength, Rainauldus escaped through the south door, quickly closing it behind him. Finding his exit barred, Old Hornie struck out at the door, leaving his claw marks scorched deep within the wood. Meanwhile the terrified parishioners had roused the rector from his bed next door, and armed with holy water and a crucifix he approached the south door, hoping to find Rainauldus, but instead he found a bubbling, stinking, tar-like mess upon the floor of the porch. This was slowly dissipating and before long all that remained of him was a dark stain with a strange skull-like flint within the centre. This flint was displayed for many years on the south wall of the church with the inscription 'Stipendia Peccati Mors' – the wages of sin is death. However, in the 1980s the flint and inscription was removed.

The village also has a holy well, sited around one and a half miles due north of the church. Known as the Running Well or Our Lady's Well, it is sited in a small dell at the boundary of three fields. Much speculation has been made over the years about this ancient well, including its influence of the origin of the village name. Runwell, is probably derived from Rune Well, meaning a well with a secret. There is a folkloresque narrative that could be traditional, but is far more likely to be the work of the imaginative and eccentric antiquarian priest, *The Most Rev. John Edward Bazille-Corbin*. In 1923, he became Rector of St Mary's church at Runwell, and held this benefice until his retirement on 30th September 1961. During his time serving the parish, he researched and wrote a book in which he published some oral traditions and folklore of the village, that he had collected from some of the older residents.

One of these tales was about the Shrine of the Blessed Virgin Mary of Running Well, and tells the tale of Sister Lucy. The folk narrative suggests that the well was looked after by a convent of nuns, and this convent stood close to the Running Well on the site where Poplars Farm now stands. The convent had its own sacred talisman or relic, called the Prioress' Ring, which was presented to the convent in a miraculous vision by the Blessed Virgin Herself. This relic, said to hold a stone of topaz, would protect the young nuns and keep them on the righteous path of purity and of the faith. One of these was Sister Lucy, who had entered the convent at the age of fourteen, but later realised that a life of chastity was not for her. She left the convent, but found that a life outside was not necessarily better, as she quickly found that she was alienated from society because of her time as a nun. One night she was particularly desperate and hungry that she decided to steal some candlesticks from the convent, which she hoped could be swapped for some food at one of the local farms. She crept into the convent whilst the nuns were at prayer, placed the candlesticks in her bag and made her way across the field and towards the lane. The night was quiet, dark, and cold, with a layer of recent snowfall covering the land. As she made her way along the snow filled lane, a strange, uncanny, and somewhat muffled noise was heard. From across the snowy landscape came a yelping and baying, which seemed to be getting closer to her position. Sister Lucy was terrified, and as the noises became louder and clearer, she witnessed three giant dogs, standing dark against the snow, with large red eyes blazing like fire, and foam dripping jaws with savage teeth that gnashed and snarled. The poor girl was overcome with fear and threw away the stolen candlesticks and ran all the way back to the convent. Running with fear and dread in her heart, she arrived first at the holy well. A cacophony of wails, barks and howls echoed across the wintry scene, as the phantom dogs continued their chilling pursuit. Lucy knew she was close to the Running Well, and as she approached the holy well and its hallowed shrine of Our Lady, she slipped on some ice, and plunged into the frozen waters. The demon dogs encircled but it was too late. Lucy was gone deep into the well, below the holy water. However, luckily for her, the convent gardener had heard the ghostly hounds and had left his warm hearth to see what the commotion was. He witnessed Lucy falling into the dark waters of the well, and subsequently witnessed the miraculous appearance of an apparition of a glowing lady, standing by the well. She was known as the Golden Lady of the Well, and she eventually managed to save Sister Lucy. However, she had to haul her out of the icy water three times before she was rescued, and each time she was pulled out of the water, she lost seven years. Meanwhile the other sisters had arrived to help, and as they observed the miraculous scene, Lucy had reverted to the age of fourteen. As the glowing golden lady faded, John Bundocke, the gardener managed to revive Lucy from her ghastly ordeal, and due to the miracle, she was immediately re-admitted to the convent, stating that she would never again stray from the path of her holy vows.[55]

---

55. See the Running Well Mystery by Andrew Collins. The tale was taken from Rev. John Edward Bazille Corbin's unpublished collection of folktales and customs entitled 'Runwell St Mary: A farrago of History, Archaeology, Legend and Folk-lore, collected and pieced together during an incumbency of many years.' The MS is held by Essex Record Office.

part 4: thames

Bats flitted over his head and followed him as he tramped the steadily-rising path, but no other living thing came near till he stood on higher ground than the castle hill and was within stone-throw of Hadleigh street. For the dark castle lane was no popular resort after dusk. One might meet the White Lady, or perhaps her victim, Wryneck Sal, and there was the man that hanged himself in the castle barn.

'Cunning Murrell' Arthur Morrison

The expansive tidal Thames stretches wide along the southern shore of Essex. The river defines this region of stark contrast, where we have our most urban of shorelines, but paradoxically, also the remotest of islands. Where the islands sit, strange tales emerge of monsters, devils, and witches and even the broad estuary hides a secretive sea serpent. This is Thameside Essex; a brackish zone where a brasher style of waterway emerges alongside the urban and suburban landscapes. This is a district of contradiction, defined in the less populated northern areas by the promontory formed by the two rural rivers of the Crouch and Roach. Immediately east of this, lies the flat muddy islands and in the south the more urban shore is completely dominated by the mighty estuary of London's great river, where viscous mud, dark clay and grey sand form a boundary, where the sea spirits and old gods dance at the confluence of the alchemical waters of sacred river and wild open sea.

The folklore of south-eastern Essex is dominated by the more famous witches and cunning men of the county. However, there is still so much more to discover among the wooded hills, saltings and farmland that still manages to creep inwardly between the urban sprawl running westwards from Shoeburyness, along the tidal mire, to the Rainham Marshes. Beyond Rainham is where Essex and London begin to blur in the east-west spread of the so-called *Thames Corridor*, and where the boundaries become hidden in a geographic mire of oblivion. Yet the sacred river somehow holds all this history along its northern shore, in tangible cohesiveness, and despite the decayed jetties, ruinous harbours and dismantled oil refineries, a new London gateway port has risen from the waterfront close to Stanford-le-Hope, allowing the history of merchant shipping to continue into the future, from a new deep-water harbour in the Thames.

10. mud archipelago

The islands of the Essex coast are deeply mysterious, and the archipelago where the rivers Roach and Crouch meet are the strangest of all. Foulness, Potton, Wallasea, Havengore, New England and Rushley are the six islands that make up this group. These remarkable flat and marshy islands just off the muddy foreshore, resemble a mini delta, with the silty channels that separate them, draining twice daily on the ebb tide. Here, the secretive network of creeks, rivulets and saltmarsh is still a rural and lonely retreat, where despite their proximity to the urbanisation of the south Essex coast, they manage to retain a deep solitude and isolation.

The most famous of the islands historic inhabitants was the witch called Old Mother Redcap. She lived close to the sea wall on Wallasea, in an old farmhouse called Tyle Barn. She is best remembered for her spoken charm *'Holly holly brolly brolly Redcap! Bonny bonny'*. After her death in the 1920s, the house, which was also known as the Duval's (or Devil's) house became haunted by the spirit of her familiar and people kept away. Cattle would become ill when they ventured too close to the farmhouse and anyone who stayed for too long was encouraged to kill themselves by a ghostly voice.[56] The folkloric history of the old farmhouse states that it was built under the supervision of the *Owd Davvil* himself, who had thrown the central building beam into the air and ordered the builders to erect the house where the beam fell. There is an even older belief that the Devil haunts the Essex saltmarsh, and holds court with the hobgoblins and sea-serpents that also dwell within this briny temporal abode. Mother Redcap's familiar resided in one particular room of the farmhouse, on the first floor. It would often signify its presence by the sound of huge wings beating up against the ceiling. The imp would sometimes show itself, either as a white mouse or in the shape of a monstrously hideous winged ape. The farm was first established on Wallasea during the mid-seventeenth century and was called the Demon's Tenement. Mother Redcap was the last to live there before the farmhouse was severely damaged by a second world war bomb. The final remains were washed away in the great flood of 1952.[57]

The witches in these parts never rode broomsticks,[58] and the ghostly form of Old Mother Redcap can still sometimes be seen riding a hurdle over the marshes on moonlit nights.

---

56. East Anglian Magic by Nigel Pennick. P 51
57. Witchcraft and Magic in the Rochford Hundred by Eric Maple. Folklore vol. 76 no. 3 Autumn 1965
58. The Witches of Dengie by Eric Maple. Folklore vol 73, no. 3 Autumn 1962

10. Mud Archipelego

It is interesting to note that the stretch of water on the south coast of Wallasea, where the islands of Potton and Foulness are closest, is still known as Devil's Reach, named after the Devil's House no doubt.[59] Witches were still meeting in these parts as late as the final decades of the twentieth century, to perform their strange sea rites and marsh conjurations. A favoured spot was at the point where Paglesham Reach, Paglesham Pool and the River Roach converge, immediately to the south of Wallasea Island, close to Mother Redcap's former home.[60]

An old story tells of a ghost ship that is sometimes seen floating across the saltings by the shore of Wallasea Island.[61] The ship can suddenly loom from the mist at dusk, creaking and groaning as though she still sailed upon the flowing tides, seeking a friendly port to make berth to unload her cargo of spirits.

Wallasea Island is now an RSPB reserve, and can be visited. The land here is specked with watery rivulets and grassland, where hares and little owls can be seen. Miles of untamed saltmarsh ring the island, and the shrill cry of wildfowl echo across the tides. The sea wall gives great views across the Crouch to Burnham and there are many trails across the island, where the wildlife can be experienced. This is a place to tread lightly, where you can walk in the ghostly shadow of Old Mother Redcap and her witchy collaborators from Burnham, who would often visit, sometimes using a variety of strange floating objects (such as upturned church bells) or perhaps more likely, the short ferry ride from Creeksea.

Mother Redcap was also active on Foulness Island and seems to have continually worked on both islands. However, sometime during the early 1920s, Alfred Herbert

---

59. Essex Coastline: Then and Now by Matthew Fautley and James Garon, p 161
60. Author's archive
61. Haunted Southend by Dee Gordon

Martin, an island farm labourer from Wallasea reported that one of his colleagues had witnessed a Mrs Smith, Mother Redcap of Foulness coming across the water on a hurdle in the moonlight. She had no oars but sailed as though she did. [62] This may possibly hint that there were two Mother Redcaps, one on each island.[63] Mother Redcap was almost certainly a title, given that others of the same name are recorded elsewhere in Britain; and appears to denote a woman that brews ale, practises witchcraft and promotes sorcery, and if Alfred Martin's account is accurate, it appears that Mrs Smith may have worn a red cap. Below is a segment of a first-hand account (in local dialect) of how Mother Redcap was seen crossing from one island to the next:

> *'One night my mate found hisself hulled out o' bed an' down the stairs. He never know'd what done it. That owd davvle wore strong as an hoss. Tew nights arterward he rowed over to Foulness Island across the creek. He came back late in the moonlight, bright as day that wore. "Alf" he say to me, "what do you recon I seed when I was a-rowin across the crick? I seed that owd Mrs. Smith, owd Mother Redcap from Foulness, comin' acrost the water on a wooden hurdle in the moonlight.*'[64]
>
> *Alfred Herbert Martin,*
> *Wallasea Island farmhand, circa 1920*

The forbidden isle of Foulness is still out of bounds, due to its MOD landlords. However, visitor-passes can be obtained, and there is a museum which is open on certain Sundays, when folk are permitted to cross the narrow

---

62. Essex Ghosts by James Wentworth Day, page 39

63. Daddy Witch and Old Mother Redcap: Survivals of the Old Craft Under Victorian Christendom by Nigel Pennick. Published on behalf of the Cornerstone Press by the New Propagators of Pagan Knowledge, 1985.

64. Essex Ghosts by James Wentworth Day, p 39

10. Mud Archipelego

channels which separate the otherworldly island from the mainland. This lonely isle is haunted by a headless ghost and is rumoured to have harboured a few witches and cunning folk over the centuries.[65] Several Bellarmine jars have been found buried in the sea wall over the years, probably brought in by the seventeenth century Dutch workers who reclaimed the marshes from the sea. These jars were popular as witch bottles during this time, and one may speculate whether they were buried here as counter-witchcraft protection charms. There is an intriguing paragraph in Eric Maple's paper *Witchcraft and Magic in the Rochford Hundred*, which hints of a possible witch of Foulness:

> *Mrs Bush, aged ninety-eight, late of the island and now living on the mainland, ridiculed any suggestion of witchcraft there, but as old memories were awakened, she trailed off into... 'It wasn't true what they said about my aunt. She didn't have a spirit following her about. It was a lie; she was a good woman.'*

At the eastern extremity of the isle, at Foulness Point on the sea wall and beyond, where the mud flats are revealed at each low tide, the ethereal cries of wading birds carry on the wind. The cackle of the curlew and the shrieking cry of the oystercatcher can chill the blood at dusk. Island folklore claims that the noisy chatter of the shelducks is believed to be the ghostly conversation of long dead sailors, now the eerie guardians of this foreboding shore, awaiting to receive the next poor souls to be drowned on the deadly tides and swirling currents on the desolate edge.[66] An old Saxon pagan tradition of appeasing the faeries and sea-spirits of Foulness was until relatively recently still practised by placing bowls of oatmeal on the edge of the saltmarsh after dark.

---

65. Folklore vol. 76 no. 3 Autumn 1965: Witchcraft and Magic in the Rochford Hundred by Eric Maple.
66. In Search of Ghosts by James Wentworth Day p 153

There are several old farms scattered around the island, dating from the seventeenth and eighteenth centuries. Quay Farm sits on the north-western edge of the isle and it was here that the main route off the island took the locals by foot ferry to Burnham, to stock up with provisions. In the past it was much easier to travel by ferry across the Crouch than face the age-old Broomway track across the tidal marshes to the south. This road was covered by the sea for most of the time, and many have lost their lives using it. The road from the mainland, that traverses New England and Havengore Islands, before it arrives at Foulness, was only built in the early twentieth century by the MOD, and previously, all road traffic had to arrive by the ancient and treacherous Broomway, including stagecoaches, the postman and any other deliveries. The old track was named thus, because it was marked out using long sticks, with smaller twigs added to the top, so they looked like a witch's broom or besom.[67]

The restrictions on visiting the island have certainly allowed the wildlife to flourish and wild hares roam freely here amongst the miles of deserted arable farmland and salt marsh. The island's name is derived from the Old English *fugla næsse*, meaning *bird headland*, referring to the many species of wildfowl that call the island home. Foulness is recognised as an internationally important site for migrating and breeding birds, including pied avocets, oystercatchers, little egrets and brent geese.

The small village of Church End, with its traditional weather boarded cottages is the main place of habitation, and the island's heritage centre can be found here, containing a small museum of island life.

The earliest known occupants of Foulness Island were people of the British tribe of the Trinovantes. A settlement existed on the south-west tip of the isle, near Shelford Creek. Here was found the remains of a barrow cemetery where

---

67. www.bbc.co.uk/essex/content/articles/2009/04/17/nature_trail_foulness_feature.shtml

10. Mud Archipelego

cremation urns were recovered. Excavation has revealed that farming, fishing, salt making, and the cultivation of oysters were all important industries. The pottery excavated here can be dated to the first century AD and was probably abandoned around AD 230, due to the rising sea levels. It is easy to speculate whether the barrows that were once on Foulness were similar to the Romano-British example on Mersea Island to the north.

A sea serpent was spotted in the Thames Estuary in August 1923,[68] by some of the crew of HMS Kellet, who were conducting a morning survey in one of the main shipping channels, off Foulness Point. The key witness was the ship's captain, F. D. B. Haselfoot, who noted that the serpent was seen at nine in the morning and had a long neck which rose out of the water to a height of seven feet before submerging. The mysterious dark sea monster broke the surface again shortly after; its long slimy neck and head was clearly seen emerging from the water around two hundred yards from the ship.[69] It is interesting to note that the area had been closed to all shipping for the previous eight years, maybe giving the creature a false sense of security.

Neighbouring Havengore Island was once farmed, and in the mid-1860s there were two farms on the island. However, the marshes were considered to be unhealthy, where agues, fevers and consumption were rife, and Mrs Print, Havengore's own cunning woman, made money by selling old gypsy cures.

To the west of this lonely and atmospheric group of islands, lies the village of Canewdon. Nestled on a remote hilltop setting, close to the old fleet and the southern bank of the river, the village is the folkloric epicentre of the district.

It is here, where the wind whips in across the creeks and saltings that lie between the former garrison town of Shoeburyness and the Crouch, that is found a mysterious

---

68. Modern Mysteries of Britain by Janet and Colin Bord, p 276
69. www.animalfolklore.wordpress.com/2014/06/26/sea-serpents-of-kent

land indeed, with many folktales and odd happenings having been recorded across the centuries. This was once the domain of Jop Summers, ghost hunter and hedge trimmer, whose claim to fame was that he had once amassed one of the most complete collections of historic ghost stories in Essex. Unfortunately, this seems to have disappeared from his sister's house in Maldon, not long after his death in 1952.

Jop was born at Passingford Mill, in the Roding valley, not far from Ongar, and he spent his later years living in Gosfield, near Braintree and died in Maldon, aged ninety-seven. He seems to have spent most of his working life living and working in Canewdon, and one of his most famous recorded ghost tales is from this notorious village.[70]

In 1876, four days after his twenty-first birthday, Jop was walking home along the road that heads into the village from the east, when the heel of his shoe came loose. He sat on the churchyard wall, so he could try to mend it, and after a short time, he looked up as he felt that he was being watched. Sure enough, there was a lady walking between the gravestones dressed in a crinoline gown and a poke bonnet. Jop thought nothing unusual was afoot, and thinking that she was maybe looking for something, he went and asked her if he could help. However, as soon as he spoke to her, she vanished. Soon after this inexplicable experience, Jop asked the sexton about it, and discovered that others had also witnessed her ghostly manifestation over the years since her death. The rumours were that she had died forty years previously. One local man had reported that he was walking through the churchyard one evening, and that she had appeared on the path before him, then promptly collided

---

70. Despite contacting author Raymond Lamont-Brown, I am still unable to discover who 'Jop Summers' really was, and I eagerly await the promised reply from Mr Lamont-Brown. In the meantime, 'Jop' will deservedly find his name entering the folkloric record of the Essex shore.

10. Mud Archipelego

with him. There are no reports of how this man felt as this happened, and one can only assume that the ghostly figure walked straight through him. The most sinister sighting of this lady was witnessed sometime during the 1870s in the lane leading from the west gate of the churchyard towards the River Crouch. A man was said to have followed the ghostly figure along this old route towards the river, and just before she disappeared, she looked up at him, and he saw that beneath her bonnet was a faceless head.[71]

Canewdon has a history of witchcraft which goes back to the sixteenth century. On 25th of July 1580, Canewdon resident Rose Pye was charged with the death of Johanna Snow, the one-year-old daughter of local farmer Richard Snow, from Scaldhurst Farm. It was alleged that Rose killed the child by bewitchment. She was acquitted at the local assizes, even though she was described as 'living as a witch'. Strangely, even though she was acquitted, she was never released from jail, and sadly died whilst still locked up a few months later.

Five years later, another Canewdon resident Cicely Makin was accused of witchcraft, and interestingly, she was unable to find five people within the village who would swear that she was not a practicing witch. After being given five years to mend her ways without success, Cicely was excommunicated from the church. From this we may assume that she did have a strong reputation as a village witch, and continued to practice her craft in the village, despite being excommunicated. Five years on, in 1590 another record appears to show that 'Goodwife' Makins of Canewdon was brought to trial for practising witchcraft. Was Cicely still performing her conjurations and curses? It seems so, given that there was no standard way of spelling in sixteenth century England.

---

71. An Essex Hedgetrimmer's Ghostbook by Raymond Lamont-Brown. This Essex, March 1974. This article was later republished in 'The Best of Essex: An Anthology of Memory Articles and Photographs' compiled by E. V. Scott.

We have Eric Maple to thank for first recording much of what is known today about the legends and folklore of Canewdon. There has been some controversy about the way he recorded the folklore from the village, but this type of controversy could well be applied to many folklore researchers and collectors from history, so I am happy to go with Maple's research, as it is now as much a part of the social history of the district as any other. The historic legends of the village that existed before Maple began his folklore research were as follows:

> *As long as the church tower stands, there will be six witches in Canewdon. Each time a stone falls from the tower, one witch will die, and another will take her place. One of the six will be the parson's wife, and another the butcher's wife. There will be as many in silk as in cotton. Those who walk round the tower at midnight, will be forced to dance with the witches. A Canewdon witch stole a bell from Latchingdon church, over the river, and attempted to re-cross the river with it in a wash tub, using feathers as oars. She was seen by a waterman, whom she bewitched into forgetfulness with the words "You will speak of it when you think of it". It was not until years later, when he heard the bells toll at the funeral of a reputed witch, that the incident came back to him. This legend was old when it was first recorded a century ago.*[72]

Maple's *Witches of Canewdon paper* is a fascinating piece of collected folklore and goes some way to allow us to understand the historical superstitions and fears that remote settlements would have to face during the nineteenth and early twentieth centuries. There was no public transport until after the first world war, and the area was marshy and cut off from neighbouring towns. There are some interesting folklore motifs in the document that

---

72. The Witches of Canewdon by Eric Maple. Folklore vol 71, no. 4 December 1960

10. Mud Archipelego

need a fresh look. Therefore, we will look at the church, the ghost-lore and animal traditions.

The church is central to the folklore of the village; its ghosts, traditions, witchcraft, and cunning tradition feature often. It is said that when the church tower crumbles, the last village witch will die. Contrariwise when the last witch dies the church tower will fall. If a stone falls from the tower, it signifies that one of the witches has died, but will be replaced instantly with another. Children used to dance around the church as a protective charm against witchcraft and there is also a large 'altar tomb' in the churchyard, associated with the Devil, and children also danced around this as a counter witchcraft protection ritual. Inside the church we can also find various apotropaic marks scratched into the masonry and believed to protect against malevolent magic and witchcraft.

In the second half of the nineteenth century, the churchyard was believed to be an enclave of supernatural white rabbits, which were believed to be the six witches of Canewdon, who could transform into a white rabbit at will. These witch-rabbits often appeared running down the haunted hill towards the river. It was always unlucky and even dangerous to touch a white rabbit and by doing so could bring on long term illness. Local folk would also not catch or eat rabbits for fear that they were one of the local witches.[73]

The ghost-lore of the village is intrinsically linked to the witch-lore. The most famous and oft repeated is that of the ghost of a witch that appears by the west gate of the churchyard. She begins to materialise as a shadowy cloud and she fully materialises as she moves down the hill to the west of the church. She sometimes stands by the edge of the churchyard and paralyses all who see her by the power of her eyes. Those who witness her ghostly apparition on

---

73. Modern Wicca: A History from Gerald Gardner to the Present by Michael Howard

the road are unluckier, as they are raised up by a mysterious force and thrown over the hedgerows. Her ghost also rides on a hurdle, speeding down towards the river, where she rides to the other side in a wash tub with feathers for oars. If anyone dares to speak to her, she vanishes 'like the wind'. It is tempting to suggest that this ghost could be the same one that Jop Summers witnessed in 1876, though the descriptions do not entirely match, suggesting that a second ghost haunts the churchyard and surrounding lanes.

Many of the themes in the witch ghost tale are shared in the annals of other witch folklore from the village, including being paralysed by the power of their eyes, using wash tubs as boats on the Crouch and rowing them with feathers and riding hurdles across the sky.[74]

Other witch stories of the village include an ancient tale that was told of a Canewdon girl. She went to keep house for her uncle at Woodham Ferrers, but being one of the witches, the uncle knew no peace during her stay, as nothing in the house would keep still.[75] In the sixteenth century, Ruth Poysey was charged with witchcraft and acquitted. If she had been found guilty and executed, it might have provided an explanation of the witch ghost of Canewdon who flies over fields and rivers at night in a silken gown minus her head. Local people today, still tremble at the memory of meeting this gruesome ghost on the lonely roads of Canewdon.[76]

Eliza Frost Lodwick was another suspected Canewdon witch. She lived at Lambourne Hall and along with her husband, farmed the area during the mid-nineteenth century. After her husband's death, she stepped up her practice, and was rumoured to be practising sorcery in the farmhouse.

---

74. The Witches of Canewdon by Eric Maple. Folklore vol 71, no. 4 December 1960

75. Canewdon and its Witches by Harold Adshead. Essex Countryside, vol. 2 no. 6 Winter 1953

76. Witch Lore of Canewdon by Eric Maple. Essex Countryside, vol. 10 no 58 Nov 1961

10. Mud Archipelego

One afternoon old Lady Lodwick had left her two maids preparing fruit for jam making in the kitchen, with strict injunctions that they were not to stop work till her return from Rochford.

Hardly had the sound of the carriage wheels died away, when Sarah Jane, the younger maid, was filled with a longing to eat the black currants that were dangling on the bushes outside the kitchen window. Down went her bowl as she cried, "I must go, Martha!"

"Doant 'ee be so foolish. Remember what Missus told us." replied her wiser companion.

But Sarah Jane was already out of the window, picking away like mad and stuffing the juicy berries into her mouth. Her appetite appeased, she made to return, throwing her leg over the kitchen windowsill.

To her horror, she found suddenly that she could not move. She was frozen solid there, half in and half out, 'till the sound of carriage wheels was again heard on the gravel drive. Now there came footsteps down the passage, and as Lady Lodwick appeared at the door, she saw the girl dangling on the threshold, and asked, "Why, you foolish girl, whatever are you doing there?" Immediately, Sarah Jane suddenly found that she could move and speak again.[77]

The witch's familiars or imps were an important part of their magic, allowing them to tap into the natural power of the land. The Essex marsh witches seemed to prefer white mice over other animals, and one tale from the district explains the story of how the succession of witches was so seamless within Canewdon. This tale gives us an insight into the witch cult of the day, and as is often the case, where we read of the Devil, we should probably assume that this was a localised horned god or spirit that was central to the witch's creed (who was, in this case, the Smith).

---

77. Witches over the Crouch - article in The Times, Tuesday, 27 January 1959

> *The old smith of Ballads Gore, who lived on the outskirts of Canewdon, was believed to have sold his soul to the Devil, which was probably the reason he always looked over his shoulder wherever he went. He had few friends, and these were not overly pleased to be visiting him on this occasion, as he lay dying, after many years of illness. They entered his room and saw that he was close to the end, but his eyes were very much alive, for they travelled round and round the room as if following something only he could see. Suddenly a great circular scorch mark spread slowly over the bed, then a small white mouse ran into the centre of the circle. It sat there looking at the smith, who said: "I can't die while the imp is there." Then, to the intrigue of the watchers, he begged his wife to take it, but she said: "No, no, I don't want the power." He then begged his daughter to take it, telling her that until she did so, he could not die. Weeping, she took the animal from him and crept into another room. As she left the bedside the smith fell back dead, and the watchers knew that his daughter was now a witch.*[78]

It is interesting to note that on the south wall of the church there appears to be a horned cat, so typical of other recorded witch familiars across Essex, especially from the Hatfield Peverel and St Osyth traditions.[79]

In 1896, another particularly feared witch lived on the edge of the village. This is without doubt, the daughter mentioned in the above tale. She lived at the smithy and Eric Maple recounted a story collected from her granddaughter, who remembered a scary visit where the witch revealed her bag of imps to the child. The little girl fled, and the same night whilst tucked up in her bed at home, the witch manifested like a spectre by her bed, peering at her from beneath her Dutch bonnet. The girl screamed in

---

78. Witch Lore of Canewdon by Eric Maple. Essex Countryside, vol. 10 no 58 Nov 1961

79. ASH magazine, number 8 Summer 1990: Paganism in Essex Churches (Canewdon) by Ian Dawson

10. Mud Archipelego

terror, and the witch vanished. This prompted the family to gain the services of a witch bottle from one of the village cunning folk. The bottle was duly prepared and dropped off at place where the little girl lived. The bottle was placed into the kitchen's blazing hearth, and as it boiled and bubbled, a scratching was heard at the locked front door. The old witch from the smithy had been drawn in by the bottle and was unable to escape the magic of the charm. In the morning, the witch was found dead at the crossroads.[80]

The witches of Canewdon were long thought to have gained their power from a piece of land bordering the river. On the marshy riverbank there was once a strip of land known as *The Witches' Field*, and this is where the witches would come to perpetually renew their powers. It is also a probability that Great Hydes Field at Pudsey Hall was another domain of the power of the witch, and as we discuss a bit later, there is an exceptionally good reason for this.[81]

Maple also hinted at another esoteric tradition within Canewdon. He mentions one of the old families whose business was to process the dead of the village. He hinted that these layers-out of the dead, became credited with 'supernatural understanding' and with abilities enabling them to 'pierce the veil of death' and to be able to destroy witches and their power, when all other means had failed. This 'clan' would pass on their knowledge just as the witches did. This entire statement from Maple's *Witches of Canewdon* article is frustrating, as it gives very few clues. He does not name the family, but instead calls them "The M... family".[82]

There is a strange tradition as to why witchcraft became associated with Canewdon. The church tower was built

---

80. The Dark World of Witches by Eric Maple
81. Author's personal archive, oral tradition from Dave Hunt
82. The Witches of Canewdon by Eric Maple. Folklore vol 71, no. 4 December 1960. (Could M stand for Murrell? author's note).

to celebrate the English victory at Agincourt, and legend would have it that a Canewdon coven was founded in the fifteenth century by a local landowner who fought in France and had been initiated into the French craft. Is this the real reason why the church was significant to local witches? Whichever way, the local lore always comes back to the remit that the six witches of Canewdon will always report back to the 'Master Witch'.[83]

The most famous of these 'Master Witches' was Old George Pickingill. The lore and legend surrounding this Essex farmhand and cunning man is huge. It is also complex, with stories appearing in various esoteric journals across the years making claims that seem to have no basis in the folkloric or historic archive. At best, we have the claims that George Pickingill was the greatest authority on black magic, witchcraft and satanism, which was made by Bill Liddell, who for many years wrote about this subject under the pseudonym of Lugh. Liddell also claimed that occultists and magicians came to visit him within many years, from across the world, and that Pickingill had actually founded nine covens over a sixty-year period. It is implied that these visitors included Gerald Gardner, the founder of modern Wicca, who it is claimed, was a member of one of the Pickingill covens and gained his witchcraft knowledge from this. There is much discussion about the claims and validity of George Pickingill as one of the founders of modern traditional witchcraft, through the so-called *Pickingill Craft*.[84] As the famous and well respected twentieth century witch, Doreen Valiente once said:

---

83. Legends of Canewdon by Michael Howard. ASH magazine, no. 4. Summer 1989

84. Most of this debate was published in The Cauldron journal, and these are now long out of print. However, they were collected together in the book 'The Pickingill Papers' by William Liddell and Michael Howard.

10. Mud Archipelego

Only further research can tell us whether, in fact, 'Old George' Pickingill was really the man who adapted the ancient ways of the hereditary witch cult in Britain to be perpetuated in modern times.[85]

I will leave readers to make up their own minds through the mire of interesting controversy, research, and gossip, and for those who are looking to delve deeper into this, there are a few online forums that could be worth joining.[86]

I suspect that Old George was remembered as a grumpy and scary individual, who would threaten to stop farm machinery with his eyes and would conjure his magical imps to aid the harvest. Eric Maple collected much remembered lore and history about his life and practises. In Canewdon, Pickingill was considered the last and perhaps the greatest of the wizards and was a widower with two sons. They lived in a cottage by the Anchor Hotel, which is now demolished. He openly practised as a cunning man, where he worked to restore lost property and cure warts. He would often mutter charms over folk with minor ailments and he made no charge for his services, instead preferring to gain favours and services from those he helped. Maple visited in 1959, and was told by various members of the farm-labouring community and some of the oldest families from the village, that the belief in witchcraft within Canewdon had completely survived into modern times. This cultural tradition is still referenced in the twenty-first century through the village sign, which stands at the entrance to the village by a crossroads. The sign depicts a witch riding across the sky on her broom. It also depicts Canute holding back the tide, which commemorates the folk-history where Canewdon's Beacon Hill is believed to be the site of Canute's camp, during the battle of Ashingdon in 1016. The sign also shows the old second-world-war radar

---

85. The Rebirth of Witchcraft by Doreen Valiente: Chapter 12 The Pickingill Material, pp 197 - 205
86. The Cauldron, Winter 1992: The Pickingill Papers by Mike Howard

tower, and the church of St Nicholas, proudly sited on the hilltop. Of particular interest is the signs positioning by the crossroads, where village folklore records a witch was once buried with a stake through her heart.[87]

There was always a tradition that the six witches of Canewdon had a male master, known as a wizard. During the first half of the nineteenth century this was probably James 'Cunning' Murrell, from Hadleigh, who it is said, was able to summon the Canewdon witches at will. Murrell died in 1860 and was thirty years senior to Old George Pickingill. However, from 1860 until his death in 1909, the witch master was Pickingill. Old George would use whatever magic was needed to keep him safe and to help or curse others. He often coerced villagers to fetch water or do other errands as he sought fit. He would threaten to send his legion of white mice imps to trouble the neighbours if they didn't obey him. And villagers often reported seeing the white mice running around at night, with their glowing red eyes confirming their menacing presence. The key to his magic was the use of his powerful eyes and his blackthorn walking stick. He could and did stop farm machinery with a stare and was often paid off by the farmers to leave them alone. Eric Maple does state that George was visited by people from great distances, and as previously stated, folk from the Dengie would travel by ferry to visit him. He held power over all animals and could control horses. He used his walking stick to send game from the hedgerows for miles around and it is believed that he once demonstrated his power over nature by instructing a hedgerow to dance down a field. Again, he used his blackthorn stick to conjure this. He was reputed to be able to fly across the land on a hurdle (his walking stick?) and often told others to go on ahead of him, and would be waiting for them when they arrived, such was his command of power. His imps would often assist, and

---

87. The Dark World of Witches by Eric Maple, p 177

10. Mud Archipelego

some say that when passing his cottage, ornaments could be seen flying around the house of their own accord.[88]

Old George would summon the Canewdon witches with a whistle, which would compel them to stand at their doorways for all to see. He would also summon them to meet in the churchyard where they would conduct their esoteric rituals and dance into the night. As the years advanced, George was eventually admitted to a nursing home, and on his death bed he uttered that he would demonstrate his powers for one last time from beyond the grave. On the day of his burial as the hearse drew up to the churchyard, the horses stepped from their shafts. One of his sons was thought to have inherited his powers and title, but as the years passed little was heard of him.

Apart from the Eric Maple paper, and subsequent book, *The Dark World of Witches*, which included his collection of folkloric anecdotes, memories, and cunning practices from villagers in 1950s Canewdon, what else is there in the folklore record?

In 1967, inspired by Eric Maple's work, English historian Ronald Hutton, who specialises in British folklore, pre-Christian religion and contemporary paganism, also visited Canewdon, where he spoke to villagers about the witch beliefs in the area. He states that what he found supported Maple's work and he spoke to many of those who Maple had previously met, including 'Granny' Lilian Garner, who had been Maple's chief informant. Interestingly, Hutton managed to interview Jack Taylor, a Canewdon villager who Maple appeared to have missed. Hutton later published one of his recollections, which ties in nicely with Maple's work and really helps to further illustrate the powers of a traditional village cunning man:

> *When my sister and I were children, we wanted to ride our pony and trap to Rochford Fair; but that day the beast just wouldn't move, no matter what we did with it. Then we suddenly saw George*

---

88. Witness to Witchcraft by Charles Lefebure

> *Pickingill staring at us with those terrible eyes of his. He came over and told us to put down the reins and not to interfere with the pony at all. Then he whispered in its ear for a few minutes and stood back and hit it; and it started off and found its own way down the lanes to Rochford, without our needing to touch it.*[89]

This is such an interesting and revealing piece of dialogue, and confirms that Pickingill was also a skilled horse whisperer, and this would have been one of the services rendered as a cunning man within the district. This ties in with another piece of folklore that suggested that there was also a horse whispering tradition regarding the colts that were bred on the marshes around Canewdon, where the marsh wizards of the district, possessed great and uncanny powers over these horses. They could bring an unbroken colt to the plough with only a whispered word, suggesting that the cult of the Horse Whisperer was active around the coastal marshes, islands, and creeks of Essex.

Jack Taylor was born in 1888 and became a young farm labourer alongside George Pickingill. Again, Hutton explains that 'George took an especial liking to him', which would confirm that they were friends. So, any recollections by Jack would be fondly and warmly remembered, though it is likely that he didn't work alongside him for that long, as Pickingill died in 1909. Jack is on record as saying that Old George was consulted by many clients from across the district but had no recollection of him having connections to groups of people from further afield.[90]

Author, renowned witchcraft practitioner and editor of *The Cauldron*, Michael Howard, also visited Canewdon in the search for answers. *The Cauldron* was one of the most prominent and influential witchcraft journals, and was published continuously between 1976 and 2015, when

---

89. The Triumph of the Moon: A History of Modern Pagan Witchcraft by Ronald Hutton, p 297
90. Ibid

10. Mud Archipelego

shortly after issue 156 was published in March 2015, the magazine ceased publication due to the death of its editor. In 2017, Howard's East Anglian Witches and Wizards book was posthumously published. In this book, we get some of the details of his visit to Canewdon, and the flavour and content of his meeting with 'Granny' Lilian Garner, who both Maple and Hutton had previously interviewed. Again, it is confirmed that she was one of the cunning women of the village and died in 1982. Howard met Garner in 1977, and she was also well known in the village as a witch. She lived in Vicarage Cottage with her family and had worked for the church for many years. Lilian was widely consulted in the village, for ailments such as bewitchment and the preparation of witch bottles to draw out and lift the curses of those practising malevolent magic. She was very psychic and had seen many of the traditional old ghosts of the village on more than one occasion, including one incident where she was in the church lighting the lamps ready for the evening service. A misty figure entered the church and knelt by the altar to pray. Mrs Garner described the ghost as a faceless woman wrapped in a grey shroud and stated that if the ghost was in the church, she must be an angel, and she promptly knelt beside her. However, when she looked up the ghost had gone.

'Granny' Garner had known Pickingill when she was growing up in the village and recalled him as an eccentric who once had his photo taken next to the first car in Canewdon. This was reported in the Southend Standard newspaper on the 27th of September 1908, not long before he died. Garner remembers his authority as the witch master of a coven in Canewdon, and interestingly stated that her mother was a member. She also recalled his cunning man work, where he would stem blood flow from farming accidents, find lost or stolen property and cure minor ailments. Michael Howard also states that she told him that she remembered Old George being visited by lots of people from out of the district, who came to consult him on occult matters. She described these visitors as 'people from far away'.[91]

I find it interesting to note that the two accounts, one from Hutton and the other from Howard have this one difference, that each of them seem keen to highlight from their respective visits. Hutton states that Garner told him that she had no recollection of him having connections to groups of people from further afield. Yet Howard states that Garner told him that Pickingill was often consulted about the occult by lots of visitors from far away. Both differing points appear to indicate their own beliefs on the reality of the alleged Pickingill Craft traditions. Like many others, I continue to wait for some actual proof of this with eager anticipation. In the meantime, I tend to agree with Folklore Society President, Owen Davies, when he stated that *"old George was a simple and rural cunning man, whose small world of village affairs never crossed with that of middle-class occultists."*[92]

As an interesting aside, there is only one photo currently in circulation that appears to show George Pickingill. However, in the July 1984 issue of Insight magazine, a letter was supposedly published by John Pope stating that it wasn't of Pickingill at all:

> *"The photograph purporting to be Old George Pickingill is in fact a photo of Alf Cavill, a station porter at Elstree, taken in the early 1960s. Alf is now dead, but he was no witch, and laughed over the photograph when he saw it."*

It is interesting to note that it is recorded that the original copy of this photograph was owned by Lillian Garner, who claimed that it was of George Pickingill. She allegedly showed it to Eric Maple in 1959, who subsequently published it in his book *The Dark World of Witches* in 1962. During Michael

---

91. East Anglian Witches and Wizards by Michael Howard, p 116
92. Popular Magic: Cunning-folk in English History by Owen Davies, p 194

10. Mud Archipelego

Howard's visit in 1977, she gave him her original copy of the photograph. In Michael Howard's *Witches and Wizards of East Anglia* the photograph is reproduced as a full page, uncropped version, clearly showing the words '*Pickingale 103 years old*, at the bottom. It was contemporary common belief in the village that George was the oldest man in England, and it was frequently believed that he lived to witness his 103rd birthday.

Whoever the man in the photograph was, in popular culture it has now become both an accepted image of George Pickingill, and a symbol of the historic witches and their legacy within Canewdon village.[93]

There is also a rare photograph of 'Granny' Lilian Garner standing outside Vicarage Cottage. This was published with Eric Maple's article about Canewdon, that he wrote for issue 14 of the *Man Myth and Magic* series of magazines, published in 1970. In this article he also recounts some of the traditions of later cunning folk in the village, including the practice of using witch bottles and the placing of knives and scissors under the doormat, to prevent a malevolent witch from crossing the threshold. This is undoubtedly describing the practices of 'Granny' Garner herself and backs up the similar stories that Michael Howard collected from Garner later in the same decade.

'Granny' Lilian Garner now takes her place in the historic record as one of Canewdon's many witches and cunning folk. To summarise; she is fondly remembered as the white witch of the village and she died at the age of ninety-one on the 16th of November 1982 and is buried close to the tower of the village church in an unmarked grave on the family plot. She was nineteen years old when George Pickingill died, and she had told three separate folklore researchers that she remembered him.

Her mother was also a witch and was allegedly a member of Pickingill's village coven. It is likely that she had learned

---

93. East Anglian Witches and Wizards by Michael Howard, p113

her craft from her mother, and her mother from Pickingill. Lilian recalled that *her own mother had told her that Mr. Pickingill was the leader of a local coven of witches* and that she was a member.[94]

On this point, it important to realise that Lilian Garner's mother, Lucy Higby died at the age of twenty-five in 1891 in Calcutta, India. Lilian was only a toddler of one year when this happened. Therefore, it must have been Lilian's stepmother, Susan Higby, that she was referring to when she states that her mother was a witch. This fits nicely, as Susan Higby was from Canewdon, and she married Lilian's father in 1895, when Lilian was five years old.[95]

Garner was known in the village as utilising the witch bottle as a tool of protection, and used this method to help people when they believed that they had been the victim of malevolent magic, something she had in common with the historic Hadleigh cunning man, James Murrell.

Other old traditions in Canewdon suggest that the medieval Guild of St Anne maintained a light on the church tower as a beacon to guide fishermen at the mouth of the Crouch and on the coast.[96] This would explain why the hill on which Canewdon is built is called Beacon Hill.

A field at Pudsey Hall received much attention in 1847 when a curiously large statue was dug up. This was thought to have been a Romano-British artefact, or possibly even earlier. However, others have speculated that it was a statue of a Saxon god, and as Thundersley is not too distant, speculation on a Thor statue has been raised as an idea.[97]

---

94. Modern Wicca: A History from Gerald Gardner to the Present by Michael Howard, p 58

95. William Wallworth www.deadfamilies.com/Z3-Others/Higby/Higby-Walter-Gen3.htm

96. Canewdon and its Witches by Harold Adshead. Essex Countryside, vol. 2 no. 6 Winter 1953

97. East Saxon Heritage by Stephen Pewsey and Andrew Brooks. P140

10. Mud Archipelego

The real answer here is that we may never know as the statue was broken up for use as hard core by the farmer. However, I would suggest that as only part of the statue was dug up, the rest of the mystery probably still awaits discovery under the soil of Great Hydes Field. Rochford Historian Philip Benton wrote the following piece around the time it was discovered, which may give us some clues:

> *Part of a gigantic statue, supposed to represent a heathen deity, was dug up upon Pudsey-Hall in 1847. It is still in existence and lies in a yard near the house. It was found in a field called Great Hydes (adjoining Hyde Wood), on the south side of the road leading from Canewdon to Ashingdon. A head of a battle-axe was found nearby was said to have been a Norman weapon. Beneath the statue were appearances of bones, which crumbled upon exposure to air.*

As discussed previously, this discovery of an ancient statue of a possible deity in Great Hydes Field, gives us a clue as to why this ground was believed to be another of the traditional areas of the witches' power within the village.

Before we leave the folklore and witch mysteries of Canewdon, there is one last piece of contemporary folklore to present, which suggests that a devilish horned imp or hobgoblin haunts the periphery of the village. On one occasion this imp chased a man on a motorbike. He was riding along one of the lanes on the edge of the village and the imp easily managed to keep up with the speed of the bike, a fitting tribute to the dark shenanigans, and awesome mysteries of the village.

11. Salt Marsh, Creek and Riverside

Sitting within the centre of a remote promontory with Paglesham Creek to the north and the tidal Roach in the south, is a traditional marshland village with white weatherboarded cottages and an ancient church, dedicated to the patron saint of fisherman, St Peter. The village of Paglesham has historic connections to farming, oyster fishing and smuggling, and the village name is from the old Essex dialect term '*pagle*' meaning the beautiful spring flowering Cowslip (Primula veris). Cowslips or Pagles were often also known as '*Herb Peter*' which links them to the lore of the fisherman's saint, through the pendulous clumps of flowers said to resemble St Peter's keys of heaven. These beautiful '*fairy flowers*' were also used by the cunning folk as a cure-all (high in vitamin C) and were also applied as a remedy

11. Salt Marsh, Creek and Riverside

for anxiety, to steady the nerves. Interestingly, the Cowslip is also the traditional flower of the county of Essex.[98]

The *Owd Davvil* was active in Paglesham, haunting the village and its marshes. He once kidnapped a local resident called Mr Tye, leaving a sooty footprint as evidence of his visit. A local kind of weather prophecy was worked in the village during the end of the nineteenth century. One village man predicted the great storm of 1897, which flooded miles of low-lying Essex fields, after which he was proclaimed as the mouthpiece of God.[99]

The most famous of the Paglesham smugglers was *Hard Apple Blyth, King of the smugglers*. His day job was grocer and churchwarden, but after dark he could be found at Paglesham Creek, unloading goods, and directing carts full of contraband to their hiding places. One of these hidden places of the Paglesham smugglers was known as *the old maids, or the three old widows*. These were three ancient and hollow elm trees, which once stood on a bend in the road near to East Hall. Growing on the edge of Pound Pond or the Smuggler's Pool, the hollow trunks were used to hide silk and other expensive goods, before being moved on to their final buyers. Another local tradition states that lovers would meet under the trees by moonlight to embrace and listen to the nightingales. Unfortunately, the trees were removed in the early 1980s, but their folkloric memories live on.[100]

Paglesham creek was also once the haunt of witches who would weave their salty incantations as the tide rose and an old postcard, published by Padgett's entitled 'the haunted

---

98. In 2002, the charity and conservation group Plantlife reassigned the Common Poppy (Papaver rhoeasas) as the flower of Essex, due to a vote of preference, as part of their campaign to assign a flower to every county within the UK. However, the Pagle (Cowslip) was always the traditional Essex county flower, and still is.

99. Witchcraft and Magic in the Rochford Hundred by Eric Maple, Folklore, Vol 76, No 3 (Autumn 1965)

100. Essex Lays and Legends (Taylor & Robbins, 1888).

house Paglesham' shows a derelict house somewhere in the village, though it is doubtful if the house is still standing.

During the Spring of 1964, a Neolithic jadeite axe head was discovered in a furrow turned up by the plough, in a field immediately to the south-west of South Hall Farm. Archaeologists considered the beautifully carved and polished axe was too small and delicate for regular use. However, it is likely that it was manufactured as a ceremonial or ritual object, and the folklore surrounding jadeite suggests that it was regarded as having divine powers for protection and healing. Interestingly, jadeite is not found in Britain, so it would have been imported, and maybe swapped during a trade, either as raw material, or a finished piece.[101] The site where it was discovered sits on slightly higher ground, above the marshy northern bank of the tidal river Roach.

Heading south across the river, Great Wakering sits on the edge of the old marshes, where the mainland ends, and the islands begin. There was once an old tree close to the junction of Barrow Hall Road and Little Wakering Road, where it was believed that if you ran around it one hundred times the ghost of the *Baker from Barling* would appear. The area is known as Baker's Grave, and the story tells us that a baker hanged himself from one of the trees branches. A ghostly black shuck, named *Baker's big black dog* also haunts the area. Interestingly, there was a flour windmill at Barling around the turn point between the nineteenth and twentieth centuries, and the boys of the village would take the gleanings (wheat left after threshing) along to Mr Manning, the miller. He was always very generous with the gleaners, often giving back more flour than grain handed in. It was seen as a local badge of honour for any boy who had been up to the mill when it was fully working and producing flour.[102]

---

101. Artefact held by www.southendmuseums.co.uk
102. Essex Countryside, May 1966: Barling Windmill correspondence by Mr J. A. Groves

11. Salt Marsh, Creek and Riverside

Another phantom black dog is said to walk along Star Lane on certain nights each year. The lane is named after an old inn, which once served refreshments to the marshmen, farmers and sailors of the area.[103] There is an interesting and historic black dog legend recorded at Barling, and the dog here is believed to be the restless spirit of a farm dog who was killed by a pack of wolves. This would place the origin of the story to sometime before the fourteenth century, as by that time wolves had become extinct in England. The lore states that the dog was buried the following day, but during the following two months the ghostly form of the dog was seen on the farm and across the arable pasture, so the farmer decided to move the dog's grave as he felt the spirit was restless. However, when they opened the grave, the body was gone. After this episode, the dog returned much more often, and he was seen with huge glowing red eyes and seemed to appear much bigger than he was in life. Over the next few years his glowing red eyes could be seen in the wheat fields, between dusk and dawn. In 1986 a young woman was walking back home at dusk, when she saw two red glowing lights in the fields near her house. The following morning when she opened her curtains, she saw two prints in the mist where a dog had been breathing against the glass.[104]

Just to the east of Wakering Common, on the saltmarsh between the village and Havengore Creek is the lonely spot where another ghostly dog has been seen.[105] Recounted in 1970 by Leslie Cripps, then 60 years old, who recalled some of his younger days rabbiting on the marshes. He included a few ghostly anecdotes, including one eerie incident that he had trouble believing himself. On a moonlit night around 9pm he went out to bag a duck or rabbit for his supper. Around 10pm he parked up and grabbed his gun in

---

103. A Ghost Hunter's Guide to Essex by Jessie Payne
104. www.hiddenea.com/shuckland/barling.htm
105. www.hiddenea.com/shuckland/greatwakering.htm

readiness to head to the sea wall. However, he was stopped in his tracks as he witnessed a black and white dog leaping towards him two feet above the ground. Soundlessly, the dog bounded past him and vanished towards the sea. A couple of months later, at the same spot but much later into the dark night, Mr. Cripps was in his car with his own dog when he saw the ghostly black and white hound floating towards the vehicle from behind. He later found that a friend had also seen the phantom sea-dog, but neither of them had dared tell anyone about it.[106]

Little Wakering had a sixteenth century healer and cunning woman. In 1566, local resident Margery Skelton appeared before a church court accused of practising as a 'blessing witch'. She was clearly one of the village's cunning women, who would have helped with herbal cures, dispensed remedies, made up potions and charms to heal and protect and acted as midwife. Typically, however, ten years later she was tried as a 'Black witch'.[107]

The town of Rochford has some interesting witchcraft and ghost-lore associated with it. The most famous ghost is that of Anne Boleyn, and her childhood home of Rochford Hall has some folklore associated with both Anne and the surrounding area. It is widely known that Anne Boleyn was accused of witchcraft by Henry VIII, which enabled him to have her killed. Popular belief around this quickly caught on, and folklore quickly spawned as a result. One story from the town confirmed that Anne really hated the peal of the church bells, and she ordered the immediate removal of them, which would have certainly confirmed the witchcraft rumours to the locals. Another odd tradition associated with Anne and her old home states that she had three secret oak chests hidden in Rochford Hall, which were never to be opened. The grounds and lanes around

---

106. 'Rabbiting in Great Wakering' SA/24/452/1 in the Sound Archive at Essex Record Office
107. Witchcraft Prosecutions in Essex 1560 – 1680 by Alan Macfarlane.

11. Salt Marsh, Creek and Riverside

the hall were also believed to be haunted by an unseen and nameless horror, which was particularly active during the twelve days of Christmas.[108]

Rochford town's most famous witch was Old Witch Hart, probably related to the Hart family of Latchingdon, but not to be confused with them.[109] She lived in the second cottage as you entered town from the Stambridge road, and she is best remembered for pottering around in her garden tending her white poppies and whispering to her imps. She would make a magic broth from the juice of the poppies, and she would feed this to her imps every full moon.

Old Witch Hart was also rumoured to have been a sea witch and was sometimes glimpsed floating on the tops of some of the rougher waves in the Thames estuary, by the sailors of the Corn Hoys, plying their trade to and from London. She would also frequently 'haunt' the townsfolk around Rochford.

The local historian, Philip Benton reported that Mr Hart was also a practising wizard, and both Mr and Mrs Hart were benevolent. One of the first Thameside constables, a Captain Harriott, of Broomhills, near Rochford, also suggested that they were both harmless as he and his brother had one day crossed the threshold of her cottage, an act they had previously been taught to believe would have had them both bewitched into their power.

Despite the support of local dignitaries, they were both swum in the Crouch. Mr Hart was proven to be innocent, after nearly drowning, but Old Witch Hart was strung to a boat and floated, proving to the watermen and townsfolk that she was guilty.[110] However, there is nothing negative written about either of them, so they were probably cunning folk, who helped and protected

---

108. Witchcraft and Magic in the Rochford Hundred by Eric Maple, Folklore, Vol 76, No 3 (Autumn 1965)
109. Ibid
110. The History of Rochford by Philip Benton, 1897. Pages 169, 170

their neighbours, though cunning men and women did like to keep mysterious profiles and ultimately this may have been their undoing.

There was once an old pond in Rochford known as the Bobbing Pond, where witches were swum. The pond no longer exists, as the site now lies under the north-east end of St. Clare Meadow housing estate and was filled in sometime between 1961 and 1964. The pond was marked on ordnance survey maps from 1874 up to 1961, when it disappeared under the encroaching development.[111] To the north-west of Rochford, lying on the south bank of the Crouch, you will come to the village of Hullbridge, one of the historic river crossings, where ferry and bridge once linked travellers from the Rochford Hundred to the Dengie. One of the last of the old ferryman, Dick Hyams was a bit of an old marsh wizard. His favourite and unique conjuration was to call up his chimney for whatever his needs were, and his desired items would immediately descend.[112] It is interesting to hear about this kind of wizardry from as late as the 1940s, and this may be an example of a typical piece of Essex folk-magic associated with ferrymen and bridge keepers of the past, who were frequently seen as otherworldly and magical. [113] To the west of Hullbridge lies Rawreth. It was here that a nineteenth century folk-practitioner known as the 'Dropsy Doctor' once lived. Thomas Bedloe was known for miles around the Rochford Hundred as being able to cure the 'quakes', which was a dialect term for the malarial plague of the Essex marshes. He would use apothecary lore and herbalism, and he travelled from village to village performing his cures and exhibiting a deformed pig, who

---

111. www.rochforddistricthistory.org.uk/page/the_bobbing_ponds?path=0p146p69p

112. Witchcraft and Magic in the Rochford Hundred by Eric Maple, Folklore, Vol 76, No 3 (Autumn 1965)

113. Thames: Sacred River by Peter Ackroyd

11. Salt Marsh, Creek and Riverside

was born with a miniature Elephant's trunk.[114] An idea that he may have picked up from the folktales of the witch's familiar, as a prop to aid his *'powers'*.

Rochford town also once boasted the strange custom of the Whispering Court. This lawless court was held outside King's Hill house, where a post marks the spot where the court began in 1631. This court was held yearly on the first Wednesday morning after Michaelmas. The court served the tenants across a vast estate from Rochford to Foulness, and the attendees had to kneel before their landlords at daybreak upon hearing the first cock crow. They were no-doubt fearful of what may be decreed by the landlords of the estate. Immediately after the first cock had crowed, the steward of the estate called out in a whisper "all as were bound to appear" and the tenants had to reply in the same manner, marking their visit with a piece of coal to prove their attendance. The powers of the court were considerable, and rents were doubled for any not attending.[115]

Between Hullbridge and Rochford lies the village of Hockley. The village operated as a 'Spa town' for a short while between 1843 and 1848 and the Spa building still stands, though long out of its original use. At the highest point lies the mysterious late Iron Age round barrow known as Plumberow Mount. Excavated in the 1913, the few finds from the barrow proved inconclusive as to its use. The barrow stands around seven metres in height, and stands on the summit of a prominent hill overlooking the Crouch valley. It has periodically been in use as an historic meeting place, and during the twentieth century as a clandestine meeting spot for witchcraft.[116] In 1958 on a dark winter's night a ghostly black dog was seen in the centre of the village. It apparently escorted a lady to a bus stop, where it promptly vanished

---

114. Magic Medicine and Quackery by Eric Maple, p 154
115. Essex Countryside, Vol 25 No 249, October 1977: The Rochford House Where the Whispering Court was Held by Denys Jay, p 42
116. Locally collected folklore from the author's archive.

into thin air.[117] There are also reports of this ghost dog appearing around the historic hilltop parish church of St Peter and St Paul and around Plumberow Mount.[118]

Hockley's most notorious folklore surrounds Nelly Button, the witch of Hockley, who was active in the mid-nineteenth century. She had power to hypnotize those she disliked so that they lost the use of their limbs. In one village tale, a girl offended the witch and was immediately struck down by a form of paralysis, where all her limbs were struck rigid. She was left in that state for seven days, until Witch Button arrived at her house, entered without speaking a word, and whispered something in the ear of the poor girl. Within five minutes or so, all was well again, and the girl was able to move around freely. Nelly possessed a wicked sense of humour and liked nothing better than to drive her victims almost frantic with her witchery. Once, when the village blacksmith offended her, she made his concertina play day and night for weeks on end until he became a quivering wreck from lack of sleep. She also hilariously punished a woman, by making the dumplings she was cooking in her pot dance around the stove and fly up the chimney. Quite understandably the recipient of this conjuration was a bit nervous after this. In the end however, Nelly met her match. One of the local lads remembered that witches could not cross iron and planted a hedge of old knives and scissors around her house, so that she was finally brought under control.[119] However, her escapades did not stop there, and her son continued to warn others not to come too near to Nelly's cottage as the front room was home to all of her imps.[120]

---

117. The Realm of Ghosts by Eric Maple, p 186
118. Haunted Southend by Dee Gordon
119. The Dark World of Witches by Eric Maple, 1962 Pages 171-172
120. Witchcraft and Magic in the Rochford Hundred by Eric Maple, Folklore, Vol 76, No 3 (Autumn 1965)

11. Salt Marsh, Creek and Riverside

In neighbouring Hawkwell, John Crushe was charged in the arch deacon's court in 1624 of making burnt sacrifices of lambs and for setting fire to the common, and Charlotte Craven Mason wrote about a woman from Hawkwell who wore a red cloak and a black bonnet. This lady, who Mason called *Mrs M* was a mid-nineteenth century door to door seller, who was suspected of being a witch, and was thought to have bewitched two children whose mother had refused to buy a penny broom from her. Mason concludes that the mother should have put some flowers of St John's Wort in the window, as a protection from witches and malevolent sorcery. The tale continues with an account of the bewitched children's mother, who was out one day crossing a local meadow, when she walked past a short bespectacled man. From the many descriptions she was convinced that it was Cunning Murrell. She called back to him, and once she had established that her identification was correct, she told him about the plight of her cursed children. Murrell returned home with her, and once half a shilling had been exchanged, he gathered hair, fingernails and toenails from the children and placed them in a bottle and buried it under their doorstep.[121]

The hilltop village of Ashingdon is reputed to be the site of the battle of Assendune, fought between Canute and Edmond Ironside, and it was believed that no trees would ever grow on the hillside where so much blood had been spilt. The ancient church, which sits on the summit of the hill is believed to have been built by Canute in 1020 to commemorate his victory in the battle. Canute's interest in Christianity began when he learned of the life of St Wendreda, daughter of King Anna of East Anglia. Wendreda's relics were carried by the Saxon monks during the battle, and these relics were stolen by Canute upon his victory at Ashingdon, and he later presented them to

---

121. Essex. Its Forest, Folk and Folklore by Charlotte Craven Mason. 1928, p 114

Canterbury Cathedral. However, her relics were eventually returned to her holy shrine in the fenland town of March, upon the sacred Isle of Ely. Interestingly, Ashingdon church later boasted its very own sacred shrine, dedicated to the Blessed Virgin Mary. The cult spread, and Ashingdon became a place of miracles where pilgrims crawled up the hill on their hands and knees to gain access to the sacred healing shrine in the very church built by the royal court of Canute.[122] The remnants of local memory of this ancient tradition was recorded by William White in 1848:

> *The Church (St. Andrew) stands on a bold eminence, commanding a view of nearly all the others in this and the adjoining Hundred. It is a small ancient structure, and formerly contained an image, which, in superstitious ages, was in high celebrity for the miracles said to have been wrought by it.*[123]

The churchyard has its own parish ghost, that of a girl who hanged herself from a tree amongst the graves. Here she wanders mournfully amongst the tombstones, forever haunting the place where she ended her life.[124]

---

122. This story was repeated to me by Jane Cook, a resident of Hockley in 1985, where she remembered her mother talking about pilgrims crawling up the hill on 'all fours' to gain access to the shrine.

123. History, Gazetteer and Directory of the County of Essex by William White. 1848

124. Witchcraft and Magic in the Rochford Hundred by Eric Maple, Folklore, Vol 76, No 3 (Autumn 1965)

12. URBAN SHORES

The seaside resort of Southend-on-Sea is the largest town in the county and is a lively and bustling place within one of the most densely populated areas in Essex. The town has the great honour of maintaining two world records: the longest pleasure pier and the remains of the oldest purpose-built pleasure park. The pier protrudes out into the Thames estuary for 1.34 miles (2.16 km). The first pier was built in 1830, to encourage visitors to arrive at Southend by ferry. The pier had to be over a mile in length to allow for the long tidal reach in the estuary, revealing wide mud flats as the tide drops. The pier was extended in 1833 and again in 1848. This allowed boats to dock at the lowest tide, and brought visitors from London.

In the heart of the town lies the famous *Kursaal Palace*. Built in 1901, this seminal building which once contained a ballroom, circus, dining room and an arcade, has been at the centre of the cultural life of the town for over one hundred years, and most recently housed a casino and shops. The exterior of the building is as iconic as the pier, and is instantly recognisable, with its 'palace' like features. The building is haunted by a *lady in green*, who is thought to be a former employee from the first decades of the twentieth century.[125]

The town boasts an annual whitebait festival. The feast has its origins in the Thames flood of 1707, known as the Dagenham Breach. The London, Kent and Essex gentry who had financed the repairs, were invited to an annual private dinner. The feast was revived in 1934 and moved to Southend, where the small fish were caught from traditional fishing smacks using the heavy nets of the longshoremen around the waters at the end of Southend pier. It is often said that during the 1950s the waters 'boiled' with the silvery fish.

The catch is washed and graded on the boats, apparently giving the fish the delicate Thames estuary 'Southend taste'.[126] During the festival's early revival, a service was led by local clergy who gathered at the pier head for the blessing of the catch ceremony. Nowadays the Whitebait Festival has once again become a dining affair, with tickets sold. The seafront blessing is still part of the day and a small offering of the catch is given back to the sea. The festival is held in September each year.

Apart from fish, during the days before food was mass produced, folk along the coast would have kept a local breed of pig known as the Essex Pig. This pig was an important source of food for the family unit, especially during the

---

125. Haunted Southend by Dee Gordon

126. www.britishpathe.com/video/whitebait. A superb short film from 1951, showing a traditional Southend fishing smack at work off the pier head.

12. Urban Shores

harsh winter months. An old Essex rhyme gives us a clue about the time of year when the pig was slaughtered.

At Michaelmas safely go stie up thy boar
Lest straying abrode, you see him no more
The sooner the better for Hallontide nie
And better he brawneth if hard he do lie.[127]

Hallontide, celebrated around the beginning of November, is the old Essex dialect term for the feast of All Saints, now better known as Halloween. Traditionally, this feast always marked the end of the harvest, where livestock was brought in and killed for meat. However, it was thought to be very unlucky if you looked the pig in the eye during the slaughter.

A ghostly presence holding a lantern haunts the area around The Lawn, a late eighteenth-century house sited in the Southchurch area of the town. Princess Charlotte stayed here as a child in 1801, sent by her doctors to take in the sea air, and the ghost with the lantern is somehow believed to have aided her recovery. The ghost is thought to be that of a smuggler.[128]

The town's Prittlewell Priory and its grounds are haunted by a spectral monk, who was always announced by the ducks and geese quacking and squawking on the pond. Prittlewell was once the main settlement on this stretch of coast, and the 'south end' of the village eventually grew into the large town of today. The settlement began by the Prittle Brook, and it is believed that the area has been in constant settlement since the late Neolithic.

A most important archaeological discovery was made in 2003, where an Anglo-Saxon burial was detected to the east of Prittlewell Priory. The barrow was part of the already known Anglo-Saxon cemetery and was identified just before a road widening scheme was to commence. The barrow

---

127. Folklore of Essex by Sylvia Kent p 96
128. www.paranormaldatabase.com/hotspots/southend.php

originally had a wooden burial chamber beneath its surface, which was adorned with rare and precious artefacts. This royal burial, dating from the late sixth century was possibly one of the earliest Saxon Christian burials, denoted by two gold crosses, which it is believed were placed over each eye of the body. A large gold buckle was also found within the remains of the coffin. Amongst many of the grave goods, were personal items from the middle east, including protective charms and relics from the Byzantine empire which were housed in a painted wooden box found on a raised table close to the head of the body. In this area of the tomb, the archaeologists also discovered a rare ceremonial folding stool, which acted as a portable throne; again this would indicate the high status of the deceased. Other items included the remains of a maple wood Lyre, which was originally housed in an animal skin case, drinking horns, a 625mm diameter cauldron, latticed blue glass beakers and an elaborate copper alloy flagon from Syria. This rare flagon showed a relief image of St Sergius on horseback, which would have been acquired by Christian pilgrims to the shrine of St Sergius and Bacchus at Resafa in Syria, again showing the person buried was high status and had trade links to the eastern Mediterranean. The most important item found were the remains of a highly crafted and decorated sword, a clear indication of a male royal burial. The latest research shows that the body was that of Prince Sæxa, and dates to AD 580. He was the brother of Prince Sæberht, who succeeded their father King Sledda, to the throne of the East Saxon Kingdom in AD 604. So, here we have the sacred burial site of one of very highest status members of the royal family of the ancient Kingdom of Essex, who claimed their ancestry directly from Wōden, the chief god of the Saxons. Local lore tells us that Sæberht died in AD 616, and was buried in Great Burstead, so maybe there is another horde waiting to be found.

    Heading west from Southend, towards the old port of Leigh, we traverse Westcliff and shortly beyond,

12. Urban Shores

Chalkwell, where the shoreline of Essex hosts one of its most liminal sites. Sited proudly on the foreshore lies an obelisk known as the Crow Stone, which marks the exact spot where the river officially becomes the sea. It was from this point that ships would have set their course for the world's first lightship, '*The Nore*', and once safely beyond, to the open sea. Built in 1732, the Nore floating lighthouse protected shipping from becoming grounded. The lightship isn't there anymore, and these days *Sea Reach No.1 Buoy* marks the notorious and dangerous seafaring spot. It is at this location, resting on the seabed, where the deadly remains of the SS Richard Montgomery lies. Now broken and decayed, the ship became grounded in a storm in 1944, and was carrying a massive cargo of explosives, most of which still remain within the wreck, hidden below the murky waters of the estuary.

The old fishing port of Leigh-on-Sea lies to the west of Chalkwell, and despite the urbanisation which has spread westward from Southend over the years, the old town and its waterfront is a wonderful mix of traditional cockle sheds, old sailing hostelries and a working quay. This area is known as Old Leigh, and you can still watch the daily catch of shellfish being hauled in, and then taste it, via the several sheds selling the local delicacies of cockle, winkle, whelk, and shrimp.

The oldest wharf is Alley Dock, and it is believed that it was originally built for the smugglers' pack ponies to draw alongside and quickly move the contraband up the hill to be stored at Adam's Elm. Another old tale of intrigue and suspicion is told about a ship which moored at the neighbouring Strand Quay in the late summer of 1397. A lead coffin was unloaded on the dock, and lay there all day, drawing the curious and macabre of Leigh to speculate who was inside. Rumours quickly circulated that it was the body of a royal, and an uncle of King Richard. Towards midday the casket was moved into one of the larger houses on the Strand and it was stored there until midnight. It was then collected by a horse and chariot, who transported it to Hadleigh Castle. The story eventually disclosed enough gossip to divulge that this was the body of Thomas of Woodstock, Duke of Gloucester, who had been strangled at Calais during his part in the rebellion against King Richard II. The folklore of the time stated that his body was embalmed and encased in a lead coffin ready to be transported to the castle at *Hadley upon Thameside*, and from there to his home at Pleshey Castle to the north-west of Chelmsford.[129]

It was in this old fishing port, in a tiny, dilapidated cottage by Victoria Wharf, that Sarah 'Mother' Moore, the Sea Witch of Leigh, once lived. She was described as a dirty and unwashed individual, toothless and weather-beaten, with a hooked nose and a hare lip. During the mid-nineteenth century, Sarah was famous for her curses and was feared because of them. She also practised a peculiar sort of divination and for this she used an ordinary scatter bowl, which was described as a galvanised pan with a wooden handle, as used by the local fisherman. She would take a trip out on the Thames, beyond Leigh Creek to Ray Gut, where she would collect the course silvery sand from the estuary. This would be brought back to her cottage and dried. Once nice and dry, she would allow it to trickle trough her fingers and into the pan of sea water. As the briny water clouded, she would see images form, and would receive her strange and prophetic visions.

The most famous story about Sarah Moore tells us of a time when a fishing smack from foreign shores arrived in the harbour and the sea witch's reputation had reached the crew before they had even docked. The captain was a harsh man, strict and brutal with all who sailed with him. He banned the crew from even talking to Sarah Moore, let alone buying any of her magic charms or letting her prophecies be sought. However, Sarah was plying her trade by the wharf as the smack pulled in, and she soon realised

---

129. Legends of Leigh by Sheila Pitt-Stanley, p 14

12. Urban Shores

that something was afoot, as she could always sell the wind or foretell a sailor's future using sand and brine; but the entire crew ignored her, and she became angry. The following day the vessel set sail, and still none of the crew had purchased a single charm, spell, or divination. Sarah was enraged. She watched the boat leave Strand Wharf, and as it sailed away, she muttered a spell under her breath and whistled up a storm. No sooner had the captain of the vessel raised the sails and gathered pace out in the wide estuary, than a vicious gale whipped up from nowhere. Dark menacing clouds scudded in across the water from the west, and soon the fishing smack was in serious trouble. The powerful wind was a serious threat to the wooden vessel, but the captain was suspicious, believing that the old sea witch had struck a curse on them. He grabbed an axe, and struck down the mast, and as soon as it fell, the wind instantly dissipated. They limped back to port, to gain repairs, and as they drew alongside the wharf, they saw old Sarah Moore lying dead by the quay, she had several axe marks across her body, which had no doubt finished her off.

Other tales tell of Sarah's knack of cursing unborn children, so that they were born with a hare lip; and the most remarkable feat of being able to start fires with her eyes. The hare lip curse often materialised in new-born children of the district, whose mothers had in some way offended Mother Moore, and this curse would often carry forward across the generations.

Sarah could also foretell the sex of an unborn child by alternating the sex, month by month, from the date of the mother's birth; and in the case of the second child or beyond, she would use the date and sex of the previous child. Using this method, she was never proven incorrect. Sarah had children of her own, although they all died before she did, during the cholera epidemic of the time. These terrible events led Mother Moore into even more bitterness and during one painful episode, she lit her copper and boiled up a particularly evil and devilish brew. Now bereft, by being robbed of any grandchildren of her own, she would damn her neighbours to the same fate. Fuelled on a gin frenzy, she took the kettle of stinking witch brew and delivered it to the doorsteps of five of her neighbours who were known to have babies under six months. After which, she wandered about the wharves, muttering curses and demanding to know why they had healthy babies, whilst her sons were dead and buried up in the boneyard of St Clement's. The terrible result of all of this, whether through the curses of Sarah Moore, or the virulent cholera epidemic, was that within three weeks all babies had sadly died.

Another tale tells us that Mother Moore could flash sparks from her eyes and was able to kill people with fire. One occurrence in 1852 seems to suggest that a local resident actually witnessed this. Jane Lungly claimed to have observed the death of her sister by sparks flashing from the Sea Witch's eyes, which caused her to burn to death. The tale goes something like this:

It was a cold and stormy winter's day, and a group of four children were playing in a narrow alley by Victoria Wharf. One of the old cottage doors opened, and out came Mother Moore, with her witch sack thrown over her shoulder, as was the norm. She shouted at the children to keep away, as she walked down the lane and disappeared around the back of the sail loft. The group of children had their attention drawn towards the witch cottage, as Sarah hadn't secured the latch and her front door was banging to and fro in the gale force winds. Stealthily they moved towards the doorstep and peered into the dark and gloomy interior. On the back wall came the glow of the copper that bubbled and hissed in a very peculiar way. In the centre of the room was a wooden table which had upon its surface an unfinished meal and some eerie old candlesticks. On the stairwell wall were some old shelves which contained lots of dusty corked bottles filled with all sorts of strange liquids and herbs. There was an ancient lamp, which illuminated the shelving, but seemed to throw the rest of the squalid room into a dark and ominous shadow. The children crossed the creepy threshold, and began to explore, but soon they heard footsteps in the alley outside and before they had a chance to escape, Mother Moore was standing on the doorstep, glaring at the children, and muttering an incomprehensible curse. At that point, a great gust of wind blew in, and sparks could be seen coming from Sarah Moore's incredibly angry looking eyes. Before they knew what was happening the children were on fire. Mother Moore grabbed her sack and ran towards them, but they were more frightened of the sea witch than they were of fire, so they pushed passed her and ran out into the street and towards the quay, where the wooden shrimpers were lined up ready for the turning tide. Their screams brought out the neighbours, and soon a crowd had assembled to put out the flames, and to question the children as to why they were burning. One of the girls shouted out that the sea witch had burned them with the sparks that flew from her eyes. Sadly, two of the children died from their injuries, but the remaining girl, Jane Lungly, repeatedly told the tale throughout the rest of her life.[130]

At the junction of Leighcliff Road and the Broadway there used to be a pond. This pond was once fed by a spring and was rumoured to be bottomless. The pond was also considered to be cursed and was used as a ducking pond for suspected witches. It's not surprising that tales of ghostly apparitions have developed at the site over the decades since, and it is believed that any building placed over the site of the pond will eventually sink.

One of the older houses of Leigh was called *Leigh House*, and before that *Black House*. Built in 1620, it stood west of St Clement's Church, at the top of Elm Road facing the Broadway. The house had a sinister reputation, possibly from its name, but more likely from the following grisly discovery. During some restoration work in 1860 to deepen the cellar, a human skeleton was found buried under the stairs. The body was re-interred in the nearby churchyard,

---

130. Legends of Leigh by Sheila Pitt-Stanley, pp 50 - 56

but until that time the troublesome ghost of a glowing lady had haunted the house and its grounds.[131]

The parish church of St Clement stands high above the busy fishing quays. This old church is incredibly atmospheric and on moonless nights two spectral bearers can sometimes be glimpsed, carry a coffin through the churchyard towards the church door, where they disappear. The interior of the church is haunted by dancing ghostly lights, sometimes known as shoreland lights, once believed to be the souls of drowned sailors or fisherman, eternally seeking rest.[132]

There are three historic cases of witchcraft from Leigh-on-Sea. The town was a small centre for fishing and ship building during this time and in 1574, Joan Allen was accused of being a witch. Around seventy years later another resident, Widow Joan Rowle, was accused of practising sorcery and witchcraft. Her crimes were wounding, consuming and murder by witchcraft. Luckily for her, she was acquitted of all charges. Twenty or so years previously, another Leigh resident was caught practising folk-magic, and in 1622, Alice Soles was questioned at the church courts for accusations of practising as a cunning woman.[133]

Adam's Elm was an ancient elm tree which once stood by *Three Wantz Way*, and was often described as having a girth of thirty feet or more, with a vast hollow trunk that at least a dozen men could hide inside. Inevitably it became a smuggling hideout, and a spot where illicit kegs of brandy could be stashed until ready for collection and distribution by the old free traders of the south Essex creeks and marshes. The spot is now hidden under suburbia, but the Elms public house still recalls the old tree in its name. The former tree stood by the crossroads, as is indicated by the

---

131. The History of Rochford Hundred by Philip Benton. 1867. P 334

132. Folklore, Vol 76, No 3 (autumn 1965) Witchcraft and Magic in the Rochford Hundred by Eric Maple

133. Witchcraft prosecutions in Essex 1560 – 1680, thesis by Alan Macfarlane, p 468

12. Urban Shores

old Essex dialect term 'three wantz way'. During some restoration works at the Elms pub in the 1920s an old bottle was found in the rafters, which contained a manuscript written by local farmer Lawrence Davies, and told of the harsh conditions working during the agricultural depression of the 1880s, stating that not a single profit had been made in twenty years. After a copy had been made, the bottle and its contents was returned to the roof, and hopefully it is still there today.[134]

Further west along the Thames lies Hadleigh, with its famous landmark castle, which lies on a sharp hill overlooking the wide mouth of the river. The castle is the spectacular home to some ghost lore, which was old even during the Victorian era, when most sightings were recorded. A spectral White Lady haunts the old ruins, and tradition states that she likes to dance with anyone who sees her ghostly manifestation. She is also recorded as having a violent temper, and once she is bored with her dancing, she has been known to throw the living over the castle's perimeter to see them tumbling down the hillside. Her terrifying companion spirit is the Man in Black, who also haunts the castle ruins and would offer to purchase a soul for a song. It is interesting to note that the stories often ramped up during times of smuggling activities, which were common in the district until the mid-nineteenth century.[135] The rolling downland stretches westwards from the castle, where a plethora of low hills and woodland provide a scenic rampart between civilisation and the brooding estuary. From here, the rare and lofty elevation draws the eye in an easterly direction towards Leigh, Westcliff, and Southend, and in the other, across the haunted marshes, to the former *'Oil City'* island of Canvey.

The most famous folkloric son of the village of Hadleigh must be James 'Cunning' Murrell. Murrell is the most well-

---

134. Legends of Leigh by Sheila Pitt-Stanley, p 48
135. The Realm of Ghosts by Eric Maple, p 185

known of all the cunning men of Essex, and we have previously come across him in chapter one of this book, where he visited Easthorpe to help in a case of witchcraft in the Colchester area.

Known for carrying his trademark brolly in all weathers, he was remembered throughout Essex for his occult powers and abilities as a cunning man. There are a few important sources of information regarding his life, cunning-practice and of the folklore that built up after his death.

The first of these is Arthur Morrison's article entitled *A Wizard of Yesterday*, which was published in *Strand Magazine, Volume XX, July – December 1900*. Morrison also wrote a novel entitled Cunning Murrell. Eric Maple wrote a paper on Murrell, for the March 1960 edition of *Folklore*, and Charlotte Craven Mason also recorded some interesting observations about Murrell in her 1923 book *Essex, its Forest, Folk, and Folklore: A Footnote to History*.

James Murrell was born in Rochford in 1785 and after he finished school, he took an apprenticeship with the Burnham-on-Crouch surveyor G. Emans. His brother, Edward Murrell already lived in the town, and it is likely that James stayed with Edward during the length of the employment in Burnham. At the beginning of the nineteenth century, Murrell moved to London and worked as a stillman at a chemist's shop. He married Elizabeth Francis Button on the 12th of August 1812 at St. Olave's Church, on the South Bank in Bermondsey, on the site now occupied by the art deco style St Olaf House. His wife was from Hadleigh, and the couple probably returned there shortly after they married.

Murrell's home was a terraced weatherboarded cottage, which stood in a narrow lane called Endway. The row stood where an office block now resides, and was the second dwelling in from the direction of the church, which still stands at the end of the lane. A car park sits immediately behind the site, taking up some of the garden space where Buck Murrell recovered some of his father's magical possessions which had been buried in the garden. Between 1814 and 1834, the couple produced seventeen children, many of whom died during infancy.[136]

In addition to his shoe making business, he widely practised as a cunning man and was popularly regarded as a wizard, and he frequented the shoreline around Hadleigh Ray and Leigh Marsh and also the ruins of Hadleigh Castle, perched high above the shore on rolling downland that stretched westwards along the Essex side of the Thames as far as the eye could see. These sites were important for both his smuggling interests and that of astronomy, astrology, herbalism, and his cunning craft. Murrell kept himself apart from the local community, and actively spread the word that he was The Devil's Master. Despite this claim, he was widely consulted, often seeing clients from across Essex, as well as North Kent and parts of Suffolk. It is asserted that he only travelled at night, and would always carry his brolly, a basket to collect herbs and his trusty magical telescope, which had many uses from the usual astronomy to the strangely esoteric, and Murrell claimed it would allow him to see through brick walls.

During his lifetime, he cultivated an atmosphere of mystery around himself and encouraged the dissemination of this gathering mythology and gossip, including one of him flying across the Crouch on a besom style broomstick, and another, where he dematerialised in front of a group of men on Canvey, only to reappear back in Hadleigh simultaneously.[137]

Murrell was born the seventh son of a seventh son, and made a few prophesies during his life, including that there would be witches in Leigh for a hundred years, but in Hadleigh they were to be three forever: and in Canewdon

---

136. William Wallworth: www.deadfamilies.com/Z3-Others/Murrell/Murrell-James-Gen3.htm
137. Folklore, volume 71, Number 1, March 1960: Cunning Murrell - A Study of a 19th Century Cunning Man by Eric Maple

as many as nine. He also predicted the date and time of his own death, informing his daughter of this some years before the event.

Murrell did nothing to suppress his reputation as a terrifying witch-finder and he often boasted that he could call out the Canewdon witches at will. His iron witch bottles were his main method of defence against malevolent witch practice, but when clients complained that his bottles didn't seem to be making much progress, he would reply:

'Oh, but she is a strong one, but I can get the better of her for another half-a-crown.'[138]

Murrell's regular nemesis was Nelly Button, the witch of Hockley, whom we have already discussed, and another was Mrs Elizabeth Eve who lived in a little cottage by the Wagon and Horses pub in Hadleigh. She had a reputation of harming crops and causing storms and was generally feared. When she died, locals were too scared to enter her cottage to lay out her body. Eventually a local woman agreed to take charge, and entered the cottage in readiness to begin preparations for Mrs Eve's burial. Shortly after, the late witch's son appeared and told the lady that his mother's ghost had manifested before him the previous evening as he was preparing to leave the field that he had been farming in. The apparition announced her own death and had summoned him to her cottage, in readiness to take over her occult powers, as was customary. The helpful lady tried to leave, but the witch's son bade her stay and asked her to build a huge fire on the brick hearth. He explained that his mother's secret witch powers needed to be passed on to him. However, he did not want this, and instead planned to destroy the secret ritual and witch family lineage, once and for all.

---

138. Essex Countryside, Volume 2, Number 6, Winter 1953: Canewdon and its Witches by Harold Adshead

12. Urban Shores

Once the fire was blazing hot, he took a small wooden box from the dresser. The box was moving, and was emanating strange shrieks and squeaks. He thrust the box and its contents into the fire, and even louder shrieks and screams were heard. But these quickly subsided as the box burned to ashes. By this time, the now shocked and frightened woman made a hurried escape from the hideous atmosphere of the cottage and its demonic hearth fire. However, she heard him say out loud – "The power is dead. At last, I am free!"[139]

This tale backs up many other stories of witches passing their powers on through their imps and familiar spirits, and as we have already discovered, this tradition of breaking the power was also common in other coastal districts of Essex.

Stephen Choppen, the Hadleigh blacksmith, became famous throughout the district for being the sole maker of James Murrell's iron witch bottles. Arthur Morrison met Choppen during his 1900 research visit to Hadleigh, and the blacksmith had plenty of anecdotes to pass on. Morrison was able to have a look at Murrell's goggle-like spectacles, made from iron, and with very thick rims. The narrowness between the arms proved that Murrell's head was of miniature size, and this backs up the many sources that tell how the cunning man was of a small stature.

Choppen also described how the first witch bottles would not forge properly, despite all procedures being correct. However, once James Murrell arrived and blew on the flames, all was well; and the bottles forged, cooled, and were subsequently used in the wizard's conjurations.

James Murrell's son, Edward 'Buck' Murrell was supposed to have continued the families 'cunning man' business, and there is another story from the blacksmith about this. Buck wanted to keep the family reputation alive after his father's death. Unfortunately, he was illiterate and mainly worked as a farm labourer. One day a local man approached him and

---

139. Essex Countryside, volume 9, Number 57, October 1961: Last Legends of the Essex Witches by Eric Maple

asked for help, as he believed he was bewitched. Buck had the last of his father's iron witch bottles, that he kept in his home, and he filled one up and threw it into the massive blaze stoked up within the hearth of his farm cottage. This must have been one of Choppen's strongest bottles, as it took a while to heat through. Buck and his client were about to give the spell up as no-good, when there was a massive explosion. The bottle shattered in every direction and with such force that it brought down the chimney and the cottage wall with it.[140]

On Friday 9th of November 1900, the Chelmsford Chronicle reported that, *'the lifeless body of Stephen Choppen, aged 69, was found hanging to a beam in an outbuilding adjoining his picturesque cottage at Hadleigh, near Southend.'* Sadly, it seems that Choppen was suffering from severe pain, and decided to end his life.

Charlotte Craven Mason had a bit to say about Murrell, and we have already visited the story in Hawkwell, about Mrs M and the witch bottle. Mason also recorded a story about Murrell's attempts to discover the whereabouts of a stolen horse. Murrell soon revealed that the horse was now in Suffolk, and the owner was incredibly grateful, and was able to recover the horse, and kept his word to Murrell, that he would not prosecute the thieves. Mason also recorded the well-known story of how another local wizard had boasted that he had finally killed James Murrell by his very own method of the exploding witch bottle. It is a shame that this other wizard's name is not recorded as it is an amazing tale. The mystery wizard, as I shall call him, had a donkey and one day this donkey started acting very strangely, and he believed it had been bewitched by his arch-rival, James Murrell. So, the mystery wizard made up a witch bottle from some hair from his donkey, plus some of his own nail pairings, and sealed it up tight and placed it on the roaring

---

140. Strand Magazine, July – Dec 1900, vol XX: A Wizard of Yesterday by Arthur Morrison

12. Urban Shores

hearth fire in his kitchen. The bottle soon burst and shortly afterwards Cunning Murrell came knocking at the locked door. The mystery wizard would not open the door, and shortly afterwards Cunning Murrell was dead.[141] This 'witch bottle' event would have happened on 16th of December 1860, as this was the day that James Murrell died. A date that Murrell himself had predicted with pinpoint accuracy.

James Murrell was renowned as a first-class astrologer and herbalist. He often went foraging for herbs with his wicker basket, and the front room of his home became a county-wide practice, where clients would come and sit amongst the massive amounts of drying herbs strung from the old ceiling beams. In one corner of the room was his ancient chest in which the wizard kept his magical books and charts. These included works on astrology and astronomy, plus medical books and many unbound notes on conjuration.[142] It is reputed that there was also a specific table, upon which Murrell kept the tools of his trade, including his telescope and a human skull. This is where Murrell also drew up his horoscopes, and again word quickly spread of their accuracy. One lady consulted him for a reading, only to be told that he could only make predictions for the next nine years. As predicted, she died within eight years of this consultation.

Murrell would always ask each client whether he or she wanted 'high or low' treatment. This was always in reference to either spiritual or physical help. Murrell frequently conjured a whole host of angelic presences to aid the 'high' treatments. How he did this is anyone's guess, though I fully expect it was done with a great deal of gusto, ritual and theatre, with much attention to detail. Murrell is believed to have possessed a special magical glass mirror with which he would be able to locate stolen or lost property. He was also

---

141. Essex. Its Forest, Folk and Folklore by Charlotte Craven Mason. 1928, p 116

142. Popular Magic: Cunning-folk in English History by Owen Davies, p 133

in great demand for the treatment of animals. Here he would often use more conventional treatments, but before he left, he would always mutter an incomprehensible incantation whilst running his hands over the animal. Sometimes he would hang a charm over the animals stable or bed, or in some cases it was hung around the neck of a cow or horse that needed help.

The terrible plight of Sarah Mott is a distinct tale that was conveyed by Mr Cracknell, who was landlord of the Castle Inn at the beginning of the twentieth century. It was here that Arthur Morrison gathered some of the remembered tales of Murrell, from the very heart of the place that he had lived.

> *Sarah was a young woman that was so devil-possessed and afflicted by witchcraft that she ran around tables without being able to stop. She was also seen walking across ceilings and would head down the walls like an insect. This was until Cunning Murrell destroyed the witch's power and the demon, which was believed had possessed Sarah, through the use of one of his iron witch bottles.*[143]

After his death, Murrell's antique chest was promptly buried in the back garden of the cottage by the landlord. However, Buck Murrell subsequently dug it back up. Maple suggests that the contents survived up until 1956, when they were apparently destroyed, as remarkably, they were thought to be worthless. It is through the work of Morrison that we have some idea of what Murrell used the chest for. The contents were recorded as follows: there were books on both astrology and astronomy, old medical books, a Nicholas Culpeper annotated in Murrell's own handwriting, and other books dealing with conjuration and alchemy. These books described the roles of the following angelic beings: Adonay,

---

143. Strand Magazine, July – Dec 1900, vol XX: A Wizard of Yesterday by Arthur Morrison

12. Urban Shores

Elohim, Raphael and Tetra, plus, ways of preparing amulets, along with correct metals, sigils, cabbalistic symbols and various old charms used to banish negativity and malevolent magic. Interestingly, there was also a book that had belonged to a previous seventeenth cunning man called Neoboad.[144]

Published within his *'Dark World of Witches'* book, is a rare photograph of Eric Maple standing behind Murrell's antique chest, and holding a 'holey stone'. During recent correspondence with Southend Museum, I have been able to ascertain that this old storage chest is not the one held by the social history department of Southend Museums Service. Therefore, we may possibly have a record of two historic storage chests that once belonged to Murrell, or perhaps there is another story to reveal?[145]

James 'Cunning' Murrell is without doubt, one of the most familiar and best documented cunning men within the historic records of Essex. The folklore surrounding him and his old stomping ground of Hadleigh is well established, giving us tantalising glimpses into the everyday lives of the people of late Georgian and Victorian Hadleigh. To stroll across the fields, to the ruined castle, is to walk in his footsteps. Whenever we do this, we keep his story alive; but it is more than this. To walk in the historic haunted shadows of the people who have lived on the lip of this marshy hinterland, helps to re-evaluate, and re-define the much-misinterpreted perspectives of the culture and history of the county of Essex.

In nearby Thundersley, there was once an ancient sacrificial tradition of the taking of a human life when a new graveyard was opened. This of course, has been long forgotten. However, the hilltop churchyard in Thundersley has retained a curious piece of lore, where children once commemorated this grisly practice in the form of a

---

144. The Dark World of Witches by Eric maple, p 170
145. Email correspondence with Vittorio Ricchetti, Assistant Curator of Social History, Southend Museums Service

game. In the corner of the old woodland churchyard by the thirteenth century church of St Peter are many old graves. These were once used by locals, where they would run around one of the tombs chanting a rhyme, now sadly lost. Six times they would encircle the grave, running counter-clockwise, against the sun. On the seventh course, they would break hands and run away from the grave, screaming and shrieking, as if being chased by a demon. The idea behind this esoteric folk-play is to ensure that the strange ritual is held around the oldest tomb in the far reaches of the churchyard. Once the participants disperse screaming, the bravest is required to put their ear to the ground, to hear and summon the old Devil below. It is believed that by doing this, they are helping to summon the old ghost-guardian of the tombs, who was once the sacrifice himself.[146]

In the same churchyard, there is an interesting skull-like stone, known locally as the *bird stone or skull stone*. It is sited by the south porch and may have once been a focus of pre-Christian veneration on the summit of this lofty hill, with its prominent views across the marshes to the Thames.[147] The stone was re-discovered whilst digging a grave sometime during the First World War, in the north-west corner of the churchyard where the land begins to slope rapidly.[148] The village name is fascinating and gives us clues to an older use for the hilltop upon which sits the parish church. The name is from the Old English Þunres lēah, which translates as the grove of Thunor. Thunor is the old Saxon god of thunder, and we have previously met him in an earlier chapter, where he is also remembered

---

146. The Realm of Ghosts by Eric Maple, p 182

147. Whilst visiting on the 6th May, 2021 it was discovered that the stone has disappeared from the churchyard. I have been informed by the Hadleigh and Thundersley Community Archive that the stone has been removed for safe keeping.

148. Hadleigh and Thundersley Community Archive correspondence.

12. Urban Shores

in the historic Essex Hundred of Thurstable, which is situated on the northern shore of the Blackwater estuary.

Within Thundersley Woods, close to Bread and Cheese Hill, are the Devil Steps, and there is some interesting weather-related folklore which describes how the name came about:

> *One cold and snowy winter's day, the Devil was residing in the woods which flanked the Hill of Thunor, high above the estuary. Despite the snowy weather, he decided to conjure up a fierce storm, as he thought it might blow away the snow clouds. However, he was so successful in the wildness of the storm, that he decided to take shelter in nearby Jarvis Hall, rather than reverse his conjuration. Once inside, the Devil discovered that some local priests had also taken cover in the same building, but were hiding from soldiers rather than the storm. One of the priests saw the great horned beast, and held up his crucifix in terror. This alarmed the Old Devil, and he turned and fled, running out of the hall and down the hill. Each time a cloven hoof hit the snowy ground, it left a spooky cloven print. Over the years that followed, each hoofprint left an indelible mark, and along with the haunting tale of a dark horned devil, perpetually running down the slope, a pathway was created. Over time, this path was gradually turned into the flight known as the Devil Steps, in honour of the devil haunted woods which still surround much of the hill today.*[149]

Within the same spooky woods, there are rumours that around two hundred years ago a wise-woman called 'Mother Connie Redcap' lived and worked there. From these woods she once dispensed her herbal cures, helped with birth control, and practised her cunning craft within the community around Thundersley.[150]

The church of Holy Cross at Basildon dates from the fourteenth century and has a churchyard ghost of a 'red

---

149. Secret Essex by Glyn Morgan, p 106
150. Mysterious Essex, volume 2. Heritage Films, 1992

monk' who is often seen after dark. This may possibly be one of the previous rectors, and the name red monk may be a corruption of rood monk, the keeper of the holy rood cross. In the porch on a roof spandrel is a carving of a winged dragon, maybe indicating a lost folk tale? An alternative or possibly different piece of ghost-lore explains that a floating monk has also been seen in the road outside the churchyard, where a man in clerical attire crosses the road and heads into the churchyard, where intriguingly, the story states he is looking to return to his grave, which is both unmarked and sited on the north side of the church.[151] In nearby Laindon at the hilltop parish church of St Nicholas, two dragon carvings can be found in the porch. These are said to commemorate a local dragon who once lived on the hill. One day the dragon attacked a man and gave him a fatal venomous bite. The dragon was eventually dispatched by a French knight, who was summoned by the fearful locals to rid them of the terrifying beast.[152]

On Bowers Marsh not far from the parish church of St Margaret, the shimmering ghost of a white lady can sometimes be seen floating across the mire and heading towards the fleet. This is the ghost of a bride who, in the 1950s, was jilted at the altar of St Margaret's. She was heartbroken and wandered off distraught across the marshes and ended up drowning in the creek.[153]

Directly south of Bowers Marsh lies Canvey Island, once a lonely and marshy domain of Romano-British salt production, and later the Saxon Shepherd's Isle, producing ewes' milk, cheese, and wool.

On the mudflats at Canvey Point, a ghostly figure has been observed walking along the foreshore. Legend says it is

---

151. Memories of an Essex Ghosthunter by Wesley Downes, pp 8, 9
152. ASH magazine number 3, Spring 1989: Paganism in Essex Churches (Holy Cross church, Laindon church) by Ian Dawson
153. ASH magazine number 6, Winter 1989/90: Gone Fishing with a Stranger by P. Hobbs

12. Urban Shores

a Viking soldier waiting for his ship to take him home. This tale was first recounted in the 1920s by Charlie Stamp, the fisherman, wildfowler, and longshoreman of Canvey Point. He lived in a wooden shack made from wreck-reclaimed barge timbers, and the dormer windows of the dwelling were level with the top of the sea wall. The hearth was made from red brick, and burned tangy salt drenched driftwood and bits of shipwrecked timbers, still black with tar. The ghost sighting is told something like this:

The moon was nearing full, and I lay in my bed staring out of the window at the bright moonlight. It was approaching midnight, and the tide was flowing in across the flat. Then out of nowhere I saw a figure wading ashore, knee deep and kicking up water. He climbed across the mud and seemed to be heading straight for my cottage. He jumped a couple of rills and then over the sea wall. He found the plank into my garden and before I had a chance to get out of bed he was in my room. He was a tall chap with long blond hair. He wore a short tunic with a leather jerkin and cross garterings. A broad belt and sword was strung around his waist and the moonlight flashed off his head, and I noticed he wore a silver helmet. He looked at me and said, "I've lost my ship, I want to go home, over the seas. Can you help me?"

"You need to head over to Grays or Tilbury; you can get a ship from there," I replied. But he just stared at me and said, "You don't understand, I've lost my ship, I've lost my country and I am a lost man."

At that point he climbed out of the window and headed back out to the tideline, where he walked along the water's edge under the light of the moon, and as I watched he suddenly vanished, disappearing into the calmness of the night.[154]

In the year AD 894, a Viking fleet of around two hundred ships arrived in Benfleet Creek and set up a stockaded settlement on the shore, close to where the church of St

---

154. Essex Ghosts by James Wentworth Day, pp 4 - 6

Mary now stands. Whilst the Vikings, led by Hastein, were on a campaign further inland, the Saxon army attacked the camp and set fire to many of the ships moored in the creek. This set the scene for the Vikings of long hard winter of war, and many of the survivors fled to Shoebury and set up a new camp there. Was this ghostly sailor one of Hastein's warriors, who had been left behind, and died in the vicinity? I would like to think so.

Author, Raymond Lamont Brown describes this ghost in his book *Phantoms, Legends, Customs and Superstitions of the Sea*:

> 'Wildfowlers and fishermen who have seen him say that he wears a horned helmet and a jerkin of coarse leather. As the phantom strides out over the mudflats, his long sword, hanging loose from his belt, sends a clanking sound through the ever-rustling reeds.'

Over the years many night-fishermen on Canvey have described seeing a tall and broad figure resembling a Viking warrior standing on the mudflats at The Point. Many islanders believe that he drowned at this spot after being left behind by the retreating Viking fleet.

On the 13th of August 1954, a local newspaper reported a headline that said *Fish with feet found on Canvey beach*. This started a debate about what kind of sea creature had washed up on the island's foreshore. People also started talking about sea monsters. The creature was described as four feet long, with bulging eyes, razor sharp teeth, and human feet, each with five toes. The large gaping mouth was surrounded by human flesh, and was pink in colour. Some of the locals at the time, including local resident Colin Day, who witnessed the event first-hand, have described it as a mermaid, but others think it was more like a monkfish.[155] Either way the Canvey Monster entered the strange *fortean*

---

155. canveyisland.org/history-2/memories/early-20th-century-canvey/the_rev_joseph_overs_the_canvey_island_monster

12. Urban Shores

folklore of the island. However, as is usual for cases like this, the interest didn't end there, and over the years many have tried to reinvestigate and reinterpret this strange beach anomaly. Some accounts suggest that there were two separate incidents, the first carcass being washed up in November 1954 and the second in August 1955. Many of the descriptions seem to be muddled between the two separate, but seemingly equally strange corpses. The 1954 specimen was described as two and a half feet long with thick reddish-brown skin, bulging eyes, sharp teeth, and gills. In addition, a witness also specified it as having hind legs with five toes protruding from horseshoe-shaped feet with concave arches. So, a mermaid with hooves and razor-sharp teeth?

Apparently, there was a cursory inspection by zoologists who said that it posed no danger to the public, and its remains were cremated. Did they want to cover it up, and keep it secret? One does wonder though, why an ichthyologist wasn't sought, as surely, they could have at least catalogued it.

The second fishy body to be washed up in August 1955, is described as similar to the first but much larger, being nearly four feet long and weighing approximately twenty-five pounds. It was sufficiently fresh for its eyes, nostrils, and teeth to be studied though no official explanation was given as to who studied it or what happened to the body.[156]

So, what was this creature? In 1999 a fortean journalist carried out an investigation and it was concluded that the creature was an anglerfish whose pronounced fins had been incorrectly described as being hind legs.[157]

Canvey was also once home to a sacred shrine of miracles to the Blessed Virgin Mary. Sited in Roggel Road, close to the sea front, was a small bungalow belonging to Nora Arthurs, where she had various visions of the Virgin, and

---

156. strangeanimalspodcast.blubrry.net/tag/mermaids
157. The Fortean Times, February 1999: Checks and Balances by Nick Warren, p 47

built a Marian shrine in her back garden. Eventually her home was visited by thousands, seeking divine guidance and messages. Because of this, Canvey Island was also known to some, as *England's Lourdes*.[158]

Back on the mainland, on the Thameside marshes at Fobbing, lies the local beauty spot of One Tree Hill, which is famous in folk-history for being the highest point in a straight line before you reach the North Pole.[159] St. Michael's Church is renowned for its historic association with the smuggling trade. At one time the church was near the waterfront of Fobbing Harbour. Smugglers sailed up Fobbing Creek guided by the distinctive church tower but, after the great flood of the 1st of February 1953, the creek and harbour were unfortunately sealed up and drained. Underneath the church are many tunnels which were used by smugglers in the fourteenth century. The road by the church is still called Wharf Road and the wooden porch leading to the south door of St Michael's has an interesting carving on the left-hand spandrel. It depicts a dragon or sea-serpent with a curious figure, which looks like an elf holding the serpent's mouth open.

The White Lion Inn still stands in the village, as it has done for over six hundred years. Set close to the old harbour, the building dates to the fourteenth century and was originally used as a sail loft and chandlery for local shipping. The White Lion Inn has been keeping the estuary fisherman, sailors, bargees and villagers refreshed across four centuries. During the eighteenth and nineteenth centuries, Oak Apple Day was celebrated, and it was customary to decorate the front of the inn with large boughs of oak. Many of the sailing barge crews would anchor their traditional craft in Fobbing Creek, and would assemble at the White Lion, where the bargee fiddle players would gather to play for the folk dancers. This celebration was originally brought to life in the village by

---

158. www.canveyisland.org/people-2/2-characters/nora-arthurs/marys-house

159. The Essex Village Book by the Federation of Essex Women's Institutes

12. Urban Shores

former rector, the Rev. John Pell, who reconstituted the old May celebrations and other rural festivities after the restoration of the monarchy.[160] Many customers have sat within the bars of the marsh side inn, where farm hands, marshmen and sailors have sought refreshment across the years. The pub is haunted by an eighteenth-century landlord's daughter, who was murdered in the building for dating one of the sail makers in the village.[161]

It was at One Tree Hill, between Fobbing and the old village of Vange, that the Vange Water Company once sold its *magical well water*. During the first two decades of the twentieth century, the mineral water was sold at outlets across South Essex and London. Extra wells were dug during this time and classical style architecture appeared around them, giving the area a feel of a traditional spa. A tuberculosis outbreak finished the business off, along with the death of the founder in 1924. Some of the neo-classical structures can still be seen close to the One Tree Hill entrance to Langdon Hills country park, and there are one or two contemporary reports that these ruins are haunted. To the south-west lies the pretty village of Horndon-on-the-Hill with its curious hot cross bun custom. Every Good Friday, since around 1900, the oldest villager has been invited to hang a freshly baked bun from one of the old oak beams in the bar of the fifteenth century Bell public house. The village is also haunted by the ghostly form of a lady called Mrs Osman, who rides her spectral donkey, mysteriously emerging out of the village pond on certain dark nights of the year. This remarkable ghostly spectacle eventually disappears into a wild copse near to Rookery Corner. Another equine ghost and male rider haunts Orsett Road and Blackbush Lane.[162]

---

160. Essex Countryside, Vol 9 No 57, October 1961: An Essex Innkeepers Notebook of 1850 by F. Z. Claro p 495

161. www.thewhitelionfobbing.com/about-us

162. The Essex Village Book by the Federation of Essex Women's Institutes

At East Horndon, is the legend of the Horndon Dragon. The story tells us of a dragon-like serpent which escaped from a ship docked on the Thames, and roamed the parish terrifying the locals. Sir James Tyrell hunted the beast and eventually cut off its head. This dragon can be seen carved into the woodwork of St. Nicholas church in nearby Laindon, which upon closer inspection, looks remarkably like a crocodile. Could it have been one of these creatures, brought back from the tropics, that escaped into the woods at Horndon?[163]

An interesting story was recorded by folklorist Charlotte Craven Mason concerning a farmhouse somewhere in Laindon where we may have a rare remnant of the old belief in fairies and the little folk in Essex. The account is a bit muddled, and has been misrepresented over the years, but seems to describe a farmhouse in Laindon which belonged to the father of Ms Mason's Rayleigh correspondent. The farmer had a lodger who was a parson and a wizard who kept three imps. These magical creatures had been handed down to the parson-wizard from his own father, which suggests that he came from a family of cunning men. The farmer's daughter used to wait on the parson-wizard, and was instructed to never take a light into his room, as it would illuminate the creatures. However, one night she entered the room with a candle, and saw the three mysterious imps standing by a table. They were as tall as the table, but it seems no other description was recorded by her. One of the farmer's sons also saw the creatures and he described them as looking like black cats, though they were also described by others as looking like a mole. One of these creatures was also seen by one of the farmer's family whilst in bed one night. It was seen standing by the foot of the bed and, as he tried to sit up, the imp held him down by his ears. One of the farm labourers also saw one of the imps walking across

---

163. Beyond the Dragon's Lair by Ian Dawson. ASH magazine, Autumn 1988

12. Urban Shores

some nettles, but the nettles remained standing. Apparently, the labourer was so frightened by this he fled from the farm, never to return. After this episode, the farmer ordered the parson to leave, stating that he would sooner have the Devil lodge at the farm.[164]

The account does have similarities with other 'little people' accounts from other areas of Britain, especially the description of how the imp walked across the nettles without bending them. There are other scattered stories from across Essex, of how farmers would leave offerings to the Brownies as thanks for helping around the farm.[165]

Other Essex fairy lore states that bakers hung Echinoid fossils by their ovens as amulets and called them 'fairy loaves'. These were used as charms to ensure you would never be short of bread. They were also known as thunderstones and if left on your windowsill would protect your house from lightning.[166]

Just north of Tilbury docks lies Hangman's Wood at Little Thurrock. The name derives from *Hanging Wood* to denote a wood which once appeared to hang over the marshes.[167] Within this old wood are the remains of medieval chalk and flint mining. These pits are known as *Dene Holes* and were once thought to be Saxon hiding places from Danish coastal raids. There were once over seventy *Dene Holes* in the wood, but only a few holes now survive as visible earthworks. The pits appear to be concentrated towards the northern part of the wood, most surviving as shallow depressions, grassed over and overgrown. The larger holes are surrounded by fencing. Hangman's Wood is the remains of a much larger ancient woodland and lies on the higher ground that was once the northern limit of the Thames marshes. Despite the

---

164. Essex. Its Forest, Folk and Folklore by Charlotte Craven Mason. 1928
165. Essex Folk Tales by Jan Williams, p 145
166. Museum of Witchcraft & Magic archive, Boscastle, Cornwall. Item 834: Twenty-one Fossilised Sea Urchins
167. Forgotten Thameside by Glyn H. Morgan, p 38

dense urbanisation, the wood still provides a leafy respite from the bustle of the southern shore. Local folklore tells us that the Dene Holes were *Cymbeline's gold mines*. Later lore, records that King Henry IV requested that *'information of a concealed mine of gold in Essex should be brought to him and to bring the gold of the mine before him.*'[168]

There is a local tradition that states that these 'mines' were reworked periodically between the fifteenth and eighteenth centuries to look for gold, but all that was found was the 'fool's gold' of pyrite.

Cymbeline or more correctly Cunobelinus, was a late Iron Age tribal king of the Catuvellauni. The area around Little Thurrock was once the Iron Age borderland between the Catuvellauni and Trinovantes tribal lands, and local folklore tales tell us that these underground chambers were built as both hiding places and traps for the border raids of the two tribal regions.

At nearby Grays Thurrock, the bend in the river is known as Fiddlers' Reach, named after the legend that three fiddle players were drowned here and their ghostly music still sometimes resonates from deep below the dark waters.[169]

It was at Tilbury, that Queen Elizabeth made her famous speech and quasi-mythic appearance to her troops on the 9th of August 1588; and descriptions of her deity-like presence add to the mythology of the sacred Thames, where she is believed to have appeared in a voluptuous glowing white satin gown, covered with a shimmering velvet cloak. Her hair was festooned with fantastic flowing plumes, as she gracefully sat upon her great white horse, brandishing a symbolic silver truncheon, riding confidently through the weighty throng of soldiers that had been gathered to defend her Tudor realm.

---

168. 'Household Words: A Weekly Journal' by Charles Dickens, January 19th, 1856, p.541.

169. Thames: Sacred River by Peter Ackroyd, p 445. Chattos & Windus. 2007

12. Urban Shores

Away from the Thameside romance of the Tudor Queen, we travel north-west, and close to the M25, we arrive at the Ockendons, both North and South. In South Ockendon, the thirteenth century round towered parish church of St Nicholas sits adjacent to the village green and displays one of the best Essex examples of a green man. He sits in all his foliate splendour on the north wall, just to the east of the porch overlooking the green.[170] At North Ockendon lies the holy well of St Cedd. This ancient holy well is dedicated to the very same holy man, who arrived on the north-east coast of the Dengie in the sixth century to build his chapel. He had another religious house at nearby Tilbury, and it is believed that he used this holy well to baptise the converted. Local tradition tell us that the old name for North Ockendon was *Wokindun Set Funteines*, alluding to the folklore of the seven springs of North Ockendon, of which the holy well of St Cedd was one. All seven of these mythic springs were believed to have once been revered in some way. One of the seven is considered to rise at Hobbs Hole, where it forms a small pond. Place names containing hobb or hob are often linked to forgotten traditions of old English hobgoblins or other fairy folk, and can be interpreted as an important remnant of the ancient fairy faith within the county. It is also suggested that a former well canopy which once covered St Cedd's well, sported a horned male head alongside a representation of St Mary Magdalene, to whom the nearby parish church is dedicated.[171]

As we end our journey along the long and winding coast of Essex, we arrive at one of the most mysterious enigmas of our entire journey. It was here on Rainham Marshes that a Neolithic wooden figure was excavated in 1922, during the construction of the Ford motor plant. The Dagenham Idol, as it became known, is a most remarkable and fascinating

---

170. ASH magazine, number 5 Autumn 1989: Paganism in Essex Churches (South Ockendon) by Ian Dawson
171. Hidden Heritage: Discovering Ancient Essex by Terry Johnson, p 137

object from the late Neolithic period. Discovered deep within the mud of the ancient marsh, the figure is carved from scots pine, and is believed to be around 4,300 years old. The Dagenham Idol is an exceptional and unique artefact, and is probably a representation of a local deity, which was deposited as a sacrificial offering to the marshes by Neolithic hunter-gatherers. Interestingly, it was found buried close to the skeletal remains of a deer, all of which may show that even in the more distant past, the Thames was a sacred and much revered waterway, once celebrated and reimagined through votive offerings and ritual sacrifices to the alluvial riverbank of the liminal shore.

Selected Bibliography

Thames: Sacred River by Peter Ackroyd. Chatto & Windus, 2007

Mehalah by Sabine Baring Gould. Smith Elder & Co, 1880
Essex Witches by Peter C Brown. The History Press, 2014

The Running Well Mystery by Andrew Collins. The Supernaturalist, 1983

Essex: Its Forest, Folk and Folklore by Charlotte Craven Mason. J. H. Clarke & Co, 1928

Popular Magic: Cunning folk in English History by Owen Davies. Hambledon Continuum, 2003

The Supernatural Coast by Peter Haining. Robert Hale, 1992
The Township of Hatfield Peverel by Teresa M. Hope. J. H. Clarke & Co, 1930

East Anglian Witches and Wizards by Michael Howard. Three Hands Press, 2017

Folklore of Essex by Sylvia Kent. The History Press, 2009
Witchcraft Prosecutions in Essex 1560 – 1680 by Alan Macfarlane, 1967. Available online through Oxford University Research Archive.

Cunning Murrell - A Study of a 19th Century Cunning Man by Eric Maple, Folklore, volume 71, Number 1, March 1960

Witchcraft and Magic in the Rochford Hundred by Eric Maple. Folklore vol. 76 no. 3 Autumn 1965

The Witches of Canewdon by Eric Maple. Folklore vol 71, no. 4 December 1960

The Witches of Dengie by Eric Maple. Folklore vol 73, no. 3 Autumn 1962

The Dark World of Witches by Eric Maple. Robert Hale, 1962

The Realm of Ghosts by Eric Maple. Robert Hale, 1964

Secret Essex by Glyn Morgan. Ian Henry Publications, 1982

Essex Witches by Glyn H Morgan. Spur Books, 1973

A Wizard of Yesterday and Cunning Murrell by Arthur Morrison; both now republished as one volume – Spirit of Old Essex, edited and introduced by Steven Kay. 1889 Books, 2014

Legends of Leigh by Sheila Pitt-Stanley. Privately published, 1989.

Index

A
Adam's Elm, 209, 214
Addedomaros, 78
Ague, 17, 156
Alchemy, 28-29, 42, 222
Alresford, 35, 79
Anglo-Saxon, 64, 126, 207
Apotropaic symbols, 88, 179
Ascension Day, 76
Ashingdon, 185, 193, 203-204
Astrologer, 221

B
Barling, 23, 196-197
Baring Gould, Sabine, 8, 23, 99
Battle of Maldon, 95, 126-128
Battlesbridge, 131, 158, 162-163
Barn Hall, 103-104
Barrow, 78, 98-100, 111-112, 128, 149, 174, 196, 201, 207
Basildon, 225
Bazille-Corbin, John Edward, 164
Beating the Bounds, 27, 76
Beacon Hill, 25, 131, 185, 192
Beaumont-cum-Moze, 62
Bedizened, 158-159, 161
Beeleigh Abbey, 115, 117, 119
Bell, 48, 60, 133, 153, 155, 178, 231
Bellarmine jars, 173
Benfleet, 227
Benfleet Creek, 227
Bennet, Elizabeth, 68-69
Bird, Fanny, 160
Bird stone, 224
Bird, Thomas, 160
Black Dog, 14, 26, 30, 56, 65-66, 108-110, 119, 146-147, 196-197, 201
Black shuck, 56, 98, 108, 110, 196
Blacksmith, 202, 219
Blackthorn stick, 186
Blackwater, river, 25, 62, 95-96, 107-108, 111-113, 121-123, 130-132, 134, 136, 139, 143, 145, 225
Blessing and Reclaiming of the Waters, 76
Blessing witch, 198

Bobbing Pond, 200
Boleyn, Anne, 198
Bonfire Boys, 54
Boudica, 78, 95
Boy bishop, 83
Bradwell-on-Sea, 119, 147
Bradwell-juxta-Mare, 21, 143
Bridgemarsh Island, 159
Bright, Edward, 125
Brightlingsea, 36, 74-76, 83, 97
British, 86, 91-92, 95, 98, 131, 174-175, 187, 192, 226
Briton, 91
Bronze Age, 18, 92, 99, 111, 123
Broomway, 14, 174
Brownie, 32, 36, 120-121, 233
Burnham-on-Crouch, 21, 54, 158, 216
Burnham wart charm, 159
Button, Nelly, 202, 218
Buzzy of Latchingdon, 156
Byrhtnoth, 95, 126-127

C
Camulodunon, 79, 91
Camulodunum, 19, 79
Camulos, 78
Canewdon, 90, 154, 157, 175-189, 191-193, 217-218
Canewdon church tower, 178-179, 183, 192
Canute, 185, 203-204
Canvey Island, 226, 230
Canvey Monster, 228
Cat, 30, 40, 57-58, 93, 110, 121, 182
Catchpole, Bessie, 55
Catholic, 69, 125
Cauldron, 92, 148, 188, 208
Celtic, 18, 37, 78, 91, 95, 144
Charm, 67-68, 88, 109, 120, 156-157, 159, 170, 179, 183, 211, 222
Chaundler, Alice, 118
Chelmer, river, 18, 28, 113, 115, 134
Chelmsford, 32, 45, 61, 68, 73, 113, 125, 144, 210, 220
Choosing Day, 75-76
Christmas, 39, 52, 83, 138, 199

240

Index

Church bells, *62, 75, 154, 171, 198*
Cinque Ports, *75*
Clacton-on-Sea, *17, 63*
Clacton spear, *17*
Clarke, Elizabeth, *39-40*
Claudius, Emperor, *79-80*
Cobmarsh Island, *103*
Cockley, Mary, *160-162*
Colchester, *16, 25, 59, 70, 73, 77-80, 82-84, 87-88, 92-93, 216*
Colchester legend, *80*
Colne, river, *35, 74, 78-79, 96, 111*
Collyne, Thomas, *117-119*
Conjuror, *119*
Conjuration, *155, 200, 202, 221-222, 225*
Cooper, Anne, *63*
Cooper, Joan, *63*
Copford, *85, 89*
Cheese, *92, 225-226*
Choppen, Stephen, *219-220*
Coppin, Mary, *61*
Corpse candle, *62*
Court Farm, *140*
Covens, *184*
Cowslip, *143, 194-195*
Craven Mason, Charlotte, *15, 23, 203, 216, 220, 232*
Creeksea, *131, 140, 159, 161, 171*
Crossroads, *76, 149, 183, 185-186, 214*
Crouch, river, *21, 130-132, 154, 158-159, 162, 168-169, 171, 174-175, 177, 180, 192, 199-201, 217*
Crow Stone, *209*
Cunning Barnard, *134*
Cunning Burrell, *85*
Cunning Cocke, *68*
Cunning Collyne, *117-118*
Cunning folk, *24, 29, 33, 65, 110, 120, 133, 153, 157, 173, 183, 191, 194, 199*
Cunning Hawes, *140*
Cunning Hovye, *39*
Cunning man, *84, 117, 119-120, 156, 159-160, 184-185, 187-190, 192, 216-217, 219, 223*
Cunning Murrell, *22-23, 167, 203, 216, 221-222*

Cunning woman, *29, 33, 34, 39-40, 44, 67-68, 147, 155, 175, 198, 214*
Cunobelinus, *234*
Curse, *39, 58, 104, 124, 137, 186, 211, 213*

D

Dagenham Idol, *235-236*
D'Arcy, Bryan, *73*
Danbury, *18, 131-134*
Dæningas, *132*
Dee, John, *117-118*
Deer, *236*
Dene Holes, *233-234*
Dengie, *21, 23, 44, 111, 126, 130-132, 136-138, 140, 147, 149-151, 153-158, 161, 170, 186, 200, 235*
Devil, *14, 27, 39-41, 60, 63, 88-90, 102-106, 108, 120, 132-133, 139-140, 146-147, 149-150, 157, 159-160, 163-164, 170-171, 181-182, 217, 222, 224-225, 233, 236*
Devil's claw mark, *163*
Devil's door, *90*
Devil's handprint, *139*
Devil's Marsh, *139*
Devil Steps, *225*
Devil's thistle, *157*
Devil's Wood, *103, 105*
Dialect, *25, 122, 172, 194, 200, 207, 215*
Divination, *91, 210-211*
Dovercourt, *57-58*
Dragon, *64, 66, 77-78, 82-83, 226, 230, 232*
Dropsy Doctor, *200*
Druid, *91-92, 108*
Druid of Camulodunon, *91*

E

East Mersea, *98, 100*
Edmond Ironside, *203*
Edward I, *117*
Edward VI, *115*
Elementals, *93, 121*
Elen, *86-87*
Elizabeth I, *29*
Elm tree legend, *214*
ELUI, *86-87*
Enchanter, *120, 133*
Eve, Elizabeth, *218*

Evil eye, 87-88
Exorcisms, 86
Eyes, 13, 25, 45, 58, 77, 108, 110, 132, 137, 146, 153, 155-156, 165, 179-180, 182, 185-186, 188, 197, 211-213, 228-229

F

Familiar, 32, 41, 50, 61, 118, 156, 170, 219
Familiar spirits, 118, 156, 219
Farming, 22, 31, 77, 84, 92, 101, 123-124, 152, 175, 189, 194, 218
Farrah, Stewart, 42
Faerie, 15, 36, 120-121, 173
Fairy, 32, 36, 93, 120, 156, 194, 233, 235
Fairy flowers, 194
Festival of the gooseberry pie, 107
Fiddlers' Reach, 234
Fingringhoe, 76-77
Fingringhoe Oak, 76
Fobbing Creek, 230
Folk magic, 84, 101, 120
Francis, Elizabeth, 32-33, 216
Free-traders, 146
Fishing, 22, 44, 55, 57, 76, 83, 107, 122, 145, 160, 175, 194, 206, 209-211, 214, 226
Foulness Island, 171-172, 174
Frinton-on-Sea, 72

G

Gardner, Gerald, 184
Gardner, Goody, 61
Garner, Lilian, 187, 189, 191-192
Gate, Sir John, 115
Genius loci, 156
Ghost, 13, 15, 23, 26, 40-41, 55, 60, 63, 65, 78, 86, 100, 108, 110, 115-116, 128, 130, 145-147, 149, 154, 159-160, 163, 171, 173, 176, 179-180, 189, 196, 198, 202, 204, 207, 214, 218, 224-228, 231
Ghost barge, 130
Ghost lore, 146, 149, 215
Ghost-laying, 86
Ghost ship, 171
Ghost yacht, 101
Gifford, George, 119
Gleaners, 196

Gnomes, 32, 93
Goddess, 43, 57, 86-87
Goldhanger, 110, 127-129
'Granny' Garnr, 189, 191
Grays, 227, 234
Grey, Lady Jane, 115
Great Bentley, 64-65
Great Clacton, 63-64
Great Hydes Field, 183, 193
Great Holland, 63
Great Wakering, 196
Great Wigborough, 78
Green Man, 77, 148, 235
Grew, Margery, 61

H

Ha'penny Pier, 56-57
Hadleigh, 10, 22, 39, 85, 88, 167, 186, 192, 210, 215-220, 223
Hadleigh castle, 210, 217
Halstead, 70
Hallontide, 207
Halloween, 207
Hamford Water, 36, 62
Hanby, Elizabeth, 43
Hard Apple Blyth, 195
Hare, Elizabeth, 63
Hares, 171, 174
Hart, Harriet, 154-156
Hart, Mary, 44
Hart witch family, 154
Harvest, 65, 77, 84, 105, 124, 147, 151-152, 185, 207
Harvest Horns, 152
Harwich, 21, 25, 43-46, 48, 50-58, 74
Hatfield Peverel, 24-33, 182
Haunting, 58, 71, 160, 195, 204, 225
Havengore Island, 175
Hawkwell, 203, 220
Headless ghost, 173
Headless horseman, 26, 163
Headless Horror of the Sea Wall, 130, 149
Herbalist, 221
Herb Peter, 194
Henry IV, 28, 234
Henry V, 29
Henry VIII, 29, 75, 115, 198
Heybridge, 113-115, 123
Heybridge Basin, 113-115

Higby, Susan, 192
Hillfort, 132
Hobgoblin, 62, 193
Hockley, 201-202, 218
Holey stone, 101, 223
Holy well, 66, 82, 163-165, 235
Hope, Teresa, 33
Hopkins, Matthew, 38-39, 41
Hoppin' Tom, 106-107
Horn, Diddy, 147
Horned cat, 182
Horned God, 181
Horned One, 160
Horndon-on-the-Hill, 231
Horse whisperer, 188
Horsey Island, 36
Hot cross bun, 231
Howard, Michael, 188-191
Hunt, Edmund
Hullbridge, 117
Hustling, 157
Hutton, Ronald, 187
Hyams, Dick, 200

I
Idol, 86, 235-236
Imp, 30-32, 63, 118, 157, 170, 182, 193, 232-233
Ingelrica, Maud, 27
Iron Age, 18, 78, 90-92, 123, 132, 201, 234

J
Jadeite, 196
Jones, Christopher, 21
Jones, Rebecca, 63
Jordan's Green, 109

K
Kemp, Ursula, 22, 67-73
King Cole, 58
Kirby-le-Soken, 61
Kitchel throwing ceremony, 56
Kursaal Palace, 206

L
Laindon, 32, 226, 232
Langenhoe, 106-107
Latchingdon, 153-157, 178, 199
Lawford, 39-40, 56
Layer Marney Towers, 134
Leigh-on-Sea, 209, 214
Lenkiewicz, Robert, 71

Lexden Barrow, 78
Liddell, Bill, 184
Lindisfarne, 82, 143-144
Linnett, Walter, 145
Little Holland, 64
Lodwick, Eliza Frost, 180
Lord of Misrule, 52
'Lord of the sea', 46

M
Macleod, George, 143
Magic, 10, 21-23, 29-30, 33, 57, 61, 65, 69-70, 84-86, 88-89, 91, 101, 107, 109-110, 120, 148, 153, 155-156, 160, 162, 173, 179, 181, 183-184, 186, 189, 191-192, 199-200, 210, 214, 223
Makin, Cicely, 177
Maldon, 18, 21, 24-26, 29, 95, 113-115, 117-128, 136, 138, 148, 176
Man in Black, 215
Manningtree, 25, 38-39, 41-42, 54-55, 93
Maple, Eric, 15, 23, 130, 153, 156, 161, 173, 178, 182, 185-187, 190-191, 216, 223
Marsh Samphire, 127
Marsh magic, 65
Marsh Wizard, 84, 89, 140, 200
Martyr Stone, 124
Maxwell, Donald, 45
May Eve, 111
May Day, 151
Mayflower, 21
Mayland, 149, 154
May Pole, 111
Mermaid, 228-229
Mersea Island, 23, 96, 99, 106, 175
Mice, 110, 147, 155, 181, 186
Michaelmas, 45, 68, 102, 201, 207
Mistley, 10, 39, 41-42, 56
Mistley Heath, 41
Mistress Hart, 154-155
Mock lord, 124
'Mock' office, 83
Molly Dancers, 124
Moone, Margaret, 61
Moore, Sarah, 210-213
Morrison, Arthur, 15, 23, 167, 216, 219, 222

243

Morton, William, 28
Mother Barnes, 68-69
Mother Cocke, 67
Mother Connie Redcap, 225
Mother Eve, 29-30, 33
Mother Ewstace, 68
Mother Kemp, 67-68
Mother Moore, 211-213
Mother Redcap, 22, 155, 170-172
Mother Saunder, 148
Mother Stookes, 134
Mother Waterhouse, 32
Motley, Norman, 143
Mrs Mole, 84-85
Mrs Print, 175
Mud Race, 125
Mugwort, 91
Mundon, 138-139, 151, 154
Murrell, Edward 'Buck', 219
Murrell, James 'Cunning', 84, 88-89, 186, 215, 223

N
Neolithic, 18, 196, 207, 235, 236
North Fambridge, 154
North Ockendon, 235
Northey Island, 95, 126-127

O
Oak Apple Day, 230
Oder, George, 117
Old George, 158, 184-190
Old Mother Redcap, 170-171
Old Knobbley, 42
Old Shuck, 147
Old Witch Hart, 199
One Tree Hill, 230-231
Orsett, 231
Osea Island, 127
Ostend, 160-161
Othona, 21, 143-146
Othona Community, 143-146
Owd Davvil, 106-107, 139, 170, 195
Oyster, 74, 83-84, 107, 110, 122, 173-175, 194
Oyster feast, 83-84

P
Paglesham, 159, 171, 194-196
Parkeston, 48, 54
Peldon, 100, 102-103, 108
Perry, Grayson, 42

Pewet Island, 148
Phantom dogs, 165
Phantom Seadog, 108
Pickingill Craft, 184, 190
Pickingill, George, 157, 184, 186, 188, 190-191
Pirate, 76-77
Pitchbury Ramparts, 78
Ploughboys Ale, 124
Plough Monday, 123-124
Plumberow Mount, 201-202
Poles, Humfrey, 119
Potton Island, 169, 171
Prince Sæxa, 208
Prittlewell Priory, 207
Protestant Reformation, 39
Purleigh, 151
Pye, Rose, 177

Q
Queen Elizabeth, 43, 69, 234

R
Ramsey Island, 127, 131
Rat, 118, 156
Rawreth, 200
Ray Island, 97
Rayleigh, 232
Rituals, 155, 160, 187
River witches, 131
Roach, river, 159, 168-169, 171, 194, 196
Rochford, 23, 44, 157, 173, 181, 187-188, 193, 198-201, 216
Rollicking Bill, 121
Roman, 16, 18-19, 26, 62, 75-76, 78-80, 83, 91, 95, 99-100, 122-123, 143, 145-146
Roman, river, 76, 78
Ropeyard Gang, 158-159
Rowhedge, 77
Runwell, 163-164
Rush Bearing ceremony, 115

S
Salcott, 103-105, 109, 236
Salt making, 122-123, 175
Samphire, 127, 143
Saxon, 16, 64, 95, 113, 126, 128, 132, 173, 192, 203, 207-208, 224, 226, 228, 233
Sea Serpent, 36, 168, 175

Sea Witch, 57-58, 110, 199, 210-213
Sell the wind, 211
Selletto, John, 74
Serpent, 36, 64-65, 168, 175, 230, 232
Shaen's Shaggy Dog, 25-26
Sheela-na-Gig, 43, 86-87, 89
Shipwright's Carnival, 53
Shoeburyness, 18, 168, 175
Shuck, 42, 56, 65, 98, 108, 110, 147, 196
Smuggling, 21-22, 54-55, 62-63, 65, 98, 146, 158-159, 194, 214-215, 217, 230
South Fambridge, 154
Southend-on-Sea, 22, 205
Southend Pier, 206
South Ockendon, 235
South Woodham Ferrers, 180
'Silly Bill' Spearman, 156
Skelton, Margery, 198
Smith, Ellen, 118-119
Smythe, John, 133
Sorcery, 29, 41, 44, 63, 68, 84, 101, 132, 148, 162, 172, 180, 203, 214
Spectral donkey, 231
Spell, 48, 57, 61, 94, 104, 109, 156, 211, 220
Spillman, Susan, 134
Spirits of place, 87, 143
Springfield, 18, 134
Springfield cursus, 18
Stearne, John, 39
St Agnes Eve, 162
St Anne, 192
St Cedd, 145, 235
St Dennis Fair, 84
St Helen, 21, 80-81, 86-87
St Helena, 81, 86
St John's Eve, 133
St John's Wort, 67, 203
St Lawrence, 131
St Michael, 66, 77, 102, 230
St Nicholas, 43, 46, 52, 83, 112, 186, 226, 235
St Osyth, 22, 63, 66-70, 72-73, 182
St Peter, 107, 125, 128, 194, 202, 224
St Peter-ad-Muram, 21
St Roger, 117
Stamp, Charlie, 227
Stanford-le-Hope, 168
Stanway, 90
Stansgate Abbey, 139
Steeple, 139-140
Stick, 155, 157-158, 174, 186
Stour, river, 35, 37, 39, 42-43, 46, 48, 50, 54, 56, 58, 60, 93
Summers, Jop, 16, 176, 180
Supernatural, 55, 88, 97, 126, 140, 149, 179, 183

T

Tarpaulin muster, 122
Tar Barrels, 54, 158-159, 161
Tendring, 35, 60, 63-64, 93
Ter, river, 34
Terling, 26
Thames barge, 84
Thames, river, 16, 21-22, 42, 75-76, 79, 84, 121, 167-168, 175, 199, 205-206, 210, 215, 217, 224, 232-234, 236
The Curren, 153, 155-157
The Devil's Master, 88-89, 217
The Ranters, 150
The Tin Shed Parliament, 122
The Witches' Field, 183
The Wizard of the North, 84, 89
Three crowns, 81-82, 87
Thor, 112, 192
Thorpe-le-Soken, 61-62
Thundersley, 10, 192, 223, 225
Thunor, 112, 224-225
Thurrock, 233-234
Thurstable Barrow, 111-112
Tilbury, 227, 233-235
Tillingham, 149-150
Time-slip folklore, 136
Tinker's Hole, 159-160
Tiptree, 102
Toad, 30, 68-69, 118, 150
Tollesbury, 73, 107-111, 161
Tolleshunt D'Arcy, 108, 110-111
Tolleshunt Knights, 104-105
Tolleshunt Major, 112
Trinovantes, 18, 78-79, 87, 91, 95, 99, 128, 131, 174, 234
Tryggvason, Olaf, 126

U
Ulting, 28
V
Vampire, 109, 115-116
Vange, 231
Viking, 64, 95, 99, 126, 128, 227-228
W
Walking stick, 155, 157-158, 186
Wart, 41, 151, 159
Waterhouse, Agnes, 29, 32-34
Waterhouse, Joan, 29
Wallasea Island, 22, 155, 171-172
Walton-on-the-Naze, 36, 62
Weather magic, 160
Weaver, Bridget, 45
Well, 66, 82, 87, 102, 163, 164-166, 231, 235
Were-wolves, 126
Westcliff-on-Sea, 208, 215
West Mersea, 101, 119
West, Anne, 40
Weymarks beach, 145
Whitebait festival, 206
White horse, 63, 149, 234
White Lady, 109, 167, 215, 226
White rabbit, 110, 179
White stallion, 159
Wicca, 184
Wickham Bishops, 25
Wildfowling, 22
Wiggins, Jane, 44-45
William the Conqueror, 27
Williamson, Cecil, 70-71
Wiseman, Margaret, 119, 148
Wise-woman, 150, 225
Witch, 15, 17, 21, 23, 29-30, 32-34, 38-45, 57-58, 60-61, 63, 67, 71-72, 78, 84-86, 88-89, 100, 109-110, 114, 118-119, 129, 134, 147-148, 151, 154-157, 160-163, 170, 173-174, 177-187, 189-193, 198-199, 201-203, 210-214, 218-222
Witch bottles, 85, 173, 189, 191, 218-220, 222
Witchcraft, 10, 14-15, 22, 29-30, 32, 34, 40-41, 43, 61, 63, 67-68, 70, 72, 84-86, 88-89, 109-110, 117-119, 148, 151, 155, 157-158, 172-173, 177, 179-180, 183-185, 188, 198, 201, 214, 216, 222
Witch Hart, 154, 199
Witch-rabbits, 179
Wivenhoe, 35
Wix, 60
Wōden, 208
Woodham Walter, 150, 159
Wool, 38, 69, 92, 118, 226
Wrabness, 42
Z
Zodiac, 90

Lightning Source UK Ltd.
Milton Keynes UK
UKHW010625210322
400370UK00002B/56